CONTEMPORARY'S

PRE-GED

LANGUAGE ARTS, WRITING

McGraw Hill Wright Group

Executive Editor: Linda Kwil
Creative Director: Michael E. Kelly
Marketing Manager: Sean Klunder
Production Manager: Genevieve Kelley

Interior Design by Think Design Group LLC

 **Wright Group**

ISBN: 0-07-252763-3

Send all inquiries to:
Wright Group/McGraw-Hill
130 East Randolph Street, Suite 400
Chicago, IL 60601-6213

Printed in the United States of America.

5 6 7 8 9 10 QPD 07 06

The **McGraw·Hill** Companies

Table of Contents

To the Student

Contemporary's Pre-GED Language Arts, Writing will help you to strengthen the skills you need to pass the Language Arts, Writing Test. To answer some questions successfully, you will need to focus on sentence structure, grammar, and mechanics. For others, you will need to concentrate on the organization of sentences within a paragraph. These skills are also important for success on the essay portion of the test.

Before beginning this book, you should take the **Pretest**. This test will help you identify which skill areas you need to concentrate on most. Use the chart at the end of the Pretest to pinpoint the types of questions you have answered incorrectly and to determine in which skills you need special work. You may decide to concentrate on specific areas or to work through the entire book. We strongly suggest you do work through the whole book to build a strong foundation in the areas in which you will be tested.

Contemporary's Pre-GED Language Arts, Writing is divided into eight chapters:

- **Chapter 1: Sentence Basics** instructs you in the fundamentals of a sentence, including the parts of a simple sentence, types of sentences, and nouns and pronouns.

- **Chapter 2: Verbs** teaches you types of verbs, different verb tenses, and subject-verb agreement.

- **Chapter 3: Modifiers** teaches you how to distinguish between adjectives and adverbs, how to use them, and how to work with phrases as modifiers.

- **Chapter 4: Sentence Structure** shows you how to combine ideas in sentences. You will also study sentence problems, style, and diction.

- **Chapter 5: Mechanics** teaches you the rules of capitalization and punctuation. You will also learn how to use a comma and to distinguish between homonyms.

- **Chapter 6: Paragraph Organization** teaches you the basics of paragraph structure, including effective topic sentences, correct text divisions, unity and coherence, and tone and diction.

- **Chapter 7: Patterns of Organization** teaches you the ways in which writers organize information. You will learn about order of importance, time order, cause-and-effect order, and comparison-and-contrast order.

- **Chapter 8: The Writing Process** introduces you to the main steps involved in the process of writing an essay: prewriting, writing, and revising.

In addition, *Contemporary's Pre-GED Language Arts, Writing* has a number of features designed to familiarize you with and prepare you for the GED Test.

- **Pre-GED Practice** exercises appear at the end of every major section in Chapters 1–7 to test your knowledge of fundamentals as you answer items in GED-format. The Pre-GED Practice at the end of these chapters serves as a review of the skills you have learned.

- **Mind on Mechanics** boxes present information on capitalization and comma usage.

- **Editing Tips** highlight important information about sentence structure and correct sentence usage.

- **Evaluate Your Progress** charts allow you to periodically check your knowledge of skill areas you have learned so far.

- **Writing a GED Essay** exercises lead you through the steps in the writing process.

- The **Answer Key** gives answers and explanations for all the questions in this book. Use the Answer Key only after you have attempted to answer a set of questions in an exercise.

- The **Glossary** contains a list of key terms found throughout the book.

- The **Index** provides easy access to important rules and terms.

After you have worked through the book, you should take the **Posttest.** The Posttest will help you to see how well you have learned the skills presented in this book. The Posttest consists of 50 questions—the same amount that will appear on Part I of the Language Arts, Writing Test.

Good luck with your studies! Keep in mind that knowing how to use grammar correctly and how to write well will help you succeed on the GED Test and in other future writing tasks as well.

Language Arts, Writing Part I

The Pretest is a guide to using this book. It has two parts. Part I consists of 25 multiple-choice questions that test the grammar, usage, and organization skills covered in this book. Part II contains an essay topic.

Directions: Choose the <u>one best answer</u> to each question. Some of the sentences contain errors in organization, sentence structure, usage, or mechanics. A few sentences, however, may be correct as written. Read the sentences carefully and then answer the questions based on them. For each question, choose the answer that would result in the most effective writing of the sentence or sentences.

Pretest Answer Grid

1 ① ② ③ ④ ⑤	10 ① ② ③ ④ ⑤	19 ① ② ③ ④ ⑤
2 ① ② ③ ④ ⑤	11 ① ② ③ ④ ⑤	20 ① ② ③ ④ ⑤
3 ① ② ③ ④ ⑤	12 ① ② ③ ④ ⑤	21 ① ② ③ ④ ⑤
4 ① ② ③ ④ ⑤	13 ① ② ③ ④ ⑤	22 ① ② ③ ④ ⑤
5 ① ② ③ ④ ⑤	14 ① ② ③ ④ ⑤	23 ① ② ③ ④ ⑤
6 ① ② ③ ④ ⑤	15 ① ② ③ ④ ⑤	24 ① ② ③ ④ ⑤
7 ① ② ③ ④ ⑤	16 ① ② ③ ④ ⑤	25 ① ② ③ ④ ⑤
8 ① ② ③ ④ ⑤	17 ① ② ③ ④ ⑤	
9 ① ② ③ ④ ⑤	18 ① ② ③ ④ ⑤	

When you have completed the test, check your work with the answers and explanations on page 9. Use the evaluation chart on page 10 to determine which areas you need to study the most.

1. **Every four years, in the summertime, the presidential candidates travel East to west, trying to earn support for their campaigns.**

   What correction should be made to this sentence?

   (1) change *summertime* to *Summertime*
   (2) change *presidential* to *Presidential*
   (3) change *East* to *east*
   (4) change *west* to *West*
   (5) no correction is necessary

2. **A womens' magazine has a survey this month asking its readers if they would like to change jobs.**

   What correction should be made to this sentence?

   (1) change *womens'* to *women's*
   (2) change *has* to *have*
   (3) change *its* to *it's*
   (4) change *readers* to *readers'*
   (5) no correction is necessary

3. **The carpenter called to her apprentice "Tony, will you be able to work late tonight?"**

   What correction should be made to this sentence?

   (1) change *carpenter* to *Carpenter*
   (2) add a comma after *apprentice*
   (3) remove the comma after *Tony*
   (4) add a period after *tonight?"*
   (5) no correction is necessary

4. **A recent <u>weather study of thunderstorms and tornadoes show</u> that parts of the Midwest are frequently hit by severe storms.**

   Which is the best way to write the underlined portion of the text? If the original is the best way, choose option (1).

   (1) weather study of thunderstorms and tornadoes show
   (2) weather study of thunderstorms and tornadoes shows
   (3) whether study of thunderstorms and tornadoes show
   (4) weather study, of thunderstorms and tornadoes show
   (5) weather study of thunderstorms, and tornadoes show

5. **Either John or his sister pick up the children whenever their parents work the second shift.**

   What correction should be made to this sentence?

   (1) change *his* to *him*
   (2) change *pick* to *picks*
   (3) change *their* to *they're*
   (4) change *parents* to *parents'*
   (5) no correction is necessary

6. **In terms of experience, we think that Ms. Tucker is a worse choice than him.**

   What correction should be made to this sentence?

   (1) change *we* to *us*
   (2) change *think* to *will think*
   (3) change *worse* to *worst*
   (4) change *him* to *he*
   (5) no correction is necessary

7. **Ho Kye and his wife were upset when they <u>learned that they forgot their</u> travelers' checks.**

   Which is the best way to write the underlined portion of the text? If the original is the best way, choose option (1).

   (1) learned that they forgot their
   (2) had learned that they forgot their
   (3) learned that they had forgotten their
   (4) learned that they forgetted their
   (5) learned that they forgot there

8. **The best mechanic in the shop does really good at repairing the transmissions of the largest trucks on the road.**

   What correction should be made to this sentence?

   (1) change *best* to *better*
   (2) change *really* to *real*
   (3) change *good* to *well*
   (4) change *largest* to *larger*
   (5) no correction is necessary

9. **The managers have divided the work equally between you and she.**

   What correction should be made to this sentence?

   (1) change *have divided* to *has divided*
   (2) change *equally* to *equal*
   (3) change *between* to *among*
   (4) change *she* to *her*
   (5) no correction is necessary

10. **Boston will have no public transportation <u>tomorrow. Because</u> bus drivers are going on strike.**

    Which is the best way to write the underlined portion of the text? If the original is the best way, choose option (1).

    (1) tomorrow. Because
    (2) tomorrow; because
    (3) tomorrow because
    (4) tomorrow, and because
    (5) tomorrow, because

11. **The car starts only on dry <u>days, therefore we</u> leave it in the garage on rainy days.**

    Which is the best way to write the underlined portion of the text? If the original is the best way, choose option (1).

    (1) days, therefore we
    (2) days, when we
    (3) days; therefore, we
    (4) days, however we
    (5) days; therefore we

12. **The speaker was interesting, conversational, and gave a lot of information.**

    What correction should be made to this sentence?

    (1) change *and* to *but*
    (2) change *gave a lot of information* to *informative*
    (3) change *conversational* to *conversation*
    (4) change *gave* to *had given*
    (5) no correction is necessary

13. **This application must be completed <u>before beginning to work here.</u>**

    Which is the best way to write the underlined portion of the text? If the original is the best way, choose option (1).

    (1) before beginning to work here
    (2) before new employees begin to work here
    (3) before work begins here
    (4) before working here
    (5) until beginning to work here

14. **Mr. Rodriguez gave the delivery boy a letter as he passed by.**

    What correction should be made to this sentence?

    (1) change *gave* to *gives*
    (2) change *he* to *they*
    (3) change *he* to *the boy*
    (4) change *passed* to *past*
    (5) no correction is necessary

15. **Byron went to cooking class so that <u>the meals that are cooked by him would be meals that taste much better.</u>**

    Which is the best way to write the underlined portion of the text? If the original is the best way, choose option (1).

    (1) the meals that are cooked by him would be meals that taste much better
    (2) the meals that he could cook would be better tasting meals
    (3) he would be able to create artistic and delicious meals
    (4) he could cook better-tasting meals
    (5) he could cook

16. **<u>The frozen pizzas are for the boys that are in the freezer.</u>**

    Which is the best way to write the underlined portion of the text? If the original is the best way, choose option (1).

    (1) The frozen pizzas are for the boys that are in the freezer.
    (2) The frozen pizzas are for the boys.
    (3) The frozen pizzas are for the boys; that are in the freezer.
    (4) The frozen pizzas that are in the freezer are for the boys.
    (5) The pizzas, frozen for the boys are in the freezer.

17. **The company cannot deliver your furniture <u>today there will be</u> no delivery tomorrow.**

    Which is the best way to write the underlined portion of the text? If the original is the best way, choose option (1).

    (1) today there will be
    (2) today, however; there will be
    (3) today; as a result, there will be
    (4) today; furthermore, there will be
    (5) today, there will be

18. **She would have been happier if she will choose a better school.**

    What correction should be made to this sentence?

    (1) change *would have been* to *would of been*
    (2) insert a comma after *happier*
    (3) change *will choose* to *had chosen*
    (4) change *better* to *more better*
    (5) no correction is necessary

PRETEST

Questions 19–25 refer to the following memo.

To: All SoftCo Employees

From: Human Resources Dept.

Re: Family Picnic

(A)

(1) SoftCo is hosting its annual picnic for all employees and their families next Saturday, August 24, but join us for a good time. (2) The location is the same as in past years: Oakwood Heights Amusement Park. (3) The park offers amusement rides for the children and musical entertainment for everyone. (4) All in an atmosphere of tree-lined country beauty. (5) SoftCo will provide a picnic supper.

(B)

(6) Nick Jenkins of the accounting department will be in charge of the barbecue. (7) There will also be watermelon and other summer fruits. (8) Maria Alvarez, our company president is making vast quantities of her special broccoli pasta, which you may remember from last year. (9) Several people from our department have volunteered to bring desserts.

(C)

(10) And this year we have more to celebrate than ever before. (11) SoftCo has always made a point of celebrating with our employees to show how much we appreciate them. (12) Thanks to you're hard work, the company has enjoyed its biggest earnings this past year. (13) Some companies are in a slump. (14) Come on out and share the food, fun, and festivities on Saturday.

19. Sentence 1: SoftCo is hosting its annual picnic for all employees and their families next Saturday, August <u>24, but join us for a good time.</u>

Which is the best way to write the underlined portion of the text? If the original is the best way, choose option (1).

(1) 24, but join us for a good time
(2) 24 but join us for a good time
(3) 24, but join us, for a good time
(4) 24, so join us for a good time
(5) 24, therefore join us for a good time

20. Sentences 3 and 4: The park offers amusement rides for the children and musical entertainment <u>for everyone. All in</u> an atmosphere of tree-lined country beauty.

Which is the best way to write the underlined portion of the text? If the original is the best way, choose option (1).

(1) for everyone. All in
(2) for everyone, but all in
(3) for everyone but all in
(4) for everyone, all in
(5) for everyone. All is in

21. Sentence 5: **SoftCo will provide a picnic dinner.**

    Which revision should be made to sentence 5?

    (1) move sentence 5 to the beginning of paragraph A
    (2) move sentence 5 to the beginning of paragraph B
    (3) move sentence 5 to follow sentence 6
    (4) move sentence 5 to the end of paragraph B
    (5) no revision is necessary

22. Sentence 8: **Maria Alvarez, our company president is making vast quantities of her special broccoli pasta, which you may remember from last year.**

    What correction should be made to sentence 8?

    (1) change *our* to *are*
    (2) remove the comma after *Alvarez*
    (3) insert a comma after *president*
    (4) change *her* to *hers*
    (5) no correction is necessary

23. Sentence 10: **And this year we have more to celebrate than ever before.**

    Which revision should be made to sentence 10?

    (1) move sentence 10 to the end of paragraph A
    (2) move sentence 10 to the end of paragraph B
    (3) move sentence 10 to the end of paragraph C
    (4) move sentence 10 to follow sentence 11
    (5) no revision is necessary

24. Sentence 12: **Thanks to you're hard work, the company has enjoyed its biggest earnings this past year.**

    What correction should be made to sentence 12?

    (1) change *you're* to *your*
    (2) remove the comma after *work*
    (3) change *has enjoyed* to *will enjoy*
    (4) change *its* to *their*
    (5) no correction is necessary

25. Sentence 13: **Some companies are in a slump.**

    Which revision should be made to sentence 13?

    (1) move sentence 13 to the beginning of paragraph C
    (2) move sentence 13 to the end of paragraph C
    (3) move sentence 13 to follow sentence 11
    (4) remove sentence 13
    (5) no revision is necessary

    Answers are on page 9.

Language Arts, Writing Part II

This part of the Pretest is designed to find out how well you write.

Essay Directions and Topic:

Look at the box on the following page. In the box is your assigned topic.

Write a short essay on the assigned topic. Keep track of how long it takes you to complete your essay. Remember that you will have only 45 minutes to write your essay for the GED Test.

Pay attention to these features as you write:

- Well-focused main points
- Clear organization
- Specific development of your ideas
- Control of sentence structure, punctuation, grammar, word choice, and spelling

As you work, be sure to do the following:

- Write legibly.
- Write on the assigned topic.
- Write your essay on a separate sheet of paper.

PRETEST

TOPIC

What is your favorite movie?

In your essay, state your favorite movie. Explain why you like it so much. Use your personal observations, experience and knowledge.

Part II is a test to determine how well you can use written language to explain your ideas.

In preparing your essay, you should take the following steps:

- Read the **DIRECTIONS** and the **TOPIC** carefully.

- Plan your essay before you write. Use scratch paper to make any notes.

- After you finish writing your essay, reread what you have written and make any changes that will improve your essay.

- Make sure your essay is long enough to develop the topic adequately.

Evaluation guidelines are on page 11.

PRETEST

Answer Key

1. (3) Do not capitalize names of directions when they refer to general directions.

2. (1) *Women* is a plural noun, so to form the possessive, add the apostrophe before the *s*.

3. (2) Use a comma to set off a direct quote.

4. (2) The subject of the sentence is the singular noun *study*. Since the verb must agree in number with the subject, *shows* is correct.

5. (2) When a compound subject is joined by *either . . . or*, the verb should agree with the closer part of the subject, in this case the singular noun *sister*.

6. (4) Mentally put the understood verb after the pronoun—*a better choice than he is*. *Him* is an object pronoun, but a subject pronoun is needed.

7. (3) This sentence says that two actions occurred in the past. To show that losing the travelers' checks occurred first, use the past perfect tense for that action and the simple past for the action that followed it.

8. (3) *Good* is an adjective, but the word being modified here is the verb *does*, which takes the adverb *well*.

9. (4) *You* and *she* are objects of the preposition *between*, so the object pronoun *her* is needed instead of the subject pronoun *she*.

10. (3) *Because bus drivers are going on strike* is not a complete sentence. Choice (3) turns it into a dependent clause that is written correctly.

11. (3) *Therefore* is a conjunctive adverb between two complete thoughts. It must be preceded by a semicolon (at the end of the first complete thought) and followed by a comma.

12. (2) Using the adjective *informative* makes the sentence structure parallel.

13. (2) The underlined phrase is a dangling modifier. There is no noun or pronoun in the sentence for it to refer to. It actually says the application is beginning to work here. Choice (2) adds the necessary subject, *new employees*.

14. (3) You can't tell whether *he* refers to the boy or Mr. Rodriguez. Choice (3) makes the pronoun reference clear.

15. (4) The underlined phrase is wordy and repetitious. Choice (4) keeps the meaning without the wordiness.

16. (4) The phrase *that are in the freezer* should be placed next to the word it modifies, *pizzas*. The original sentence implies the boys are in the freezer.

17. (4) This sentence is a run-on. Choice (4) adds a conjunctive adverb with correct punctuation to connect the two main clauses.

18. (3) This sentence contains a dependent clause beginning with the conditional word *if*. Since the verb form in the first part of the sentence is *would have been*, the *if* clause must be in the past perfect—*had chosen*. No comma is needed when the dependent clause comes after the independent clause.

19. (4) The two clauses joined here have a cause-effect relationship. The conjunction *so* is a better choice than *but*, which shows contrast.

20. (4) Sentence 4 is a fragment. Changing the period to a comma correctly makes it part of sentence 3.

21. (2) Sentence 5 belongs at the beginning of paragraph B because it is the topic sentence for the paragraph about the picnic supper.

22. (3) *Our company president* is a renaming phrase, so it needs to be set off by commas before and after it.

23. (4) Sentence 10 doesn't make sense on its own. The information in sentence 11 must come before it so the reference to celebrating is clear.

24. (1) *You're* is a contraction meaning *you are*. The possessive pronoun *your* is needed here.

25. (4) A sentence about other companies' slumps does not belong in this paragraph about SoftCo's appreciation of its employees.

Part I Evaluation Chart

On the following chart, circle the number of any item you answered incorrectly. Next to each group of item numbers, you will see the pages you can review to learn how to answer the items correctly. Pay particular attention to reviewing skill areas in which you missed half or more of the questions.

Skill Area	Item Number	Review Pages
ORGANIZATION		
Text divisions		162–164
Topic sentences	21	159–161
Unity/coherence	23, 25	165–171
SENTENCE STRUCTURE		
Complete sentences, fragments, and sentence combining	10, 20	13–18, 101–110
Run-on sentences/comma splices	11, 17	103–104
Wordiness/repetition	15	121–127
Coordination/subordination	19	102–110
Modification	8, 13, 16	81–100, 111–112
Parallelism	12	113–114
USAGE		
Subject-verb agreement	4, 5	67–77
Verb tense/form	7, 18	53–66, 115–117
Pronoun reference/antecedent agreement	6, 9, 14	30–47, 118–119
MECHANICS		
Capitalization	1	133–138
Punctuation (commas)	3, 22	20, 139–148
Spelling (possessives, contractions, and homonyms)	2, 24	27–28, 149–152

P R E T E S T

Part II Evaluation Guidelines

If at all possible, give your instructor your essay to evaluate. You will find his or her objective opinion helpful in deciding whether you are ready to begin preparing for the actual GED. If this is not possible, have another student evaluate your essay. If you cannot find another student to help you, review your essay yourself. If you do this, it is usually better to let your essay sit for a few days before you evaluate it. This way you will have similar views as someone reading your essay for the first time. No matter which way you review your work, use the checklist on the next page to review your essay.

After you have evaluated your essay in terms of the criteria in the checklist, look at the number you checked for each question. Pay attention to the questions where you checked a 2 or a 1—these scores indicate that you need some extra practice in certain writing skills. Studying the following sections will help you to raise your score:

1. If you had trouble answering the question that is asked in the writing prompt, pay attention to pages 195–196.

2. If you had trouble organizing your ideas, pay attention to Chapter 7 and page 197.

3. If you had trouble supporting your main idea with details or examples, pay attention to pages 196 and 202–203.

4. If you had trouble writing grammatically correct sentences and paragraphs, pay attention to Chapters 1–6.

5. If you had trouble using words correctly, pay attention to Chapters 4 and 6.

If possible talk to your instructor, another student, or a friend about your feelings as you wrote. Together you will be able to identify your current writing strengths as well as any weaknesses. Based on this combined evaluation, review the sections in this book that will help you most in improving your writing.

Essay Scoring Checklist

A. Does your essay answer the question that is asked in the writing prompt?

- ☐ 1. No, my essay refers to the question, but it doesn't really discuss it or develop a main idea that answers the question.
- ☐ 2. My essay addresses the question with a main idea, but it also includes some ideas that are not directly related to the question.
- ☐ 3. Yes, my essay has a main idea that is based on the question, but the main idea could be stated in a better way.
- ☐ 4. Yes, my essay clearly answers the question with a main idea.

B. Are the ideas in your essay well organized?

- ☐ 1. No, the ideas in my essay are mixed up in order and are hard to follow.
- ☐ 2. Most of the ideas in my essay are clear and easy to follow, but there are some ideas that are hard to follow.
- ☐ 3. Yes, the ideas in my essay are clearly organized, but some of the ideas could be organized in a better way.
- ☐ 4. Yes, the ideas in my essay are clearly organized and easy to follow.

C. Does your essay contain details or examples that support the main idea?

- ☐ 1. No, many of the paragraphs in my essay contain details or examples that don't support the topic sentence, or many of the paragraphs don't have any details or examples at all.
- ☐ 2. Some of the paragraphs in my essay have a topic sentence and supporting details and examples, but the details and examples could be stronger and more abundant.
- ☐ 3. Yes, each paragraph in my essay contains a topic sentence and details or examples, but some of the paragraphs have more details or examples than others.
- ☐ 4. Yes, each paragraph in my essay contains a topic sentence with specific details and examples that support the topic sentence.

D. Are the sentences and paragraphs in your essay grammatically correct?

- ☐ 1. No, the sentences and paragraphs in my essay are not worded correctly, and a majority of the sentences contain errors in grammar and spelling.
- ☐ 2. Some of the sentences and paragraphs in my essay are worded incorrectly, and there are a noticeable amount of errors in grammar and spelling.
- ☐ 3. Yes, the sentences and paragraphs in my essay are mostly worded correctly, and there are only a few small errors in grammar and spelling.
- ☐ 4. Yes, the sentences and paragraphs in my essay are worded correctly, and there are practically no errors in grammar or spelling.

E. Does your essay display a wide range of words that are used correctly?

- ☐ 1. No, my essay displays a very limited choice of words, which are often reused or used incorrectly.
- ☐ 2. My essay doesn't display a very wide range of word choice, and there are a few words that are used incorrectly.
- ☐ 3. Yes, my essay displays a word choice that is appropriate to the topic but could be more complex.
- ☐ 4. Yes, my essay displays a wide range, in which all words are used correctly.

CHAPTER 1

Sentence Basics

What Is a Sentence?

When you're talking with friends, you probably don't worry much about speaking in complete sentences.

"Saw a movie today."

"Any good?"

"Not great. Fantastic special effects. A weak plot, though."

You've probably had conversations like this one. The meaning is clear because you know the situation and understand the subject being discussed. Besides, if you don't immediately know what your friend has said, you can just ask, "What do you mean?"

When you write, though, single words or phrases are not enough to make an idea clear. This is why it's so important for you to write in complete sentences. A sentence makes your ideas clear. Your reader isn't forced to guess what you really mean.

A **sentence** is a group of words that contains a subject and a predicate and that expresses a complete thought.

The **subject** is *whom* or *what* the sentence is about. Whom or what is the following sentence about?

The young woman bought two tickets to Friday's rock concert.

This sentence is about the young woman. Therefore, the subject is *the young woman.*

The **predicate** of a sentence tells what the subject *is* or what it *does.* Everything in the sentence that is not part of the subject is part of the predicate. Find the predicate in the sample sentence above.

You should have identified the predicate as the words *bought two tickets to Friday's rock concert.*

Besides having a subject and a predicate, a sentence must also express a complete thought. When you finish a sentence you should not be asking questions such as *Who did it? What is this about? What happened?*

The sample sentence below has a subject and a predicate and expresses a complete thought.

| The young woman | bought two tickets to Friday's rock concert. |
| SUBJECT | PREDICATE |

EDITING TIP

A group of words must pass three tests in order to be called a sentence:

1. It must have a subject that tells *whom* or *what* the sentence is about.

2. It must have a predicate that tells what the subject *is* or *does*.

3. It must express a complete thought.

EXERCISE 1

Directions: In each of the following sentences, first find the predicate and underline it twice. Then underline the subject once.

Example: Karen Wong drove to Ohio for the weekend.

1. Sarah attacked the chores with enthusiasm.

2. Indira's kitchen table was piled high with fresh-baked bread.

3. High winds broke several windows in downtown buildings.

4. Jevon raced to the telephone in the living room.

5. Mr. Zimmer's house will always be our least favorite.

6. The woman answered the police officer carefully.

7. The doctor arrived at the office at 8:30 A.M.

8. Soon Young prepared a huge meal for her parents.

9. The forest fire had destroyed several thousand acres of trees.

10. Marek's grandmother will turn eighty-five this year.

Answers are on page 223.

Parts of a Simple Sentence

Simple Subjects and Verbs

The **simple sentence** is the most basic, or simple, form of the complete sentence. It has at least one subject and one predicate.

The subject of a sentence tells *whom* or *what* the sentence is about. The **simple subject** is a part of the sentence's subject. It tells *what* or *whom* the sentence is about but does not include the descriptive words that are part of the subject.

Look at the following example. Which key word tells *what* or *whom* the sentence is about?

An angry, thin man	walked up the courthouse steps.
SUBJECT	PREDICATE

The simple subject is *man*. It tells *whom* the sentence is about.

Sometimes the subject includes more than one word. A subject that has more than one part connected with words like *and* and *or* is called a **compound subject.** In the following sentence, the compound subject is *my brother and his wife.*

My brother and his wife rented a car for the day.

The predicate is what the subject *is* or *does*. A **verb** is the most important part of the predicate. It is the key word that tells what something *is* or *does*. A verb does not include the descriptive words found in the predicate. Often, but not always, the verb shows action, as in the following sentence.

Mary Rios	walked onto the stage of the comedy club.
SUBJECT	PREDICATE

In this sentence, the verb is *walked.* It tells what the subject, Mary Rios, *does.*

Often a verb needs two or more words to express an action or state of being. This is a way of showing whether the action or state of being occurs in the past, present, or future. In the following sentence, the words *had waited* are the verb.

The photographer	had waited	patiently for the bear to wake up.
SUBJECT	VERB	

EXERCISE 2

Directions: In the following sentences, first find the verb and underline it twice. Then underline the simple or compound subject once.

Example: The crisp, autumn leaves and berries had crunched under our feet.

1. The team's manager should win an award.

2. Everyone has ordered something different to eat.

3. Andrej fumbled in his pockets for his car keys.

4. Mr. and Mrs. Hastings complained about the defective lamp.

5. The run-down old bus pulled slowly out of the station.

6. The previous receptionist had been more efficient.

7. Pak Ku runs during his lunch hour every Friday.

8. Christy and Jan became good friends last year.

9. My brother's apartment was burglarized recently.

10. The brilliant writer of this movie has created a suspenseful plot.

Answers are on page 223.

Fragments

A group of words that does not have a subject and a predicate and does not express a complete thought is called a fragment. A **fragment** is an incomplete sentence. Look at the following group of words. Is it a sentence or a fragment?

The party last night.

The group of words has a subject, *party,* but there is no predicate. The sentence doesn't express a complete thought. What is it about the party last night? What happened? What was it like? If we add the predicate *was very crowded,* the sentence now expresses a complete thought.

The party last night was very crowded.

Other fragments can result when a group of words begins with a connecting word such as *because, when,* or *if,* and the thought is not completed.

If you leave on the earlier train.

This group of words does not tell what will happen if you leave on the earlier train. An easy way to fix the fragment is to combine it with another sentence.

If you leave on the earlier train, I will drive you to the station.

Now the sentence is complete, The subject is *I* and the predicate is *will drive you to the station.*

EDITING TIP

There are two ways to correct a fragment:

1. Attach the fragment to the sentence before or after it.

2. Reword or add words to the fragment to give it a subject and a predicate.

EXERCISE 3

Directions: Read each group of words below. Decide whether each group is a sentence or a fragment. Write *S* for sentence or *F* for fragment in the space provided.

Example: ___*F*___ Went to St. Louis for a ball game.

1. _____ You need three stamps on that envelope.

2. _____ Yesterday, Sam and his nephew fished all morning.

3. _____ When that thick magazine fell off the sofa.

4. _____ This room is a mess!

5. _____ My client in Dallas will send you the brochure.

6. _____ Rattled and chugged all the way down the street.

7. _____ My former next-door neighbor and good friend.

8. _____ The workers walked carefully through the construction area.

9. _____ Because you and your co-workers are dependable.

10. _____ Florentia received dozens of cards during her illness.

Answers are on page 223.

Parts of a Simple Sentence

Directions: Choose what correction should be made to each sentence below. If you think the sentence is correct, choose option (5).

1. <u>People with homes</u> on the Mississippi's floodplain.

    (1) People fled their homes
    (2) People in homes
    (3) Living in homes
    (4) Because of record-high levels
    (5) no correction is necessary

2. <u>Migrated hundreds of miles south</u> from Canada.

    (1) While migrating south
    (2) Migrating wolves
    (3) Packs of wolves
    (4) Wolves migrated hundreds of miles south
    (5) no correction is necessary

3. <u>Because the air pollution</u> was so bad.

    (1) Because, the air pollution
    (2) Laws were enacted because the air pollution
    (3) Air pollution, which
    (4) A source of air pollution that
    (5) no correction is necessary

4. During the rain, the car's <u>electric window</u>.

    (1) electric window on the driver's side
    (2) electric window and windshield wipers
    (3) electric window became jammed
    (4) jammed electric window
    (5) no correction is necessary

5. In high school, <u>my grades in biology were poor</u>.

    (1) my first two grades in biology
    (2) my grades in biology
    (3) my grades on biology tests
    (4) my grades on biology experiments
    (5) no correction is necessary

6. Yesterday at the beach, <u>the sun shone brightly</u>.

    (1) the sun in my eyes
    (2) the sun and sand
    (3) the sun above the clouds
    (4) the sun's harsh rays
    (5) no correction is necessary

Answers are on page 224.

Types of Sentences

There are four types of sentences: statements, questions, commands, and exclamations. Each type of sentence is used for a different purpose.

Statement

A **statement** gives information or tells something. All of the example sentences used so far have been statements.

> The young woman bought two tickets to Friday's rock concert.

Question

A **question** asks for or about something.

> Where is my math book? Will you go to the concert with me?

In most cases, the subject comes before a predicate in a sentence. In a question, though, this order is reversed. It can make it more difficult to find the subject. You can find the subject more easily if you change the order of the words in a question into a statement.

> Where is my math book? ⟶ | My math book | is where. |
>   SUBJECT   PREDICATE

In some questions, the subject falls between parts of the verb. To find the subject, change the order of the words to form a statement.

> Will you go to the concert? ⟶ | You | will go to the concert. |
>   SUBJECT   PREDICATE

Command

A **command** states an order or a request.

> Shut the door.
>
> Move, please.
>
> Get away from there this minute.
>
> Don't go near the edge of the cliff.

These sentences seem to have predicates but no subjects. The subject is actually *you. You* is understood without being directly stated.

> You + shut the door.
>
> You + move, please.
>
> You + get away from there this minute.
>
> You + don't go near the edge of the cliff.

Exclamation

An **exclamation** is an expression of excitement or surprise. As in a command, certain words that are understood may be left out of an exclamation. As in a question, changing the order of the words in an exclamation may help you find the subject.

Fire! ⟶ There is a + fire.

Wonderful! ⟶ This is + wonderful.

Is that a great movie! ⟶ That is a great movie.

MIND ON MECHANICS

Endmarks

Once you've written a complete sentence, be sure to punctuate it (put in the endmarks) correctly. All sentences begin with a capital letter and end with an endmark. The punctuation you use at the end of a sentence depends on the type of sentence it is.

- A statement ends with a period.

    Mount McKinley is North America's highest mountain.

    Too much fat in your diet is unhealthy.

- A question ends with a question mark.

    Who will be our new senator next year?

    Are you running in the Boston Marathon?

- A command ends with a period. It has *you* as the understood subject.

    Turn on the air conditioning.

    Move that bike out of my way.

- An exclamation ends with an exclamation point.

    What a fantastic game!

    We won!

Directions: Punctuate each sentence below with the correct endmark.

Example: Watch out for that other car ___!___

1. Brian slowly got to his feet _____
2. Be careful with that lawn mower _____
3. Smoke is coming from the roof _____
4. Where did you find the book _____
5. Stop jumping on the bed _____
6. The train stops here every fifteen minutes _____
7. Have you seen my radio _____
8. Ms. Luna left here at least twenty minutes ago _____
9. What a nightmare _____
10. Can you see her yet _____

Answers are on page 224.

PRE-GED PRACTICE
Types of Sentences

Directions: Choose what correction should be made to each sentence below. If you think the sentence is correct, choose option (5).

1. **Watch out for that falling ladder.**
   (1) add a subject
   (2) change the period to an exclamation point
   (3) change the period to a question mark
   (4) add a verb
   (5) no correction is necessary

2. **Who would like to attend the concert.**
   (1) change the period to an exclamation point
   (2) change the period to a question mark
   (3) add the word *you* to make the subject clear
   (4) restate the sentence as a command
   (5) no correction is necessary

3. **Will you take this book back to the library for me?**
   (1) change the question mark to a period
   (2) change the question mark to an exclamation point
   (3) add a verb to the sentence
   (4) add a subject to the sentence
   (5) no correction is necessary

4. **The grizzly bear is the most dangerous animal!**
   (1) change the exclamation point to a question mark
   (2) change the exclamation point to a period
   (3) add a subject to the sentence
   (4) add a verb to the sentence
   (5) no correction is necessary

Answers are on page 224.

Nouns

What Are Nouns?

Read the following paragraph. Pay attention to the words in dark print as you read.

> **Teresa Rivas** pulled her **car** into the small parking **lot.** About fifteen **miles** to the **south** lay the **town** of **Taos, New Mexico. Teresa** walked up a **path** to the **top** of a **hill.** A concrete **building** marks the **grave** of **D. H. Lawrence.** It is a **place** of **solitude** and **beauty.** This famous English **novelist** had lived here in the early twentieth **century. Lawrence's ranch** now belongs to the **University of New Mexico.**

What do the words in dark print have in common? They are nouns.

Nouns are words that name people, places, things, or ideas.

People:	Teresa Rivas, Teresa, D. H. Lawrence, novelist, Lawrence's
Places:	lot, south, town, Taos, New Mexico, top, hill, building, grave, place, ranch, University of New Mexico
Things:	car, miles, path, century
Ideas:	solitude, beauty

Directions: Underline the nouns in each sentence below.

Example: Bryan's only wish is to have a new car.

1. Hilda says she will return home soon.

2. Construction of the Alaska Highway began in 1942.

3. Superman's first home was Cleveland, Ohio.

4. Two high school students created the superhero.

5. Last year, Louis Padilla moved into an apartment in Washington, D.C.

6. Padilla visits the Smithsonian Institution at least twice a month.

7. The Smithsonian is one of the largest museums in the world.

8. Toni is learning to paint landscapes.

9. William wants to capture the beauty of the outdoors in his photos.

10. Shawna captured the colors of the morning sky in her painting.

Answers are on page 224.

Common and Proper Nouns

There are two main types of nouns: proper nouns and common nouns. **Proper nouns** name a specific person, place, thing, or idea. Proper nouns are always capitalized. **Common nouns** name a whole group or general type of person, place, thing, or idea. Common nouns are not capitalized.

	Proper Nouns	**Common Nouns**
People:	Billie Smith, Toya Greene, Jay Hawk Wind	artist, mechanic, mayor, writer, police officer
Places:	Grand Canyon, Kentucky, Empire State Building	city, mountains, train, valley, restaurant
Things:	Sports Illustrated, Compton's Encyclopedia, Space Shuttle Columbia	newspaper, table, pencil, diploma, computer
Ideas:	Modernism, Zionism, Roaring Twenties	politics, justice, happiness, religion, patriotism

EXERCISE 6

Directions: Underline each common noun once in the sentences below. Underline the proper nouns twice. The proper nouns have not been capitalized. Cross out the small letter at the beginning of each proper noun and write a capital letter above it.

Example: As they crossed the street, <u><u>A̶nna</u></u> grabbed her daughter's hand.

1. The two friends traveled to chicago and visited the sears tower.

2. The salesperson showed melanie two navy blue jackets.

3. While riding on the train, an attorney read the *st. louis post-dispatch*.

4. The nurse took james's blood pressure and recorded the numbers on the form.

5. My friend yolanda wants to learn more about hinduism.

6. Many people go out of town over memorial day weekend.

7. A chef from france prepared a fabulous meal for the special event.

8. Let's go into the museum when mark and noriko arrive.

9. There are geysers and hot springs in yellowstone national park.

10. Can jeremy stop at the quikstop food store and pick up some milk?

Answers are on page 224.

Plural and Singular Nouns

Nouns that name more than one person, place, thing, or idea are called **plural nouns.** Nouns that name only one person, place, thing, or idea are called **singular nouns.** The nouns in boldface in the passage below are plural.

> Our **lives** are constantly enriched by the unusual **people** around us. Marcia, for example, has entertained many **people** with her taste in **clothing.** As a child, other **children** laughed at Marcia's way of dressing. She thought nothing of mixing **colors** and **fabrics** in unusual **ways.** She might mix **plaids** with **stripes** or **corduroys** with **silks.** Now in her **thirties,** Marcia still dresses in her own style. Her **dresses** still do not match her **shoes.** She delights in wearing **shirts** with contrasting **cuffs** and **collars.** Now, however, both **women** and **men** say she is a trendsetter.

Fill in the blanks below with the correct plural form. Several of the plurals are used in the passage above.

1. Most nouns are made plural by adding *s*.

   color ⟶ colors (line 4)

   fabric ⟶ _____ (line 4)

   stripe ⟶ _____ (line 5)

2. Nouns ending in *s, ch, sh,* or *x* are made plural by adding *es*.

   dress ⟶ _____ (line 7)

   match ⟶ matches

   dish ⟶ dishes

   box ⟶ boxes

3. Nouns ending in *y* are made plural in two ways. If the final *y* follows a vowel *(a, e, i, o,* or *u)*, make the noun plural by adding an *s*. If the *y* follows a consonant (any letter but *a, e, i, o,* or *u*), form the plural by changing the *y* to *i* and adding *es*.

   Following a Vowel   **Following a Consonant**

   way ⟶ _____ (line 5)   thirty ⟶ _____ (line 5)

   corduroy ⟶ _____ (line 5)   penny⟶ _____ pennies

4. Many nouns ending in *f* or *fe* are made plural by changing the *f* to *v* and adding *es*.

   Change   **No Change**

   knife ⟶ knives   cuff ⟶ _____ (line 8)

   leaf ⟶ leaves   roof ⟶ roofs

5. A few nouns do not change form when they are made plural.

   clothing → _____ (line 3)   fish → fish

6. Some nouns take special forms when they are made plural.

   woman → _____ (line 8)   foot → feet

EXERCISE 7

Directions: Look at the plural nouns after each number below. If one plural noun is incorrect, underline it. If all the plural nouns in a group are correct, choose option (5).

Example: (1) chiefs   (2) beef   (3) <u>loafs</u>   (4) shelves   (5) correct

1. (1) batches   (2) taxes   (3) scratchs   (4) addresses   (5) correct

2. (1) dictionaries   (2) turkeys   (3) alloys   (4) supplies   (5) correct

3. (1) deer   (2) scissors   (3) sheeps   (4) trousers   (5) correct

4. (1) leaves   (2) knives   (3) beliefs   (4) lifes   (5) correct

5. (1) babies   (2) spys   (3) butterflies   (4) alleys   (5) correct

6. (1) judges   (2) officers   (3) women   (4) salespersons   (5) correct

7. (1) feet   (2) trouts   (3) pants   (4) teeth   (5) correct

8. (1) cities   (2) countries   (3) monkeys   (4) skys   (5) correct

9. (1) boxes   (2) nieces   (3) dishs   (4) messes   (5) correct

10. (1) handkerchieves   (2) grooves   (3) halves   (4) wives   (5) correct

Answers are on page 224.

Possessive Nouns

The way to show ownership or possession is by using a **possessive noun.**
Form a possessive noun by adding an apostrophe and an *s* to a noun.

The dog's name is Griffin.　　　Carla's shirt is red.

MIND ON MECHANICS

Apostrophes in Possessive Nouns

1. For singular nouns, add an apostrophe and an *s*.

   the lawyer's opinion　　Dino's truck

2. For plural nouns ending in *s*, add only an apostrophe.

   the Bergs' home　　my parents' gifts

3. For plural nouns not ending in *s*, add an apostrophe and an *s*.

   people's traditions　　the children's shoes

It is easy to confuse plural and possessive nouns. You need to read a
sentence carefully to decide if the noun is singular or plural and if it shows
possession. If it does not show possession, it should not have an apostrophe.
Which sentence is correct?

That **singer's** shirt is white.

That **singers** shirt is white.

The word *that* shows there is only one singer. That singer owns the shirt.
So the noun is both singular and possessive. *Singer's* is the correct form to use.

Which of the following two sentences is correct?

Those **singers** shirts are white.

Those **singers'** shirts are white.

The word *those* shows there is more than one singer. Those singers own the
shirts. So the noun is both plural and possessive. *Singers'* is the correct form to use.

Which of the following sentences is correct?

All the **singers'** have white shirts.

All the **singers** have white shirts.

The word *all* indicates there are several singers. However, the verb *have*
already shows possession. So there is no need to add an apostrophe to the
plural noun *singers*.

EXERCISE 8

Directions: Read each of the following sentences. If the underlined noun is correct, write *C* on the line. If the noun is incorrect, write the correct form of the word on the line.

Example: _artists'_ The five <u>artists</u> paintings were already framed.

1. _____ Some people believe that our <u>countrys</u> greatest problem is the economy.

2. _____ For increased sales, the prices of <u>womens'</u> clothing must be reduced.

3. _____ <u>Benjamin's</u> favorite food is spaghetti and meatballs.

4. _____ The <u>Millers'</u> have four red chairs in their kitchen.

5. _____ Mrs. Chan has trouble sleeping because of her <u>husband's</u> snoring.

6. _____ In spite of all my studying, these Spanish <u>books'</u> are still too difficult.

7. _____ The <u>owners</u> of this restaurant serve great salads.

8. _____ High stacks of paper always cover my <u>bosses</u> desk.

9. _____ Rebuilding downtown will require several <u>years</u> planning.

10. _____ Thomas Jefferson wrote about <u>citizens</u> rights.

Answers are on page 225.

Nouns

Directions: Choose what correction should be made to each sentence below. If you think the sentence is correct, choose option (5).

1. **The Panthers' coach watched his teams' star forward sink two three-point baskets to win the game.**

   (1) change *Panthers'* to *Panther's*
   (2) change *teams'* to *teames*
   (3) change *baskets* to *baskets'*
   (4) change *teams'* to *team's*
   (5) no correction is necessary

2. **Four churchs' were located along Olive Street on the town's south side.**

   (1) change *churchs'* to *churches*
   (2) change *Olive Street* to *olive street*
   (3) change *town's* to *towns*
   (4) change *town's* to *townes*
   (5) no correction is necessary

3. **Can you guess what dark mysteries' lie hidden in Lake Superior's depths?**

   (1) change *mysteries'* to *mystery's*
   (2) change *mysteries'* to *mysteries*
   (3) change *Lake Superior's* to *lake superior's*
   (4) change *depths* to *depthes*
   (5) no correction is necessary

4. **Two boxs in the corner of Bess's room contained the last of her worldly possessions.**

   (1) change *boxs* to *boxes*
   (2) change *Bess's* to *Bess*
   (3) change *Bess's* to *Besses*
   (4) change *possessions* to *possessions'*
   (5) no correction is necessary

5. **Piri's face grew sad as she watched the suns last rays gleam on the Golden Gate Bridge.**

   (1) change *Piri's* to *Piris'*
   (2) change *suns* to *sun's*
   (3) change *rays* to *rayes*
   (4) change *Golden Gate Bridge* to *golden gate bridge*
   (5) no correction is necessary

   Answers are on page 225.

Pronouns

Nouns make writing precise. They tell the reader specifically who or what is being discussed. Occasionally, however, too many nouns can make writing dull.

> Jevon is an excellent mechanic. Jevon has worked at Boyer's Garage for six years, and the other mechanics there often come to Jevon with problems that the other mechanics cannot solve. Jevon's wife is very proud of Jevon and Jevon's work. Jevon's wife supports and encourages Jevon, even when Jevon works late.

In this paragraph, two nouns, *Jevon* and *mechanics,* are overused. The writing is repetitive and dull. The writing can be improved by replacing some of the nouns with pronouns. Look how pronouns can improve the paragraph.

> Jevon is an excellent mechanic. **He** has worked at Boyer's Garage for six years, and the other mechanics there often come to **him** with problems that **they** cannot solve. Jevon's wife is very proud of **him** and his work. **She** supports and encourages **him,** even when **he** works late.

A **pronoun** is a word that replaces and refers to a noun. It is used in exactly the same way as the noun it replaces.

There are four kinds of pronouns: subject pronouns, possessive pronouns, object pronouns, and reflexive pronouns.

Subject Pronouns

A **subject pronoun** replaces a noun that is used as a subject.

> The Cowboys | are my favorite football players.
> SUBJECT   PREDICATE

> They | are my favorite football players.
> SUBJECT   PREDICATE

Pronouns have singular and plural forms. These are the forms for subject pronouns.

Subject Pronouns	
Singular	**Plural**
I	we
you	you
he, she, it	they

Nouns and pronouns are often joined with *and* or *or.* Sometimes it may be difficult to know what kind of pronoun to use with the noun. (Remember, subject pronouns are used only to replace a subject or part of a subject.)

EDITING TIP

If you're not sure which type of pronoun is correct when a pronoun appears with a noun, try thinking of the pronoun by itself in the sentence.

Lee and Frank are absent today.

(He, Him) and Frank are absent today.

He is absent today.

He and Frank are absent today.

Subject pronouns are also used to rename the subject following a verb of being *(am, are, is, was, were,* and verbs with *be* and *been*). Remember that these verbs act as equal signs. So if the pronoun that follows the verb of being is the same as the noun before the verb, use the subject pronoun.

The director has been **Marie Tso.**

The director has been **she.**

Subject pronouns also replace nouns that give more information about the subject of the sentence.

The two people we hired, **Barry and Sharon,** are former teachers.

The two people we hired, **Barry and she,** are former teachers.

EXERCISE 9

Directions: In each of the following sentences, underline the correct choice in parentheses.

Example: (Him and Gloria, <u>He and Gloria</u>) both enjoy going to movies.

1. The only guests who arrived on time were *(they, them)*.

2. *(Him and I, He and I)* eat supper together every Friday.

3. My two friends, *(Julian and she, Julian and her)*, planned a surprise party for me last week.

4. Did *(they, them)* sell more tickets to the benefit than the rest of us?

5. Since we had such a terrific time together, *(you and he, you and him)* should plan to visit us again soon.

6. In the beginning, *(we, us)* learned the most from the class.

7. It is *(I, me)*.

8. Although it seems as if we moved in only yesterday, *(the Porters and we, the Porters and us)* have lived in this area for several years now.

9. Our most humorous co-worker is *(he, him)*.

10. Although you and *(I, me)* both love baseball, I go to more games.

11. *(We, Us)* invited the Greens to the play on Friday night.

12. Tina and *(I, me)* are in the same classes together.

13. *(He, Him)* often asks his friend Todd for advice.

14. William and *(her, she)* both have similar interests.

15. *(You and he, You and him)* both did very well on the test.

Answers are on page 225.

Possessive Pronouns

A **possessive pronoun** replaces a noun that shows ownership.

There are two kinds of possessive pronouns. One type is used along with a noun. The other type is used by itself.

My favorite pastime is fishing.
(The pronoun *my* goes with the noun *pastime*.)

Mine is bowling.
(The pronoun *mine* stands alone.)

Possessive Pronouns		
	Singular	**Plural**
Used with a Noun:	my	our
	your	your
	his, her, its	their
Standing Alone:	mine	ours
	yours	yours
	his, hers, its	theirs

Note that possessive pronouns never take an apostrophe.

Incorrect: The old blue car is her's.

Correct: The old blue car is hers.

Possessive pronouns are sometimes confused with contractions. *It's,* for example, is a contraction meaning "it is." *Its* is a possessive pronoun.

EDITING TIP

If you are unsure whether or not to use an apostrophe, substitute *it is* or *it has* for *its* and see if the change makes sense.

(It's, Its) hinges are rusty.

Incorrect: *It is* hinges are rusty.

Correct: *Its* hinges are rusty.

EXERCISE 10

Directions: Choose the correct word to fill each blank.

Example: _yours_ Is this suitcase (*your, yours, your's*)?

1. _____ They were dazzled by (*her, her's, hers*) knowledge.

2. _____ Is this cap (*you'res, yours, your's*)?

3. _____ Sheila said the umbrella by the door was (*her, her's, hers*).

4. _____ You seem very certain of (*your, yours, you're*) opinion.

5. _____ When I opened the book, I noticed that (*its, it's, its'*) binding needed to be repaired.

6. _____ Your family's kitchen table is much larger than (*ours, our, our's*).

7. _____ The workers wanted (*they, their, theirs*) break time extended.

8. _____ I'm not sure whether this coat is Carol's or (*mines, my, mine*).

Answers are on page 226.

Object Pronouns

An **object pronoun** is used when the pronoun is not the subject of a verb.

Object Pronouns	
Singular	**Plural**
me	us
you	you
him, her, it	them

Generally, object pronouns follow a preposition or receive the action of a verb. In the following example, the pronoun *him* replaces the proper noun *Shen*. It is the object of the preposition *to*.

Please give this magazine to **Shen.**

Please give this magazine to **him.**

In the following example, the pronoun *him* replaces the noun *Robert*. In this case, Robert receives the action of the verb *hired*. The object pronoun is correct.

Mr. Schwartz hired **Robert** for the job.

Mr. Schwartz hired **him** for the job.

EDITING TIP

If a pronoun is joined to a noun in a sentence, it may not always be clear which pronoun is correct. Think of the pronoun by itself.

This book would be helpful to Rosa and *(she, her).*

This book would be helpful to **her.**

This book would be helpful to Rosa and **her.**

When two or more pronouns are joined and one is *me, me* goes last.

Incorrect: The astronomy lecture was interesting to **me and her.**

Correct: The astronomy lecture was interesting to **her and me.**

Using the wrong pronoun after the word *between* is a common error. Because it is a preposition, *between* always takes an object pronoun.

Incorrect: We can split this newspaper between **you and I.**

Correct: We can split this newspaper between **you and me.**

Directions: Choose the correct word to fill each blank.

Example: Please send the tickets to Mr. Arocha or _____me_____ (me, I).

1. The manager wants to begin regular meetings between himself and _____ (us, we).

2. The stray dog followed Arnold and _____ (she, her) all the way home.

3. The receptionist was apologetic when she spoke to _____ (me and him, him and me).

4. The clerk asked two customers, Donald and _____ (her, she), if they ever used credit cards.

5. There is certainly enough food here for you and _____ (they, them).

6. Between _____ (you and me, you and I), I think our best course of action is no action at all.

Answers are on page 226.

Reflexive Pronouns

Reflexive pronouns show action done by the subject to himself or herself.

We can finish the work by **ourselves**.

Bill left **himself** a note.

Reflexive Pronouns	
Singular	**Plural**
myself	ourselves
yourself	yourselves
himself, herself, itself	themselves

Reflexive pronouns are also used to emphasize the subject. They stress that the subject alone performed the action of the verb.

They wanted to do the work **themselves.**

Reflexive pronouns are sometimes used incorrectly in place of object or subject pronouns.

Incorrect: **Jan and myself** are painting the house.

Correct: **Jan and I** are painting the house.

Incorrect: The lawyer spoke to **Aaron and myself.**

Correct: The lawyer spoke to **Aaron and me.**

Certain forms of reflexive pronouns are also incorrect: *hisself, ourself, theirself, theirselves,* and *themself.*

EXERCISE 12

Directions: In the following sentences, underline the correct pronouns in parentheses.

Example: Stanley filled out the application (*himself*, *hisself*).

1. We planned last year's vacation (*ourself, ourselves*).

2. Lonnie and (*her, herself, she*) freeze their own vegetables every year.

3. (*I, Myself, Me*) am responsible for meeting the deadline.

4. The second-shift workers built those benches (*theirselves, themselfs, themselves*).

5. The bus driver gave Alicia and (*me, I, myself*) transfers that had already expired.

6. The Morrisons repaired the broken furnace (*themself, theirselves, themselves*).

7. Yulian made all the arrangements for the party (*her, herself, she*).

8. Gary and (*I, myself, me*) met at the mall for lunch.

Answers are on page 226.

Special Pronoun Problems

Some of the most common problems in the use of pronouns have to do with a few specific pronouns. The following guidelines will help you avoid these errors.

Who or Whom and Whoever or Whomever

These pronouns frequently cause confusion. Which words would you use in the following sentences?

> **(Who, Whom)** is that child?

> **(Who, Whom)** are you calling?

The correct choice is easier if you remember which are subject pronouns and which are object pronouns.

Subject Pronouns: who, whoever (he)

Object Pronouns: whom, whomever (him)

If you have trouble remembering when to use the subject or object pronouns, try substituting *he* and *him*. If the subject pronoun *he* works in the sentence, then use *who* or *whoever*. If the object pronoun *him* fits in the sentence, use *whom* or *whomever*.

> **(Who, Whom)** is that child?

Incorrect:	**Him** is that child.
Correct:	**He** is that child.
So:	**Who** is that child?

Rearranging the subject and verb in a question will sometimes help you make the right choice.

> **(Who, Whom)** are you calling?

> You are calling **(who, whom)**?

Incorrect:	You are calling **he**?
Correct:	You are calling **him**?
So:	**Whom** are you calling?

If the sentence is more complicated, look just at the group of words beginning with the pronoun. (You may have to rearrange the words in normal subject-verb order.)

I know that **(whoever, whomever)** the coach picks will help our team.

Rearrange: the coach picks **(whoever, whomever)**

Incorrect: the coach picks **he**

Correct: the coach picks **him**

So: I know that **whomever** the coach picks will help our team.

Pronouns After *Than* or *As*

Than and *as* are used to compare two people or two things.

Tomás walks faster **than** Marcia.

Marcia is as tall **as** Tomás.

These sentences have parts that are understood but not stated.

Tomás walks faster than Marcia *(walks)*.

Marcia is as tall as Tomás *(is tall)*.

Because part of the sentence is not stated, choosing the correct pronoun is more difficult.

Tomás walks faster than **(she, her)**.

Marcia is as tall as **(he, him)**.

To chose the right pronoun, mentally complete the sentence.

Tomás walks faster than **she** *(walks)*.

Marcia is as tall as **he** *(is tall)*.

We or *Us* Followed by a Noun

The pronouns *we* and *us* sometimes cause problems when they are followed by a noun.

Car dealers are offering better deals to **(we, us)** Americans.

To choose the correct pronoun, mentally drop the noun. Then decide which pronoun is correct. (<u>Remember</u>: *we* is a subject pronoun; *us* is an object pronoun.)

Incorrect: Car dealers are offering better deals to **we.**

Correct: Car dealers are offering better deals to **us.**

So: Car dealers are offering better deals to **us Americans.**

EXERCISE 13

Directions: Three pronouns have been underlined in each sentence. If one of them is incorrect, circle the error. Then write the correct pronoun in the blank. If there is no error, write *Correct*.

Example: *Ted and me* Nancy and he watched me and Ted do our imitation of their dancing.

1. _____ Amy is just as qualified for the job as him, but they did not promote her as quickly.

2. _____ We voters wanted both he and her to run on the ticket.

3. _____ I thought our plans were just between you and myself.

4. _____ Michael and Sarah gave we parents a chance to get away from them and their noise this weekend.

5. _____ You should pay me more than you pay Janet; I work harder than her.

6. _____ The administrators of mine company did not notify us workers of their decision.

7. _____ Would you please tell whoever Marla brings home that we will be home to greet Marla and her?

8. _____ Whomever would like to see our production should buy tickets from either Jean or her.

9. _____ After we left, I and Ted continued laughing at that joke of theirs.

10. _____ We bowlers didn't know that Franco and he had not reserved our lanes.

11. _____ Jodie and me are as excited about our trip to Florida as our husbands are.

12. _____ Manny said that he would go to the store for his mother since herself was too busy to go.

Answers are on pages 226–227.

Noun-Pronoun Agreement

Pronouns must always agree with their **antecedents.** These are the nouns or pronouns they refer to.

> **Yolanda** and **Gary** both went to work, but **she** drove a car and **he** rode a bicycle.

In this example, *she* refers to *Yolanda. Gary* is the antecedent of *he.* Each pronoun has the same characteristics as its antecedent. There are four pronoun agreement characteristics: *use, number, gender,* and *person.*

Pronoun Characteristics	
Use:	Does the pronoun function as a subject, object, possessive, or reflexive pronoun?
Number:	Is the antecedent singular or plural?
Gender:	Is the antecedent masculine, feminine, or neither?
Person:	Is the pronoun referring to the person speaking, the person spoken to, or the person spoken about?

Use

For more about how pronouns are used in their subject, object, possessive, and reflexive forms, review pages 30–37.

Number

If the pronoun refers to a singular noun (one thing or person), use a singular pronoun. If the pronoun refers to a plural noun (more than one thing or person), use a plural pronoun. Making pronouns agree with their antecedents is usually simple. However, be alert for the following situations.

1. When the pronoun replaces two or more nouns that are joined by *and,* use the plural form of the pronoun.

    Patty and Laura ate **their** meals together.

2. When the pronoun replaces two or more nouns joined by *or, nor, either … or, neither … nor,* or *not only … but also,* the pronoun should agree with the last noun in the series.

    Neither Dale nor **Gordon** likes **his** sandwich.

    Neither Nancy nor her **sisters** liked **their** sandwiches.

3. Some words always require a singular pronoun. These include all words ending in *one, body, other,* and *thing*. Some of these words look like they are plural, but they are actually all singular.

anyone	everyone	no one	someone
anybody	everybody	nobody	somebody
anything	everything	nothing	something
one	another	each	either
much	person	every	neither

Incorrect: **Everyone** should be careful of **their** health.

Correct: **Everyone** should be careful of **his or her** health.

4. Some nouns name a group of people or things. These are called **collective nouns.** Examples include the following:

audience	class	family	group
committee	jury	crowd	staff
faculty	team	band	army

Sometimes a collective noun is replaced by a singular pronoun. Sometimes it is replaced by a plural pronoun.

The jury returned **its** verdict.

The jury took **their** seats.

To decide whether a pronoun that refers to a collective noun should be plural or singular, look at the meaning of the whole sentence. Ask yourself, Is the collective noun acting as a group or individually? In the examples above, there was only one verdict, but more than one person sat down.

5. Some nouns look plural but are singular. Always use a singular pronoun to replace them. The following nouns are singular.

athletics	economics	measles	politics	news
diabetes	mathematics	mumps	physics	United States

Mathematics has **its** own set of symbols.

6. A few nouns have only a plural form even though they name only one thing. Always use a plural pronoun with these nouns.

scissors   eyeglasses   pants   trousers

I need to sharpen my **scissors** because **they** are dull.

EDITING TIP

When pair of is used with one of these types of plural nouns, use a singular pronoun. In this case, pair is the subject.

That **pair** of pants has **its** zipper broken.

Gender

Masculine Pronouns	Feminine Pronouns
he, him, his, himself	she, her, hers, herself

Incorrect:	The actress seems quite unhappy with **its** role.
Correct:	The actress seems quite unhappy with **her** role.

Certain pronouns can be used only in certain ways.

Pronoun	Usage
which	animals and things
who, whom	people only
that	people, animals, and things

Incorrect:	The waiter **which** works at Zippos is very clumsy.
Correct:	The waiter **who** works at Zippos is very clumsy.
Correct:	The waiter **that** works at Zippos is very clumsy.

Hint: If a pronoun refers to a person who may be either male or female, the pronoun should refer to both.

Incorrect:	Every baseball fan brought **their** glove.
Incorrect:	Every baseball fan brought **his** glove.
Correct:	Every baseball fan brought **his or her** glove.

Person

Pronouns change forms in order to agree with their nouns.

First person: agrees with the person or persons *speaking*

Second person: agrees with the person or persons *spoken to*

Third person: agrees with the person or persons *spoken about*

FIRST PERSON | SECOND PERSON | THIRD PERSON
I asked **you** to see **him.**

There are singular and plural forms for each person.

Singular and Plural Pronouns		
	Singular	**Plural**
First Person	I, me, my, mine	we, us, our, ours
Second Person	you, your, yours	you, your, yours
Third Person	he, she, it, him, her, it, his, her, hers, its	they, them, their, theirs

EDITING TIP

When checking pronoun agreement in a sentence, make sure the person used is consistent.

Incorrect: When you runners train, they should get enough rest.

Correct: **When you** runners train, **you** should get enough rest.

Directions: In each of the following sentences, underline the correct pronoun choice given in parentheses. Then underline its noun or pronoun antecedent twice.

Example: People who fall asleep easily should not waste (his, _their_) time on boring movies.

1. Someone who forgets to pay (his or her, their) electric bill may end up without lights.

2. The woman (which, who) plays the guitar used to play the drums.

3. When Sergeant York tells you to do something, he expects (him, you) to do it.

4. The players must have (his, their) luggage on the bus by noon.

5. Although I've had (it, them) for years, this pair of scissors is still sharp.

6. If people want to succeed in life, (you, they) must make plans now.

7. The group was sure (its, their) performance would win first prize.

8. The couple giving this party have plenty of food for (his, their) guests.

9. Frank put his sunglasses back in (its, their) case.

10. Everything must be put in (its, their) place before the guests arrive.

11. Everyone should sign (his or her, their) name to register for the workshop.

12. Politics has (its, their) own set of rules.

13. The pair of pants is missing (its, their) belt.

14. The tailor (which, who) altered the suit did an excellent job.

15. Neither Velma nor I can work any harder no matter how hard (I, we) try.

Answers are on page 227.

EXERCISE 15

Directions: Three pronouns have been underlined in each sentence. If one of them is incorrect, underline the error. Then write the correct pronoun in the blank. If there is no error, write *Correct*.

Example: *themselves* Peter and he taught ~~theirselves~~ to play basketball, and both of them became good players.

1. _____ They have a cat who is always following them.

2. _____ Us lazy people cannot understand why he works whenever the boss asks him.

3. _____ She and I told him that everyone should be well organized.

4. _____ He told us that having three jobs made his life hectic.

5. _____ Just between you and me, Sam, whoever gets this job deserves it.

6. _____ If you were him, would you want this job?

7. _____ When the United States elects its president, your vote will count as much as his.

8. _____ I left me a note so I would remember to write a letter.

9. _____ He will give a ticket to whomever wants to attend his comedy act.

10. _____ On their vacation, they sent greetings to we slaves still on the job.

11. _____ That baby showed his parents that it was ready to walk by pulling himself up to a standing position.

12. _____ She proved herself the person which is most qualified.

13. _____ They claimed the money that was on the table was theirs.

14. _____ Do you remember when you and me visited Washington, D.C.?

Answers are on page 227.

Pronouns

Directions: Choose what correction should be made to each sentence below. If you think the sentence is correct, choose option (5).

1. **They're not going to like what I have to tell them about my pet monster and it's enormous appetite.**

   (1) change *They're* to *Their*
   (2) change *them* to *they*
   (3) change *my* to *mine*
   (4) change *it's* to *its*
   (5) no correction is necessary

2. **Our friends, Alicia and her, met them at the train station and brought them to his house.**

   (1) change *Our* to *Ours*
   (2) change *her* to *she*
   (3) change *met them* to *met they*
   (4) change *her* to *him*
   (5) no correction is necessary

3. **Just between you and I, whoever takes that job will have problems working with him.**

   (1) change *you* to *your*
   (2) change *I* to *me*
   (3) change *whoever* to *whomever*
   (4) change *him* to *he*
   (5) no correction is necessary

4. **Harry wants me and you to go to the festival with him and her.**

   (1) change *me and you* to *you and me*
   (2) change *me and you* to *you and I*
   (3) change *him and her* to *he and she*
   (4) change *him and her* to *him and she*
   (5) no correction is necessary

5. **Maria and myself are building a doghouse ourselves. Then our two dogs will have a home for themselves and can stay out of ours.**

   (1) change *myself* to *me*
   (2) change *myself* to *I*
   (3) change *ourselves* to *ourselfs*
   (4) change *themselves* to *theirselves*
   (5) no correction is necessary

Answers are on page 227.

Chapter Review

Directions: Choose the <u>one best answer</u> to each question. Some of the sentences may contain errors in sentence basics. A few sentences, however, may be correct as written. Read the sentences carefully and then answer the questions based on them. For each question, choose the answer that would result in the most effective writing of the sentence or sentences.

1. **<u>While thousands of ducks</u> rose from the lake.**

   Which is the best way to write the underlined portion of the text? If the original is the best way, choose option (1).

   (1) While thousands of ducks
   (2) Because the ducks were nervous and
   (3) Feeding on seeds
   (4) Thousands of ducks
   (5) After a brief rest

2. **<u>Gave himself</u> a pepperoni pizza as a reward for his hard work.**

   Which is the best way to write the underlined portion of the text? If the original is the best way, choose option (1).

   (1) Gave himself
   (2) Jevon gave hisself
   (3) Jevon gave himself
   (4) After finishing the job
   (5) Feeling great, ate

3. **<u>Because his cold</u> was so bad.**

   Which is the best way to write the underlined portion of the text? If the original is the best way, choose option (1).

   (1) Because his cold
   (2) Because, his cold
   (3) John stayed home from work because his cold
   (4) Feverish and weak, which
   (5) A cough that

4. **During that cold <u>night around the fire.</u>**

   Which is the best way to write the underlined portion of the text? If the original is the best way, choose option (1).

   (1) night around the fire
   (2) night sitting around the fire
   (3) night, the fire kept them warm
   (4) night as the snow fell
   (5) night without any food

5. **Eric and his brother both have their own businesses. Eric replaces old roofs. His brother builds tables, chairs, and bookshelfs.**

   What correction should be made to these sentences?

   (2) change *roofs* to *rooves*
   (3) change *chairs* to *chaires*
   (4) change *bookshelfs* to *bookshelves*
   (5) no correction is necessary

6. **The zookeeper told me to be careful when returning to my car. The ferocious lions had freed themselves. Had jumped over a wall.**

   What correction should be made to these sentences?

   (1) change *me* to *I*
   (2) change *my* to *mine*
   (3) change *themselves* to *theirselves*
   (4) add the subject *They* to the last sentence
   (5) no correction is necessary

7. **As soon as he drove the car off their lot, it began coughing. People pointed at him and his car. Smoke rose from under it's hood.**

   What correction should be made to these sentences?

   (1) change *their* to *their's*
   (2) change *it* to *his*
   (3) change *him* to *he*
   (4) change *it's* to *its*
   (5) no correction is necessary

8. **Will she go to their party with he?**

   What correction should be made to this sentence?

   (1) change *she* to *her*
   (2) change *their* to *theirs*
   (3) change *their* to *they*
   (4) change *he* to *him*
   (5) no correction is necessary

9. **Carla and three of her friends went bowling. When her friend dropped a bowling ball, she yelled, "Watch out!"**

   What correction should be made to these sentences?

   (1) change *her friends* to *hers friends*
   (2) change *she* to *Carla*
   (3) add a subject before *"Watch out!"*
   (4) change the exclamation point to a period
   (5) no correction is necessary

10. **Mercedes and she were both hungry. They split a pizza between themselves. Whom do you think ate the most?**

    What correction should be made to these sentences?

    (1) change *she* to *her*
    (2) change *themselves* to *theirselves*
    (3) change *Whom* to *Who*
    (4) change the question mark to an exclamation point
    (5) no correction is necessary

11. **Fire.**

    What correction should be made to this sentence?

    (1) add a subject to the sentence
    (2) add a verb to the sentence
    (3) change the period to a question mark
    (4) change the period to an exclamation point
    (5) no correction is necessary

12. **Karen wants her son to be a basketball player. She teaches him herself. Already he shoots better than her.**

    What correction should be made to these sentences?

    (1) change the first *her* to *hers*
    (2) change *She* to *Herself*
    (3) change *him* to *he*
    (4) change the second *her* to *she*
    (5) no correction is necessary

13. **Us Americans like our cars. We know public transportation is great, but whoever can afford a car has one, sometimes two.**

    What correction should be made to these sentences?

    (1) change *Us* to *We*
    (2) change *our* to *ours*
    (3) change *We* to *Us*
    (4) change *whoever* to *whomever*
    (5) no correction is necessary

14. **Somebody lost their keys at the drugstore. The manager will give the keys to whoever claims them.**

    What correction should be made to these sentences?

    (1) change *their* to *his*
    (2) change *their* to *his or her*
    (3) change *whoever* to *whomever*
    (4) change *them* to *it*
    (5) no correction is necessary

Answers are on pages 227–228.

Evaluate Your Progress

On the following chart, circle the number of any item you answered incorrectly in the Chapter 1 Review on pages 46–49. Next to each group of item numbers, you will see the pages you can review to learn how to answer the items correctly. Pay particular attention to reviewing skill areas in which you missed half or more of the questions.

Skill Area	Chapter 1 Review Item Number	Review Pages
SENTENCE STRUCTURE		
Complete sentences, fragments, and sentence combining	1, 2, 3, 4, 6	13–18
USAGE		
Pronoun reference/ antecedent agreement	8, 9, 10, 12, 13, 14	30–47
MECHANICS		
Punctuation (commas)	11	20
Spelling (possessives, contractions, and homonyms)	5, 7	27–28

CHAPTER 2

Verbs

Types of Verbs

In Chapter 1, you learned that every sentence is made up of a subject and a predicate. The key word in the predicate is the verb. It tells what the subject *is* or *does*. Verbs are divided into two types: action verbs and linking verbs.

Action Verbs

Action verbs are verbs that tell what the subject *does*.

Paul **hunts** for his car in the huge parking lot.

Hunts is an action verb that tells what Paul does. Here, the action is physical. Other action verbs tell what mental action the subject does. These can be more difficult to identify. *Know, wish, realize,* and *hope* are common verbs that tell about mental action.

Helena **knows** where her car is parked.

Linking Verbs

Linking verbs tell what the subject *is* or link the subject with a word or words that describe it.

When Toshi **became** a father, he **felt** proud.

Note that some sentences, as in the example above, contain more than one verb. Verbs may also be made up of more than one word. *Has been* and *did run* are examples.

Sometimes the words in a verb may be separated by other words. These other words are not part of the verb. In the example below, the verb is *has watched. Always* is not part of the verb.

Harrison **has** always **watched** boxing on television.

EDITING TIP

Words in a question are often in a different order than they are in a statement. Usually, the parts of verbs are separated.

Does Julie **play** the guitar better than Juan?

EXERCISE 1

Directions: Underline all the verbs in the following sentences.

Example: Julian <u>was</u> sick, so he <u>stayed</u> home from work.

1. Sidney will come to the table when you call him.

2. Did you know that my aunt is still living in Canada?

3. When Veronica saw the picture, she was very surprised.

4. I will be coming to work early tomorrow.

5. When can you come and see my new baby?

6. During our vacation, we camped, cooked, and hiked.

7. By the time we finish this job, our boss will have found two new ones for us.

8. Can you describe the man who just left the store?

9. Although her manager rarely talked to her, Akiko liked her job.

10. Cindy has never missed an Elvis Presley movie that has been shown on television.

11. I will always be grateful that I got a good education.

12. Since she came back from her trip, Raisa has felt much more relaxed.

13. After cleaning, shopping, and fixing lunch, Ida took a nap.

14. What will it be like when we arrive in Florida, I wonder?

Answers are on page 228.

Verb Tenses

In addition to telling what something *is* or *does,* verbs also tell the time of the action.

The time shown by a verb is called its **tense.**

Simple Tenses

There are three basic or simple tenses.

Present tense:	Traci plays soccer on Wednesday.
Past tense:	Traci played soccer on Wednesday.
Future tense:	Traci will play soccer on Wednesday.

Infinitive and Base Form

Read the following sentence. Pay special attention to the underlined words.

Jim wants <u>to borrow</u> our barbecue grill.

The underlined words, *to borrow,* make up a verb form called an **infinitive.** The infinitive almost always begins with the word *to.* The verb form following *to* is called the base form. The **base form** is what you begin with when you form all verb tenses.

Simple Present Tense

Verbs in the **simple present tense** are used in three situations. First, present tense verbs tell what is happening or is true at the present time.

Andrea **gets** herself a second cup of coffee.

Second, present-tense verbs show actions that are performed regularly.

We **walk** for an hour every day.

Third, present tense-verbs tell about an action that is always true.

The Sonoran Desert **is** hot and dry.

The simple present tense is formed in three ways: base form (sometimes plus *s*), base form plus *ing*, and base form with *do* or *does*.

Base Form or Base Form plus *s*

Almost all verbs form their simple present tense from the base form of the verb or from the base form plus *s*. Study the following chart showing the simple present tense of the verb *walk*.

Simple Present Tense	
Singular	**Plural**
I walk	we walk
you walk	you walk
he, she, it walks	they walk

The only time a regular verb changes its form in the present tense is when the subject is *he, she, it,* or a singular noun. When the subject is one of these, we add *s* (or *es* if the verb ends in *s, x, ch,* or *sh*).

Pedro plays basketball every evening.

Kathy pushes the pedal to the floor.

Base Form or Base Form plus *ing*

Present Tense with *ing*		
I	am	
He, She, It	is	walking
We, You, They	are	

When the present tenses of verbs are formed in this way, they are used to tell about actions that are true now and are ongoing

I **am working** too hard.

Evelyn and John **are planning** the company picnic.

Base Form with *do* or *does*

The present tense can also be formed by combining *do* or *does* with the base form of the verb. *Do* or *does* gives added emphasis to the verb.

My dog **does eat** at the table with everyone else.

Do you **know** what time it is?

Simple Past Tense

The **simple past tense** shows actions that occurred at a specific time in the past.

> Ms. Chavez **asked** me for a ride home from work.

> I **hoped** for a promotion.

The simple past is formed by adding *ed* or *d* to the base form.

Simple Past Tense	
Singular	**Plural**
I walked	we walked
you walked	you walked
he, she, it walked	they walked

Simple Future Tense

The **simple future tense** shows an action that will occur in the future.

> I will call you tomorrow.

The simple future tense is formed by using *will* with the base form of the verb.

Simple Future Tense	
Singular	**Plural**
I will walk	we will walk
you will walk	you will walk
he, she, it will walk	they will walk

EXERCISE 2

Directions: Write the correct tense of the base form in each space. Then underline any words that gave you a clue to the correct verb tense.

Example: (open) I _____ will open _____ my birthday gifts <u>tomorrow,</u>

1. (call)   We _____ your daughter yesterday.

2. (wait)   Stan _____ for his children every afternoon after school.

3. (move)   The Rosellos _____ to Columbus two years ago.

4. (enjoy)   I always _____ a good mystery book.

5. (work)   Mrs. Haynes _____ on your furnace next week.

6. (happen) What _____ to you last night?

7. (demand) Today consumers _____ higher-quality products than in the past.

8. (end)   You _____ your study of the Constitution next Tuesday.

9. (own)   Simon now _____ a car and a pickup truck.

10. (talk)   We _____ about you for hours yesterday.

11. (discuss) They _____ the issue tomorrow.

12. (park)   Marissa _____ her car at the airport last Sunday.

13. (answer) Martin _____ the phone after the third ring last night.

14. (smile)   You _____ when you open your gift next Tuesday.

Answers are on page 228.

Principal Parts of Verbs

As you have learned, there are three simple verb tenses: the past, present, and future tenses. In addition to these simple tenses, there are perfect verb tenses. To understand the perfect tenses, you must understand the principal parts of verbs. These parts are used to form the perfect tenses.

The three principal parts of verbs are the base, past, and past participle.

The following chart shows the three principal parts, or forms, of the verb *help*.

Principal Parts of Verbs		
Base	**Past**	**Past Participle**
help	helped	helped

The base form is used to form the simple present and simple future tenses. The past form is used to form the simple past tense. The past participle form is used to form the perfect tenses, which you will learn about on pages 61–62.

Regular Verbs

Regular verbs are verbs that form their past and past participle forms in a regular, or predictable, way. The majority of verbs are regular verbs.

Most regular verbs form the past and past participle by adding *ed* to the base. If the verb ends with an *e* only a *d* is added. In some cases, the final consonant is doubled. If the regular verb ends in a consonant plus *y*, the *y* is changed to *i* before *ed* is added. Here are examples:

Examples of Regular Verbs		
Base	**Past**	**Past Participle**
walk	walked	walked
praise	praised	praised
stop	stopped	stopped
reply	replied	replied

Irregular Verbs

Verbs that do not form their past and past participle forms by simply adding *ed* are called **irregular verbs.** There are no simple rules for forming the irregular forms of verbs. You will, however, notice patterns. You have to memorize the spellings of the principal parts of these verbs.

EDITING TIP

When you look up an irregular verb in the dictionary, look up the base form. The past and past participle forms will be given for irregular verbs.

Three irregular verbs are so common and so important they need special attention.

Have, Do, and Be			
Base	**Present**	**Past**	**Past Participle**
have	has, have	had	had
do	do, does	did	done
be	am, is, are	was, were	been

The following list gives the principal parts of common irregular verbs. Some verbs have more than one correct form for some parts.

Common Irregular Verbs		
Base	**Past**	**Past Participle**
awake	awoke, awaked	awaked, awoken
become	became	become
bend	bent	bent
bet	bet	bet
bid	bid	bid
bind	bound	bound
bite	bit	bitten
blow	blew	blown
build	built	built
burst	burst	burst
buy	bought	bought
cast	cast	cast
catch	caught	caught
cost	cost	cost
creep	crept	crept
cut	cut	cut
deal	dealt	dealt
dig	dug	dug

Common Irregular Verbs		
Base	**Past**	**Past Participle**
draw	drew	drawn
dream	dreamed, dreamt	dreamed, dreamt
drive	drove	driven
fall	fell	fallen
feed	fed	fed
feel	felt	felt
fight	fought	fought
find	found	found
fly	flew	flown
forget	forgot	forgotten
keep	kept	kept
lay	laid	laid
lead	led	led
leave	left	left
lend	lent	lent
lie	lay	lain
lose	lost	lost
make	made	made
mean	meant	meant
meet	met	met
pay	paid	paid
prove	proved	proved, proven
put	put	put
read	read	read
rid	rid	rid
ride	rode	ridden
rise	rose	risen
say	said	said
sell	sold	sold
send	sent	sent
set	set	set
shake	shook	shaken
shine	shone, shined	shone, shined
shoot	shot	shot
sit	sat	sat
sleep	slept	slept
spend	spent	spent
spin	spun	spun
stand	stood	stood
strike	struck	struck
swear	swore	sworn
teach	taught	taught
tell	told	told
think	thought	thought
throw	threw	thrown
understand	understood	understood

EXERCISE 3

Directions: Write the correct form of the verb in the blank. The base form is given in parentheses.

Example: Our house _shook_ violently during last week's earthquake. *(shake)*

1. Brian _____ out the runner trying to steal second. *(throw)*

2. The rain _____ as soon as it hits the pavement. *(freeze)*

3. Please _____ this package to the delivery person. *(give)*

4. I didn't know what she _____ when she said she was skating home. *(mean)*

5. Jill's babies _____ tightly to her when she left home. *(cling)*

6. Dilip is the most helpful real estate agent I have ever _____ with. *(deal)*

7. Anna _____ another tale of horror for her young listeners as they squirmed in their seats. *(spin)*

8. If you value your life, don't _____ that can on the table. *(set)*

9. Ms. Tso _____ to the judge that she was telling the truth. *(swear)*

10. Javier leaped excitedly as he _____ the huge fish ashore. *(pull)*

11. The bread dough had _____ after a few hours. *(rise)*

12. I _____ I won the lottery. *(dream)*

13. He _____ the balloon with a pin. *(burst)*

14. Mr. Hanley was _____ by a dog. *(bite)*

Answers are on page 229.

The Perfect Tenses

The simple tenses divide time into the three natural periods: the past, present, and future. Verbs also have three perfect tenses: the present perfect, past perfect, and future perfect. Two of the perfect tenses are actually special forms of the past tense. The other perfect tense is a special form of the future tense.

The **perfect tenses** tell that an action has been completed before a certain time or will be continuing to a certain time.

Although you may think of the past as one time, there are actually three levels of past tenses. You already know about the simple past tense. The other two types of past tense are the present perfect and the past perfect.

Present Perfect Tense

The **present perfect tense** tells that an action was started in the past and is continuing in the present or has just been completed.

> Pat **has waited** for the bus since three o'clock.

> I **have walked** the entire way home.

Form the present perfect tense of regular verbs by adding either *has* or *have* to the past participle of the main verb.

Present Perfect Tense	
he, she, it	has waited
I, you, we, they	have waited

Past Perfect Tense

The **past perfect tense** tells that an action was completed in the past before another event or before a certain time in the past.

> Pat **had waited** for the bus for ten minutes before we arrived.

Form the past perfect tense of regular verbs by adding *had* to the past participle of the main verb.

Past Perfect Tense	
I, you, he, she, it, we, they	had waited

Future Perfect Tense

There are two levels or types of verbs in the future tense. You already know about the simple future. It tells what will happen in the future. The other future tense is the future perfect tense.

The **future perfect tense** shows an action that will be completed by a specific time in the future.

Pat **will have waited** ten minutes by the time we get there.

Form the future perfect tense of regular verbs by adding *will have* to the past participle of the main verb.

Future Perfect Tense	
I, you, he, she, it, we, they	will have waited

EXERCISE 4

Directions: In each of the blanks below, write the correct form of the verb in parentheses. These sentences review all six of the verb tenses: present, past, future, present perfect, past perfect, and future perfect.

Example: Ms. Luna _will explain_ the new procedure next week. (*explain*)

1. In two more weeks, I _____ my class. (*begin*)

2. A cup of tea with lunch always _____ good to me. (*taste*)

3. Frank _____ a lot of pictures before he discovered that his camera battery was dead. (*take*)

4. Jose and Molly _____ more than twenty miles by the time they finish the race. (*swim*)

5. As I _____ before, I'm not going to be talked into taking the first offer I get. (*say*)

6. Since last Tuesday, Sachi _____ the lines for the first act of the play. (*memorize*)

7. Curtis didn't reach the landlady until he _____ six times. (*try*)

8. Bill Killian _____ the train to work every day since last March. (*ride*)

9. Alexander Graham Bell _____ the telephone. (*invent*)

Answers are on page 229.

Subjunctive Mood

The **subjunctive mood** is a verb form used in three situations: in commands, to express urgency, and to express wishes or a condition that is contrary to fact.

When used for commands or to express urgency, the subjunctive is formed in two ways.

1. Use the base form of the verb. Do not add an *s* to the end of the verb.

    Be careful. *(command)*

    It is important that Lee **complete** this questionnaire. *(urgency)*

2. Use the verb *be* plus the past participle of the main verb.

    Mr. Chino insists that this project **be finished** today. *(urgency)*

To express wishes or something that is contrary to fact, the subjunctive is formed using *were*. *Were* may be used by itself or with the infinitive, past participle, or the *ing* form of the main verb.

If I **were** taller, I could dunk the ball.

If we **were to leave,** we would never know what happened.

If you **were elected** president, would you name me to the Supreme Court?

If he **were lying,** do you think he could keep a straight face?

EXERCISE 5

Directions: Underline the correct verb in parentheses in the following sentences.

Example: If I *(was, were)* a fast runner, I would enter that 10K race.

1. It is necessary that the runner *(complete, completes)* the entire form.

2. If I *(was, were)* stronger, I would run a marathon.

3. It is important that lots of water *(is drunk, be drunk)*.

4. If Naoshi *(was, were)* to see me in this race, he would be surprised.

5. The rules require that every runner *(pay, pays)* a small fee.

Answers are on page 229.

Active and Passive Voice

When a sentence is written in the **active voice,** the subject performs the action. When a sentence is written in the **passive voice,** the subject is acted upon.

Active: LeRoi poured the pancake batter onto the grill.

Passive: Steaming hot pancakes were served to the customer.

The first sentence is in the active voice. The subject, *LeRoi,* performs the action of pouring. The second sentence is in the passive voice. The subject, *pancakes,* is acted upon by being served.

Sentences in the passive voice can be written in any tense. To write regular verbs in the passive voice, use a form of the verb *be* and the past participle.

Passive Voice		
Present	I am he, she, it is we, you, they are	
Past	I, he, she, it was we, you, they were	shocked
Future	I, you, he, she, it, we, they will be	

EXERCISE 6

Directions: Rewrite each of the following passive voice sentences in the active voice.

Example: That wedding dress was worn by my grandmother sixty years ago.

My grandmother wore that wedding dress sixty years ago.

1. The old house was deserted by my grandparents.

   _____

2. The doorway is hidden by large shrubs.

   _____

3. The cellar door was jammed shut by that fallen tree.

   _____

4. The old house will be torn down by the wrecking crew.

   _____

Answers are on page 229.

Sequence of Verb Tenses

Remember that verb tenses are used to show when an action takes place. As you write, use the correct tenses so your reader is not confused. Do not change tenses within a sentence or between sentences unless it is necessary to show a change in the time of the actions.

Incorrect: Amy **picked** up the keys and **walks** to the door.

Correct: Amy **picks** up the keys and **walks** to the door.

Correct: Amy **picked** up the keys and **walked** to the door.

Sometimes a change in tense is necessary to show that two actions occur at different times.

Abraham Lincoln **had been** (past perfect) a senator before he **became** (simple past) president.

EDITING TIP

When trying to decide if two actions occur at the same or different times, look for clues. In the sentence above, for example, the word *before* signals that one event came before the other. Other clues to time include words like *now, yesterday, after, while, next, then,* and *when.*

EXERCISE 7

Directions: In each blank, write the correct form of the verb in parentheses.

Example: Before Yolanda (come) ____*came*____ to see me, she (go) ____*had gone*____ to the bakery.

1. Last year Lauren always (ride) _____ the bus to work, but now she always (ride) _____ her bike.

2. After we (buy) _____ a gas stove, we (discover) _____ we did not have a gas hookup.

3. Our company (begin) _____ a new hiring policy last month while I (be) _____ on vacation.

4. Jason (finish) _____ the book by the time class (begin) _____ next week.

5. Audrey (sweat) _____ when she (return) _____ from carrying the box of books up two flights of stairs.

6. I (hope) _____ that when you testified you (give) _____ the correct information.

Answers are on page 229.

Types of Verbs and Verb Tenses

Directions: Choose what correction should be made to each sentence below. If you think the sentence is correct, choose option (5).

1. **Javier crossed the finish line after John arrives at the track.**

   (1) change *crossed* to *will have crossed*
   (2) change *crossed* to *had crossed*
   (3) change *arrives* to *had arrived*
   (4) change *arrives* to *has arrived*
   (5) no correction is necessary

2. **Scientists will study Jupiter when the satellite reachs the planet.**

   (1) change *will study* to *study*
   (2) change *will study* to *studied*
   (3) change *reachs* to *reaches*
   (4) change *reachs* to *will reach*
   (5) no correction is necessary

3. **Before the lawyer asked any questions, the witness had swore she would tell the truth.**

   (1) change *asked* to *asks*
   (2) change *had swore* to *had sworn*
   (3) change *had swore* to *swears*
   (4) change *would tell* to *tells*
   (5) no correction is necessary

4. **Yolanda had written the address on a slip of paper while she stood at the station.**

   (1) change *had written* to *had wrote*
   (2) change *had written* to *writes*
   (3) change *had written* to *wrote*
   (4) change *stood* to *stands*
   (5) no correction is necessary

5. **It is important that Sid connects the wires properly or the battery will go dead.**

   (1) change *connects* to *connect*
   (2) change *will go* to *went*
   (3) change *will go* to *goes*
   (4) change *will go* to *will have gone*
   (5) no correction is necessary

6. **Maya exchange the purple skirt for a white one so that she could wear more blouses with it.**

   (1) change *exchange* to *exchanged*
   (2) change *exchange* to *will exchange*
   (3) change *could wear* to *has worn*
   (4) change *could wear* to *wore*
   (5) no correction is necessary

7. **After Ted gets his tax return, he bought a computer.**

   (1) change *gets* to *will get*
   (2) change *gets* to *get*
   (3) change *bought* to *will buy*
   (4) change *bought* to *buy*
   (5) no correction is necessary

8. **When Thelma was given a promotion, she will thank her boss.**

   (1) change *was given* to *gave*
   (2) change *was given* to *give*
   (3) change *will thank* to *thanks*
   (4) change *will thank* to *thanked*
   (5) no correction is necessary

Answers are on pages 229–230.

Subject-Verb Agreement

Besides knowing how to make verb tenses agree, you also need to know how to make verbs and subjects agree.

Simple Subjects

The key to making subjects and verbs agree is to look at the **simple subject**. (Remember that the simple subject is the noun or pronoun that the sentence is about.) Then look at the verb. If the simple subject is singular, the verb must also be singular. If the simple subject is plural, the verb must also be plural. How would you correct these sentences?

> Juan leap up the stairs.

> The birds flies to the feeder.

In the first sentence, the simple subject is *Juan,* a singular noun. *Leap* is the plural form of the verb, so use the singular verb *leaps*.

> Juan **leaps** up the stairs.

In the second sentence, the simple subject is *birds,* a plural noun. To correct this sentence, you must change the singular verb *flies* to the plural verb *fly*. Another way to correct this sentence would be to change the plural noun *birds* to the singular noun *bird*.

> The birds **fly** to the feeder.

> The bird **flies** to the feeder.

To check whether you have correctly matched subjects and verbs in a sentence, replace the subject noun with a pronoun. The pronoun helps you see what is correct. Look at the pattern below.

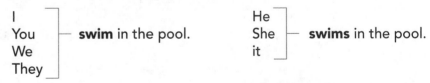

I
You
We
They
} — **swim** in the pool.

He
She
it
} — **swims** in the pool.

Adding an *s* or an *es* to a present-tense verb makes it agree with the singular pronouns *he, she,* and *it,* as well as with all singular nouns that they replace.

Special Problems with Linking Verbs

Linking verbs can cause confusion in subject-verb agreement. For example, which of the following is correct?

Our best hope **is** our children.

Our best hope **are** our children.

If you're not sure, find the simple subject of the sentence—*hope.* Since *hope* is singular, it should be used with the singular verb form *is.*

Our best hope **is** our children.

EXERCISE 8

Directions: Find the simple subject in each sentence and underline it once. Then choose the correct verb form in parentheses and underline it twice.

Example: The women across the street (*is*, *are*) my aunts.

1. Those fish (*has*, *have*) been jumping since we got here.

2. Our problem (*is*, *are*) getting the tent set up.

3. We in the jury (*believe*, *believes*) he is innocent.

4. My muscles (*ache*, *aches*) from all the exercise.

5. The security guards at the store (*want*, *wants*) a raise.

6. I (*come*, *comes*) to all my son's baseball games.

7. The order (*include*, *includes*) paper clips, folders, and tape.

8. My favorite movie (*is*, *are*) The African Queen.

9. Michiko's three huge dogs (*pull*, *pulls*) her helplessly along.

10. The price of those strawberries (*seem*, *seems*) awfully high.

Answers are on page 230.

Compound Subjects

Sentences can have two or more nouns or pronouns as their subject. These are called **compound subjects**, and they can cause confusion in subject-verb agreement. Are the following sentences correct?

Alicia and Patrick buy tickets to every concert.

Alicia or Patrick buys tickets to every concert.

Both sentences are correct. To decide which verb form to use, look at how the parts of the compound subject are connected. In the sample sentences, they are connected by *and* and *or*.

When a compound subject is connected by *and*, the subject is plural. Use the present-tense verb that does not end in *s*.

Incorrect: Juanita and George plays tennis every week.

Correct: Juanita and George play tennis every week.

Words such as *or* and *neither … nor* split the parts of a compound subject. Each noun or pronoun in the compound subject is considered separately. The verb agrees with the part closer to it.

Neither Helen nor Maria **wants** to go to the game.

Either David or the twins **take** the dog for a walk.

EXERCISE 9

Directions: Underline the correct verb in each sentence.

Example: Either Sarah or her two children (*does*, <u>*do*</u>) the dishes.

1. Mr. Fletcher and Ms. Ortega (*were*, *was*) a good sales team.

2. Not only three books but also a new CD (*appear*, *appears*) on my son's Christmas list.

3. My favorite lunch (*are*, *is*) fruit and cheese.

4. Neither the twins nor Jeffrey (*plan*, *plans*) to go to the reunion.

5. Either Veronica or they (*has*, *have*) the keys to my apartment.

6. My roommate and best friend, Mitch, often (*give*, *gives*) parties.

7. My car and Stan's pickup (*is*, *are*) in the repair shop.

8. Zelda, Pearl, and Tonya (*complain*, *complains*) constantly.

Answers are on page 230.

Interrupters

Many sentences look more complicated than they really are because they have interrupting phrases. An **interrupting phrase** is a group of words that comes between the simple subject and the verb. Because of these interrupters, it's easy to make an error in subject-verb agreement. Many interrupters are prepositional phrases.

The building **with the white shutters** needs painting.

A **prepositional phrase** is a word group that starts with a preposition and ends with a noun or pronoun. The prepositional phrase can be removed, and the sentence will still be complete.

A **preposition** is a word that connects a noun with another part of the sentence. There are many of them in English. Here are a few.

Some Common Prepositions			
above	by	into	through
at	for	near	to
before	from	of	under
between	in	on	with

When you write a sentence with a prepositional phrase, use these three steps to make sure the subject and verb agree.

1. Draw a line through any prepositional phrases.

    My mother's biscuits and barbecued chicken ~~off my father's grill~~ *(is, are)* my favorite foods.

2. Find the simple subject.

    My mother's **biscuits and** barbecued **chicken** ~~off my father's grill~~ *(is, are)* my favorite foods.

3. Choose the verb that agrees with the subject.

    My mother's **biscuits and** barbecued **chicken** ~~off my father's grill~~ **are** my favorite foods.

A special group of words can make interrupting prepositional phrases especially troublesome. These are words that seem to make the subject plural. Actually, they introduce an interrupting phrase.

as well as	besides	including	together with
along with	in addition to	like	

These words usually introduce phrases that are set off by commas. Treat the phrase as an interrupter, not as part of the subject.

My **sister**, along with my brother, **likes** horror movies.

Inverted Sentences

In most sentences, the subject comes first and is followed by the verb. Sometimes, however, the subject and verb are reversed, or inverted. **Inverted sentences** can cause confusion in subject-verb agreement. Which of the following is correct?

In her hand **is** two red roses.

In her hand **are** two red roses.

Notice that this sentence begins with a prepositional phrase, *in her hand*. The phrase is followed by the verb and the subject comes last. Often, it is easier to figure out correct subject-verb agreement in an inverted sentence by rephrasing it in normal order.

Two red roses **is** in her hand.

Two red roses **are** in her hand.

Now it is easy to see that the subject is *roses* and the correct verb is *are*.

Sentences Beginning with *Here* and *There*
Sentences beginning with *here* and *there* can also be confusing. Which of the following sentences is correct?

Here **is** my new car.   Here **are** my new car.

Neither *here* nor *there* is a noun or pronoun, so they cannot be the subject of a sentence. You know, then, that this is an inverted sentence. Rearrange the sentence in normal subject-verb order. Then choose the verb.

My car **is** here.   My car **are** here.

Car is a singular subject, so it takes the singular verb *is*.

EXERCISE 10

Directions: Underline the correct verb in parentheses.

Example: On top of the suitcase (is, <u>are</u>) my tennis shoes.

1. At the end of the dusty road (stand, stands) two old water pumps.

2. There (is, are) no clues to tell who the robber is.

3. Antonio, along with his two sons, (waits, wait) beneath the tree.

4. Across the front windows (stretch, stretches) a yellow ribbon.

5. Three lost dogs, including my collie, (walk, walks) into the yard.

6. Here (is, are) my old hiking boots.

7. Later in the day, the clouds in the west (grow, grows) thick and dark.

8. Why (do, does) those two dead plants still sit on your desk?

Answers are on page 230.

Clauses

Another group of words that often causes problems in subject-verb agreement is a clause. A **clause** is a group of words that contains a subject and a verb. Sentences often contain more than one clause.

An article **that explains the scandals** appears in today's newspaper.

When a sentence has more than one clause, you must be careful to identify which verb goes with which subject. When you're not sure, draw a line under the interrupting clause. Then check the subject-verb agreement in the main sentence and also in the clause.

In the sample sentence, *article* is the main subject of the sentence and should agree with the verb *appears*. *That explains the scandals* is a clause. *That* is a pronoun and goes with the verb *explains*.

Errors in subject-verb agreement are often caused by the pronouns that introduce interrupting clauses. Many pronouns, you recall, can be either singular or plural, depending on the nouns they replace. *That, who,* and *which* are examples. To be sure subject-verb agreement is correct, you need to know if the pronoun refers to a plural or a singular noun.

Kyoko is one of those people who love to read mystery novels.

In the sample sentence, the clause is *who love to read mystery novels*. The verb of the main sentence is, which agrees with the simple subject, *Kyoko*. The verb in the clause is *love* and its subject is *who*. In this sentence, *who* replaces *people,* a plural noun. *Love* is a plural verb, so the subject and verb do agree.

EXERCISE 11

Directions: In each of the sentences below, underline the correct verb form in parentheses.

Example: Do you know the woman who *(is, are)* selling those plants?

1. Molly is one of those people who *(argue, argues)* about everything.

2. Pak is taking all the orders that *(is, are)* placed this morning.

3. He has two lamps that *(need, needs)* new shades.

4. The solution, which *(seems, seem)* quite simple, is to hire more help.

5. Larry reads books that *(require, requires)* a lot of concentration.

6. The speakers have suggested a plan that *(appear, appears)* to be logical.

7. My niece is one of those children who *(love, loves)* being outdoors.

8. June's office has several computers that *(are, is)* no longer needed.

9. This childproof cap is one of many useful inventions that *(drive, drives)* me crazy.

10. The two brothers, who *(like, likes)* to go fishing, usually go to Beck Lake.

11. The answer, which *(appear, appears)* to be correct, is, in fact, incorrect.

12. Mr. Lee, who has several tables and chairs to refinish for his customers, *(plan, plans)* to finish them by Tuesday.

13. His nephews, who *(arrive, arrives)* next week, plan to meet Don at Metro Airport at noon.

Answers are on pages 230–231.

Special Agreement Problems

Singular Subjects that Seem Plural

One of the most common mistakes in subject-verb agreement is caused by a certain group of pronouns. They look plural but are really singular. Which sentence is correct?

Everybody on the team win.   Everybody on the team wins.

Everybody seems to refer to all people. So it's plural, right? No. What it really says is *every body,* and *body* is singular. The correct sentence is the second one, which has the singular verb *wins.* All of the following pronouns are singular.

Singular Pronouns		
another	either	no one
anybody	everybody	nothing
anyone	everyone	one
anything	everything	somebody
each	neither	someone
each one	nobody	

Here's a way you can easily remember most of these words. Look at the second part of the words. The words *one, thing,* and *body* are all singular. The words they are part of are also singular.

EDITING TIP

Many of these pronouns are often followed by a prepositional phrase. Remember to ignore the interrupting phrase when deciding on the correct verb.

Neither of the whales **is** happy living in the tank.

Each of those sharks **weighs** more than 500 pounds.

Subjects that Are Always Plural

Just as some pronouns are always singular, some are always plural.

Plural Pronouns	
both	many
few	several

I liked these books. **Both** are science fiction.

Lots of people like Lovecraft's books. **Many** have all his books.

Some nouns are always plural even though they seem to be one thing. They always take a plural verb.

Nouns That Are Always Plural		
clothes	eyeglasses	trousers
pants	scissors	

Your **clothes** are all over the house!

Those **scissors look** very sharp.

Subjects that Can Be Singular or Plural

Certain subjects can be either singular or plural, depending on their meaning in a sentence.

Words That Are Either Singular or Plural		
all	any	more
most	none	part
some	half (and other fractions)	

When these words refer to a singular noun, they take a singular verb. In the following examples, *some* refers to *cake,* which is singular. *Half* refers to *game,* which is singular.

Some of the cake **is** gone.

Half of the game **remains.**

When these words refer to a plural noun, they take a plural verb. In the following examples, *some* refers to the plural noun *people. Half* refers to the plural noun *children.*

Some of the **people** have left.

Half of the **children** arrive late.

Collective Nouns

A **collective noun** names a whole group of people or things. It may be either singular or plural. The following chart shows examples of common collective nouns.

Collective Nouns		
audience	band	class
club	collection	committee
corporation	crowd	faculty
family	group	jury
number	staff	team

A collective noun is singular when it refers to the group as a single unit. Then it takes a singular verb. The collective noun is plural when it refers to individual members of the group. Then it takes a plural verb.

The **band plays** its first concert tonight.

The **band tune** their instruments.

In the first example, the band, as a unit, plays the concert. The verb is singular. In the second sentence, each member of the band tunes his or her own instrument. The verb is plural.

EXERCISE 12

Directions: Underline the correct verb in parentheses in each sentence.

Example: One of the most popular diets (*stress, stresses*) the importance of exercise.

1. Everyone in these offices (*ride, rides*) the bus to work.

2. Most of the meat (*are, is*) grilled.

3. Everything in those shops (*look, looks*) expensive.

4. Unfortunately, this crowd (*laugh, laughs*) at all the comedian's jokes.

5. None of the voters (*are, is*) happy with any of the candidates.

6. Of all the restaurants, few (*serve, serves*) good Mexican food.

7. Each bill and coin (*was, were*) counted carefully.

8. Of all the people in the building, half (*is, are*) sick with the flu.

Answers are on page 231.

Subject-Verb Agreement

Directions: Choose what correction should be made to each sentence below. If you think the sentence is correct, choose option (5).

1. **Shen and Mike plan to visit the National Air and Space Museum, which is part of the Smithsonian Institution. Neither of them want to miss the historic airplanes. The collection includes many famous planes.**

   (1) change *plan* to *plans*
   (2) change *is* to *are*
   (3) change *want* to *wants*
   (4) change *includes* to *include*
   (5) no correction is necessary

2. **Rosa, along with her sister, jump out of the stalled car and walks the rest of the way home. The sisters, who get there at the same time, rush through the front door.**

   (1) change *jump* to *jumps*
   (2) change *walks* to *walk*
   (3) change *get* to *gets*
   (4) change *rush* to *rushes*
   (5) no correction is necessary

3. **Everybody says mass transit is a good idea. Many use the buses and trains we have. Neither Sachi nor Andrew have ever been on a bus, however.**

   (1) change *says* to *say*
   (2) change *is* to *are*
   (3) change *use* to *uses*
   (4) change *have ever been* to *has ever been*
   (5) no correction is necessary

4. **John and Sarah Kelly have all the food. This barbecue, which they planned, starts the moment they arrive. Here is the Kelly family now.**

   (1) change *have* to *has*
   (2) change *starts* to *start*
   (3) change *arrive* to *arrives*
   (4) change *is* to *are*
   (5) no correction is necessary

5. **Here is your tickets. When the band plays tonight, it will be before a full house. José and Kathy, as well as the Tucker family, seem eager to hear it. Everyone wants to hear this hot band.**

   (1) change *is* to *are*
   (2) change *plays* to *play*
   (3) change *seem* to *seems*
   (4) change *wants* to *want*
   (5) no correction is necessary

6. **The choir, which perform its first concert tonight, is quite excited. Everybody says it will sing well.**

   (1) change *perform* to *performs*
   (2) change *is* to *are*
   (3) change *says* to *say*
   (4) change *will sing* to *sang*
   (5) no correction is necessary

7. **Jed, along with his brother Thomas, run ten miles a day. They plan to compete in the marathon and win.**

   (1) change *run* to *runs*
   (2) change *plan* to *plans*
   (3) change *compete* to *competed*
   (4) change *win* to *will win*
   (5) no correction is necessary

8. **The committee, which meets every Friday, decide the company's policies and how to carry them out.**

   (1) change *meets* to *meet*
   (2) change *meets* to *would have met*
   (3) change *decide* to *decides*
   (4) change *carry* to *carries*
   (5) no correction is necessary

   Answers are on page 231.

Chapter Review

Directions: Choose the <u>one best answer</u> to each question. Some of the sentences may contain errors in verb form and agreement. A few sentences, however, may be correct as written. Read the sentences carefully and then answer the questions based on them. For each question, choose the answer that would result in the most effective writing of the sentence or sentences.

1. **The security guard who walks the long halls is exhausted at the end of his shift.**

   What correction should be made to this sentence?

   (1) change *walks* to *walked*
   (2) change *walks* to *had walked*
   (3) change *is exhausted* to *are exhausted*
   (4) change *is exhausted* to *had been exhausted*
   (5) no correction is necessary

2. **The computer class will start next week. Everyone who is interested in computers are welcome. A fee of $25.00 has been set.**

   What correction should be made to these sentences?

   (1) change *will start* to *will have started*
   (2) change *who is* to *who are*
   (3) change *are welcome* to *is welcome*
   (4) change *has been* to *was*
   (5) no correction is necessary

3. **Lucinda arrived at the store after the sale has ended.**

   What correction should be made to these sentences?

   (1) change *arrived* to *has arrived*
   (2) change *arrived* to *arrive*
   (3) change *has ended* to *had ended*
   (4) change *has ended* to *ends*
   (5) no correction is necessary

4. **Somebody whom I do not know send me a birthday card every year.**

   What correction should be made to this sentence?

   (1) change *do not know* to *does not know*
   (2) change *do not know* to *do not knows*
   (3) change *send* to *will send*
   (4) change *send* to *sends*
   (5) no correction is necessary

5. **Ana had given the package to Curtis while they stood at the door talking.**

   What correction should be made to this sentence?

   (1) change *had given* to *had give*
   (2) change *had given* to *gave*
   (3) change *stood* to *have stood*
   (4) change *stood* to *stand*
   (5) no correction is necessary

6. **Everybody says athletics are a great way to stay healthy. Something that results in bruises and broken bones does not seem healthy to me.**

   What correction should be made to these sentences?

   (1) change *says* to *say*
   (2) change *are* to *is*
   (3) change *results* to *result*
   (4) change *does not seem* to *do not seem*
   (5) no correction is necessary

7. **It is necessary that the club manager signs this contract or the band will quit.**

   What correction should be made to this sentence?

   (1) change *is* to *will be*
   (2) change *signs* to *sign*
   (3) change *will quit* to *will have quit*
   (4) change *will quit* to *quits*
   (5) no correction is necessary

8. **Sonia, along with her two little brothers, were given tickets to the game.**

   What correction should be made to this sentence?

   (1) change *were given* to *were give*
   (2) change *were given* to *was given*
   (3) change *were given* to *are give*
   (4) change *were given* to *were gave*
   (5) no correction is necessary

9. **Shawna has overslept. She hurries to leave so she will not be late for work. Her little daughter has hid her car keys.**

   What correction should be made to these sentences?

   (1) change *has overslept* to *had overslept*
   (2) change *hurries* to *had hurried*
   (3) change *will not be* to *is not*
   (4) change *has hid* to *has hidden*
   (5) no correction is necessary

10. **Not only Maya but also her two cousins lives in those apartments. Maya moved in last September, after she had taken the job at the bank.**

    What correction should be made to these sentences?

    (1) change *lives* to *live*
    (2) change *lives* to *has lived*
    (3) change *moved* to *has moved*
    (4) change *had taken* to *had took*
    (5) no correction is necessary

11. **Before the amusement park had opened, neither Martha nor Kim had ever seen such a large roller coaster.**

    What correction should be made to these sentences?

    (1) change *had opened* to *have opened*
    (2) change *had opened* to *opened*
    (3) change *had ever seen* to *had ever saw*
    (4) change *had ever seen* to *have ever seen*
    (5) no correction is necessary

12. **The jury do not look happy as they enter the courtroom. They stand as the judge takes her place.**

    What correction should be made to these sentences?

    (1) change *do not look* to *does not look*
    (2) change *enter* to *enters*
    (3) change *stand* to *have stood*
    (4) change *stand* to *will stand*
    (5) no correction is necessary

13. **Simon stoops to pick up the broken plate, and his eyeglasses slips down his nose.**

    What correction should be made to this sentence?

    (1) change *stoops* to *stoop*
    (2) change *stoops* to *has stooped*
    (3) change *slips* to *slip*
    (4) change *slips* to *had slipped*
    (5) no correction is necessary

14. **Beside the new garage rests three tired carpenters. They will be going home when the work is done.**

    What correction should be made to these sentences?

    (1) change *rests* to *rest*
    (2) change *will be going* to *went*
    (3) change *is done* to *was done*
    (4) change *is done* to *will be done*
    (5) no correction is necessary

Answers are on pages 231–232.

Evaluate Your Progress

On the following chart, circle the number of any item you answered incorrectly in the Chapter 2 Review on pages 78–79. Next to each group of item numbers, you will see the pages you can review to learn how to answer the items correctly. Pay particular attention to reviewing skill areas in which you missed half or more of the questions.

Skill Area	Chapter 2 Review Item Number	Review Pages
USAGE		
Subject-verb agreement 13, 14	1, 2, 4, 6, 8, 10, 12,	67–77
Verb tense/form	3, 5, 7, 9, 11	53–66

CHAPTER 3

Modifiers

Adjectives and Adverbs

Nouns and verbs give sentences their main structure. They tell you what the sentence is about and what is happening. By themselves, though, nouns and verbs make language pretty dull. Modifiers give language color. Read the following paragraph. The words in boldface are modifiers. Notice what they add to the writing.

> One of nature's **worst** storms moved **slowly** toward the **unprotected** land. **Worried** people were preparing for **this** hurricane. It would hurl **powerful** winds and **mountainous** waves at them. **Already, gigantic** waves were beating **savagely** against **that** shore. **One** town was **nearly empty. Wisely**, its people had run toward **higher** land **far away** from the **dangerous sea.**

Modifiers are words that describe other words in a sentence. There are two kinds of modifiers: adjectives and adverbs.

Adjectives

Adjectives are words that modify, or describe, a noun or pronoun.

An adjective can modify a noun in several ways. It can tell *what kind, which one,* or *how many.*

what kind	⟶	**worst** storms	**mountainous** waves
which one	⟶	**this** hurricane	**that** shore
how many	⟶	**one** town	

Often a noun is modified by more than one adjective.

safer, higher land

Adverbs

Adverbs are words that modify, or describe, a verb, an adjective, or another adverb.

modifying a verb	⟶	moved **slowly**
modifying an adjective	⟶	**already** gigantic
modifying an adverb	⟶	**far** away

Adverbs can modify words in several ways. They can tell *how, when* or *how often, where*, and *to what extent*.

how	⟶	moved **slowly**
when	⟶	**already** gigantic
where	⟶	land **far** away
to what extent	⟶	**nearly** empty

EDITING TIP

To figure out whether a modifier is an adjective or an adverb, look for the word it modifies.

EXERCISE 1

Directions: Look at the underlined modifier in each sentence below. Circle the word that is modified, or described. Tell whether the underlined modifier is an adjective or an adverb.

Example: *adjective* The snow fell on the <u>red</u> (flower.)

1. _____ The mail arrived <u>late</u> today.

2. _____ A <u>late</u> dinner was served at the restaurant.

3. _____ <u>Four</u> children came to my door this afternoon.

4. _____ Andrew moved too <u>quickly</u> in the darkness and fell.

5. _____ He made an <u>absolutely</u> amazing discovery as he got up.

6. _____ <u>This</u> chair goes over there in the corner.

7. _____ The music played <u>quietly</u> in the distance.

8. _____ Juan lives <u>here</u> with his two brothers.

9. _____ What an <u>awful</u> noise was heard in the basement!

10. _____ My <u>new</u> red sports car has a dent in it!

Answers are on page 232.

Forming Adjectives and Adverbs

Adjectives and adverbs are both modifiers, but they modify different kinds of words. Therefore, you should not use one in place of the other. Usually adjectives and adverbs are formed in different ways. By knowing how they are formed, you can be sure to use them correctly.

Adjectives do not have a special form. Many adverbs, however, are formed by adding *ly* to an adjective.

Adverbs Formed with *ly*	
Adjectives	**Adverbs**
loud screaming	scream **loudly**
warm clothes	**warmly** dressed
beautiful photograph	paints **beautifully**

Some adverbs are formed from adjectives in other ways.

If the adjective ends in

ll add only a *y*	full	⟶ fully
y change the *y* to *i* and add *ly*	happy	⟶ happily
le change the *le* to *ly*	horrible	⟶ horribly
ic add *al* before adding *ly*	frantic	⟶ frantically

Some adjectives and adverbs have the same form. The chart below shows some of these. Note especially that words ending in *ly* are not always adverbs.

Adjectives and Adverbs with the Same Form			
daily	fast	ill	right
early	hard	low	straight
far	high	near	weekly

Remember that there is not an adverb for every adjective.

EXERCISE 2

Directions: If the adjectives and adverbs in each sentence below are correct, write *C* in the blank. If an adjective or adverb is incorrect, write the correct form.

Examples: _____*C*_____ Paul spoke kindly to the frightened child.

_____*slowly*_____ The parks committee worked slow.

1. _____ The runners moved rapid toward the finish line.

2. _____ This new calculator is supposed to work easy.

3. _____ Andre willingly agreed to help me move that heavy chair.

4. _____ I fully expect you to complete this project by noon.

5. _____ The extremely heat and lack of rain is hard on the crops.

6. _____ Rico buys the paper daily.

7. _____ I read the contract careful before signing it.

8. _____ Molly hurt her foot bad.

9. _____ She looked straightly into my eyes and said it was broken.

10. _____ Susan said she had a practically solution to my problem.

11. _____ Hector lovingly gave his girlfriend Rosa a dozen roses on her birthday.

12. _____ The old road winds crooked through the hills.

Answers are on page 232.

Problems with Adjectives and Adverbs

Adverbs can often be moved around in a sentence without changing the meaning or making the sentence unclear.

Reading my favorite book relaxes me slowly.

I am relaxed when I read my favorite book slowly.

But sometimes putting an adverb in the wrong position can change the meaning of a sentence. Compare the meaning of the following two sentences.

Mia actually told me that they eat worms.

Mia told me that they actually eat worms.

When an adverb is placed too far from the word it modifies, it can make the meaning of the sentence unclear.

I'll just give you two hours to get out of town.

A reader might wonder exactly what is meant in this sentence. Moving the adverb will make it clear.

I'll give you just two hours to get out of town.

Modifiers Used with Linking Verbs

Remember that linking verbs are words like *is, are, seems, appears,* and *looks.* They connect a noun with another word that describes it or renames it.

Certain verbs can be used as either linking verbs or action verbs. These include the following:

Both Linking and Action Verbs			
appear	feel	look	smell
become	grow	seem	taste

A modifier that follows these words can be an adjective or an adverb. To know which is correct, decide what word is being modified. If the word describes the noun, it must be an adjective. A common mistake is to use the adverb because it seems to modify the verb that it follows.

Incorrect: That anvil looks **heavily.**

Correct: That anvil looks **heavy.** *(a heavy anvil)*

Incorrect: Jason grew **quick.**

Correct: Jason grew **quickly.** *(how Jason grew)*

EDITING TIP

Use this trick to help you decide whether a verb is used as a linking verb or an action verb. Mentally replace the verb with the linking verb *is* (or *are*). If the sentence still makes sense, the verb is a linking verb. The modifier should be an adjective. If the sentence doesn't make sense, it is an action verb. Then the modifier should be an adverb.

Sarah grew angry.   ⟶   Sarah is angry.

Jeremy grew tomatoes carefully. ⟶ Jeremy is tomatoes carefully.

EXERCISE 3

Directions: Read each sentence below. If the underlined modifiers are correct, write *C* in the blank. If an underlined modifier is incorrect, write the correct one in the space.

Example: *delighted*   Laura seemed delightedly to see us.

1. _____ The <u>early</u> morning sky became <u>darkly</u> with thunderclouds.

2. _____ Will you be <u>sadly</u> if you don't see him again?

3. _____ When the two dogs look <u>fiercely</u> at Gopal, he crosses <u>quick</u> to the other side of the street.

4. _____ The doctor felt Ann's swollen arm <u>careful</u>.

5. _____ Kyle seems fairly <u>surely</u> that they will take a <u>long</u> vacation <u>next</u> summer.

6. _____ I feel <u>happily</u> that you are my friend.

7. _____ The sun shone <u>bright</u> after the storm.

8. _____ The robber looked <u>evil</u> at the woman as he snatched her purse.

9. _____ Mrs. Valdez <u>lightly</u> scented her wrist with perfume.

10. _____ The volume on the radio seemed too <u>loudly</u>.

11. _____ Weeds <u>slow</u> covered our neighbor's backyard.

12. _____ Smoking is <u>harmful</u> to your health.

Answers are on pages 232–233.

Adjectives and Adverbs in Comparisons

When writing, you often want to compare different things or actions. Adjectives are used to compare people, places, things, and ideas. Adverbs are used to compare actions.

> Claudia is **tall.**
>
> Claudia is **taller** than William.
>
> Claudia is the **tallest** person in her family.

In the first sentence, the basic form of the adjective *tall* is used to describe Claudia. In the second sentence, the adjective *taller* is used to compare two people, Claudia and William. In the third sentence, *tallest* is used to compare three or more people. These are the three degrees or levels of comparison. Both adjectives and adverbs have these degrees. Here are examples of the three degrees of the adverb *quickly.*

> Hyung walks **quickly.**
>
> Sachi walks **more quickly** than Hyung.
>
> Kim walks the **most quickly** of the three friends.

Comparing Two Things or Actions

When two things or actions are compared, the correct adjective or adverb is usually formed in one of two ways. If the modifier is short—one or two syllables—you usually add *er.* If the modifier is longer—three or more syllables—use the word *more* plus the adjective or adverb. Always use *more* with adverbs ending in *ly.* If an adjective ends in a consonant plus *y,* change the *y* to *i* before adding *er.*

Adjectives

Kathy's job is **harder** than his.

This shirt is **more expensive** than that one.

Adverbs

Steve's band plays **louder** than Ken's band.

Of those two stars, that one sparkles **more brightly.**

The opposite of *more* is *less.* You can also make comparisons using *less.*

That house is **less expensive** than ours.

I clean the kitchen **less carefully** than my mother does.

EDITING TIP

Never use *more* or *less* along with the *er* ending.

Incorrect: A bicycle is **more cheaper** than a motorcycle.

Correct: A bicycle is **cheaper** than a motorcycle.

Comparing Three or More Things or Actions

There are two ways to form modifiers that compare three or more things or actions. For the short adjectives and adverbs, add *est* to the end of the word. For longer modifiers—and all adverbs ending in *ly*—use *most* plus the regular form of the adjective or adverb. For adjectives ending in a consonant plus *y*, change the *y* to *i* before adding *est*.

Adjectives

Of the three children, John is **sleepiest.**

This book is the **most interesting** one I've read all year.

Adverbs

Our team plays the **hardest** of all.

Maria works the **most carefully** of the four employees.

You can compare three or more things or actions using *least.*

What is the **least** amount of salt I can use in this recipe?

This car runs the **least dependably** of any I've ever owned.

Forming Comparisons		
Types of Modifiers	Comparing Two Things or Actions	Comparing Three or More Things or Actions
Short modifiers	add *er*: **taller, harder**	add *est*: **tallest, hardest**
Adjectives ending in a consonant plus *y*	change *y* to *i* and add *er*: **happier**	change *y* to *i* and add *est*: **happiest**
Long modifiers and all adverbs ending in *ly*	Use *more* or *less*: **more quickly, less intelligent**	Use *most* or *least*: **most quickly, least intelligent**

Irregular Forms of Comparisons

Like verbs, adjectives and adverbs have both regular and irregular forms. Most adjectives and adverbs are regular and comparisons are formed as already described. Comparisons for some of the most commonly used irregular adjectives and adverbs are given below.

Irregular Comparisons		
Describing One Thing or Action	**Comparing Two Things or Actions**	**Comparing Three or More Things or Actions**
bad	worse	worst
far	farther	farthest
good	better	best
ill	worse	worst
little	less	least
many	more	most
much	more	most
well	better	best

Comparison Problems with Modifiers

When making comparisons, check how many things or actions are being compared. If two items are being compared, always use the *er, more,* or *less* forms. If more than two items are being compared, always use the *est, most,* or *least* forms. Errors often result from not using these forms correctly.

Incorrect: Of the **two** sisters, she is the *shortest.*

Correct: Of the **two** sisters, she is the *shorter.*

Incorrect: **All** the workers do well, but Martha does **better.**

Correct: **All** the workers do well, but Martha does **best.**

Be alert to comparisons between one thing and a group of things. It may seem as though you are comparing many things. In fact, it is two things—one thing and one group.

Incorrect: He speaks **most slowly** than the **other men.**

Correct: He speaks **more slowly** than the **other men.**

EXERCISE 4

Directions: Write the correct form of each modifier in parentheses below.

Example: *hungrier* Elena is (hungry) than Margo.

1. _____ This is the (little) enthusiastic group of volunteers we have ever had.

2. _____ Rice, beans, and macaroni are the (cheap) items I buy at the grocery store.

3. _____ Everyone knows that Noriko is the (fast) of the two typists.

4. _____ I think Soon Young would be the (good) house painter among all those people who applied.

5. _____ Mark always dresses (neat) than Tamiko.

6. _____ Tony has (few) duties now than he had in his last job.

7. _____ Helena is (serious) about starting a business than I am.

8. _____ Of all the movies you've seen this summer, which was the (exciting)?

9. _____ I feel (much) relaxed after swimming than after biking.

10. _____ Susan has never been (happy) than she is now.

11. _____ Andy's has the (good) buys on fruits and vegetables in our area.

12. _____ Ben traveled (far) on his bike yesterday than Tim did.

13. _____ Anita's allergies are (bad) during the summer than during the winter.

Answers are on page 233.

More Problems with Adjectives and Adverbs

There are four common mistakes in the use of modifiers.

Well or Good; Badly or Bad

Well and *badly* are adverbs. *Good* and *bad* are adjectives. Be careful to use them correctly.

Adjectives	Adverbs
Take a **good** look at this example.	She plays **well**.
Do you think this is a **bad** idea?	The toast is **badly** burnt.

Be especially careful when using linking verbs. Remember they connect a subject to its modifier, which is always an adjective.

This book is **good.** Those rotten apples smell **bad.**

There is an important exception to this rule. When the modifier after a linking verb refers to health, use *well* instead of *good*.

Are you feeling **well?**

Double Negatives

A negative word is one that means *no* or *not*.

Negatives		
hardly	nobody	nothing
neither	none	nowhere
never	no one	*n't* in contractions
no	not	scarcely

Never use more than one negative in a clause.

Incorrect:	I do **not** want **nothing.**
Correct:	I do **not** want anything.
Correct:	I want **nothing.**

Look for words like *don't, won't, wouldn't, can't,* and *shouldn't*. These words are negatives. The *n't* stands for "not." Do not use them in a sentence with another negative.

Incorrect:	She **can't** go **nowhere.**
Correct:	She **can't** go **anywhere.**
Correct:	She can go **nowhere.**

A common mistake is to forget that *hardly* and *scarcely* are negatives.

Incorrect:	Teresa **can't hardly** see well enough to drive.
Correct:	Teresa can **hardly** see well enough to drive.
Correct:	Teresa **can't** see well enough to drive.

This, That, These, Those, and *Them*

This and *that* are adjectives used to point out singular nouns. *This* points to something that is close by. *That* points to something that is not close.

This book goes in **that** bookcase.

These and *those* are adjectives used to point out plural nouns. *These* points to things that are nearby. *Those* points to things that are not nearby.

These books go in **those** bookcases.

Because *this* and *these* mean "here," do not use *this here* or *these here.* For the same reason, do not use *that there* or *those there.*

Incorrect:	**These** pencils **here** are mine.
Correct:	**These** pencils are mine.

Them cannot be used in place of *those* to point out a noun. *Them* is always an object pronoun.

Incorrect:	Did you see **them** cars?
Correct:	Did you see **those** cars?

A and *An*

The words *a* and *an* are adjectives. They modify nouns to show they are singular. *An* is used before all words that begin with a vowel sound. (The vowels are *a, e, i, o, u.*)

an ape   **an** opinion   **an** unusual day

Use *an* before a word that begins with an *h* if the *h* is not pronounced.

an hour   **an** honor   <u>but:</u> **a** hospital

Use *a* before all other words.

a boring speech   **a** lazy dog   **a** flower

There is one vowel to watch out for. Use *a* before words beginning with a *u* that is pronounced like *you.*

a unicorn   **a** usual day   **a** union

EXERCISE 5

Directions: In each sentence below, underline the correct word or group of words in parentheses.

Example: Hilda visited (a, an) university last week.

1. I have already read (those, them) books.
2. Sarah (hadn't scarcely, had scarcely) begun to clean her house.
3. That coffee tastes (bitter, bitterly).
4. When Jon had a cold and didn't feel (well, good), who (careful, carefully) nursed him back to health?
5. There is (a, an) easier way that (wouldn't hardly, would hardly) cost any more money.
6. Jill is (a, an) ideal candidate for mayor.
7. We don't have time to sponsor (no, any) special events.
8. Slice (these, this) carrots and add (those, that) cup of peas to the pot.
9. When I'm sick, there isn't (nothing, anything) anybody can do to make me feel (best, better).
10. It's good for your health to eat (a, an) variety of fruits and vegetables each day.
11. We couldn't find the little girl (anywhere, nowhere).
12. Carry (this, these) basket over to the dining room table.
13. I (can hardly, can't hardly) wait for spring to arrive so that I can see the flowers in bloom.
14. That is (a, an) unusual house because it is the (more angular, most angular) house in the neighborhood.

Answers are on pages 233–234.

Adjectives and Adverbs

Directions: Choose what correction should be made to each sentence below. If you think the sentence is correct, choose option (5).

1. **The nervous man drove careful down the busy street. He seemed glad when he turned onto the side road.**

   (1) change *nervous* to *nervously*
   (2) change *careful* to *carefully*
   (3) change *busy* to *busily*
   (4) change *glad* to *gladly*
   (5) no correction is necessary

2. **The regular salesperson has not been feeling good. When she had good health, she rarely missed work. Now she misses more work.**

   (1) change *regular* to *regularly*
   (2) change *feeling good* to *feeling well*
   (3) change *good health* to *well health*
   (4) change *more* to *the most*
   (5) no correction is necessary

3. **I didn't hardly ever do anything fun while I lived in that city. After a few months, I moved back to this city, where I know more people.**

   (1) change *didn't hardly ever do* to *hardly ever did*
   (2) change *that* to *those*
   (3) change *this* to *that*
   (4) change *more* to *most*
   (5) no correction is necessary

4. **My manager wants our small department to be the most successful in the company. She tries to hire the better people she can find.**

   (1) change *small* to *smaller*
   (2) change *most successful* to *successfullest*
   (3) change *most successful* to *more successful*
   (4) change *better* to *best*
   (5) no correction is necessary

5. **If I were more wiser, I would quickly learn to save more and instantly forget how to spend it so well.**

   (1) change *more wiser* to *wiser*
   (2) change *quickly* to *quick*
   (3) change *instantly* to *instant*
   (4) change *well* to *good*
   (5) no correction is necessary

6. **The oak tree is highest than the maple tree in our yard. We get more shade early in the morning from the oak tree.**

   (1) change *highest* to *high*
   (2) change *highest* to *higher*
   (3) change *more* to *most*
   (4) change *early* to *earliest*
   (5) no correction is necessary

   Answers are on page 234.

Modifying Phrases

Sometimes a whole group of words acts to modify, or describe, another word in a sentence. A **phrase** is a group of words that contains either a noun (or pronoun) or a verb, but not both. A phrase also includes some other words that describe the noun or verb or that tie the group of words to the rest of the sentence.

Prepositional Phrases

As you learned in Chapter 2, a **prepositional phrase** is a group of words that begins with a preposition and ends with a noun or pronoun. In a sentence, a prepositional phrase works as an adjective or an adverb. When it serves as an adjective, it modifies a noun or a pronoun.

The water **in the pool** is clear.

When a prepositional phrase is used as an adverb, it modifies a verb, an adjective, or an adverb.

Cindy jumped **off the high board.**

She is skillful at **diving.**

Cindy began diving soon **after her older sister.**

EDITING TIP

A prepositional phrase can be placed either before or after the word it modifies. However, the sentence will be clearer if the phrase is close to the word it modifies.

Confusing:	Cindy teaches children to jump off the low board from the grade school.
Better:	Cindy teaches children from the grade school to jump off the low board.

Verb Phrases

Another group of words that acts as a modifier is a **verb phrase.** A verb phrase begins with a verb form.

Tired after a long day, José took his dog for a walk.

José used a leash **to walk his dog.**

Breaking the leash, the dog was free.

Introductory Phrases

A modifying phrase is often used to begin a sentence. When it is, use a comma to separate it from the rest of the sentence. A comma is not always needed if the phrase occurs somewhere else in the sentence.

Stumbling over the curb, Mindy almost fell.

EXERCISE 6

Directions: Underline the modifying phrase in each sentence below. Write the word it modifies.

Example: _Jan_ Walking home, Jan watched dark clouds gather.

1. _____ Louis saw the bus at the corner.

2. _____ Opening the door, Shen looked outside.

3. _____ The smell of barbecued chicken made Shawna hungry.

4. _____ The exhausted runner, seeing the finish line, speeded up.

5. _____ Julie was sorry to lose the watch.

6. _____ Jacobo left his books at the library.

7. _____ Already soaked to the skin, Ms. Atole opened her umbrella.

8. _____ The basketball game ended soon after sunset.

9. _____ The police car left the crime scene in a hurry.

10. _____ Hoping to get more customers, the store manager lowered prices.

11. _____ Locking the door, Mr. Henshaw left his apartment.

12. _____ Mrs. Cosmos crossed over the Canadian border.

13. _____ Sitting between her parents, Lenore felt quite happy.

Answers are on page 234.

Renaming Phrases as Modifiers

A **renaming phrase**, also called an **appositive,** is a group of words that gives more information about a noun in a sentence. It is made up of a noun and other words that modify it.

John Tenorio, **a truck driver,** left the warehouse at noon.

As with other phrases, a renaming phrase must be placed carefully in the sentence. Otherwise, it can be confusing or misleading. A renaming phrase usually comes directly after the noun it modifies. Occasionally, it may come before the noun.

A retired state senator, Margaret Fisher stayed active in politics.

Usually, renaming phrases are separated from the rest of the sentence by commas. If the renaming phrase occurs in the middle of a sentence, a comma comes before and after it.

EXERCISE 7

Directions: Find the renaming phrase in each sentence below and punctuate it correctly.

Example: Neil Armstrong, the astronaut, was the first person on the moon.

1. Yuri Gagarin the first human in space was from the Soviet Union.

2. Ham a chimpanzee tested the U.S. spacecraft.

3. Alan Shepard the first American in space wrote a book about the early space program.

4. Shepard went into space in *Redstone 3* a tiny spacecraft.

5. Shepard an astronaut and test pilot went to the moon years later.

Answers are on page 234.

Modifying Phrases

Directions: Choose what correction should be made to each sentence below. If you think the sentence is correct, choose option (5).

1. **Jumping up from the ground Isabel, my mother's friend, ran after the children.**

    (1) move the phrase *jumping up from the ground* to the end of the sentence
    (2) add a comma after *ground*
    (3) remove the commas after *Isabel* and after *friend*
    (4) add a comma before *after the children*
    (5) no correction is necessary

2. **Tomás watched the truck in the driveway. His neighbor, a mechanic, was busy, under the hood.**

    (1) add a comma before *in the driveway*
    (2) move *in the driveway* to the beginning of the sentence
    (3) remove the commas on each side of *a mechanic*
    (4) remove the comma after *busy*
    (5) no correction is necessary

3. **Janet, a photographer, was always on the go. Finishing one assignment, she would grab her camera an expensive Japanese model and race to the next.**

    (1) remove the commas on each side of *a photographer*
    (2) remove the comma after *assignment*
    (3) add commas before and after *an expensive Japanese model*
    (4) add a comma after *race*
    (5) no correction is necessary

4. **Losing his wallet, Jerome called the security office to report his loss. Leonard Chino, chief of security, told him the wallet had been found.**

    (1) move *losing his wallet* to the end of the sentence
    (2) remove the comma after *wallet*
    (3) add a comma after *office*
    (4) remove the commas before and after *chief of security*
    (5) no correction is necessary

5. **To rescue her cat Ann called the fire chief, an old friend. He sent a young firefighter up a long ladder to save the cat.**

    (1) add a comma after *To rescue her cat*
    (2) move *To rescue her cat* to the end of the sentence
    (3) add a comma after *called*
    (4) add a comma after *ladder*
    (5) no correction is necessary

6. **After we left the movie theater we stopped for some coffee. My friend Albert, an avid film buff, discussed the movie with me for about an hour.**

    (1) add a comma after *theater*
    (2) remove the comma after *Albert*
    (3) remove the comma after *buff*
    (4) add a comma after *me*
    (5) no correction is necessary

Answers are on page 234.

Chapter Review

Directions: Choose the <u>one best answer</u> to each question. Some of the sentences may contain errors in modification. A few sentences, however, may be correct as written. Read the sentences carefully and then answer the questions based on them. For each question, choose the answer that would result in the most effective writing of the sentence or sentences.

1. **Ann Watson, manager of the grocery store, hired two new employees. The younger one will help Sid the produce manager.**

   What correction should be made to these sentences?

   (1) change *new* to *newer*
   (2) change *younger* to *youngest*
   (3) change *younger* to *more young*
   (4) add a comma after *Sid*
   (5) no correction is necessary

2. **Noriko can't hardly go to work today. Her car, a beat-up old jalopy, won't start. It has seen better days.**

   What correction should be made to these sentences?

   (1) change *can't* to *can*
   (2) change *hardly* to *scarcely*
   (3) remove the commas before and after *a beat-up old jalopy*
   (4) change *better* to *best*
   (5) no correction is necessary

3. **After I put them cans in the cooler, I added a big bag of ice. In this hot weather, the ice melted fast.**

   What correction should be made to these sentences?

   (1) change *them* to *those*
   (2) change *this* to *these*
   (3) remove the comma after *weather*
   (4) change *fast* to *faster*
   (5) no correction is necessary

4. **To buy that new car, Sheri signed a application for a loan.**

   What correction should be made to this sentence?

   (1) change *that* to *these*
   (2) remove the comma after *car*
   (3) change *a application* to *an application*
   (4) change *a loan* to *an loan*
   (5) no correction is necessary

5. **Taro's car looks much shinier than it did. That there wax really makes it look good.**

   What correction should be made to this sentence?

   (1) change *much* to *more*
   (2) change *shinier* to *shiniest*
   (3) remove *there*
   (4) change *good* to *well*
   (5) no correction is necessary

6. **The letter carrier looks nervous at the dog. It is the most ferocious of all the dogs on that street.**

   What correction should be made to these sentences?

   (1) change *nervous* to *nervously*
   (2) change *most ferocious* to *more ferocious*
   (3) change *most ferocious* to *ferocious*
   (4) change *that* to *these*
   (5) no correction is necessary

7. **Those steaks smell bad. They looked fresh when I picked them out.**

   What correction should be made to these sentences?

   (1) change *Those* to *Them*
   (2) change *bad* to *badly*
   (3) change *bad* to *more bad*
   (4) change *fresh* to *freshly*
   (5) no correction is necessary

8. **The funnier book I have ever read is *Roughing It*. Mark Twain, a nineteenth-century writer, is the author.**

   What correction should be made to these sentences?

   (1) change *funnier* to *most funny*
   (2) change *funnier* to *more funnier*
   (3) change *funnier* to *funniest*
   (4) remove the commas around *a nineteenth-century writer*
   (5) no correction is necessary

9. **Lee Chung did not feel very good yesterday. He feels even worse today.**

   What correction should be made to these sentences?

   (1) change *good* to *well*
   (2) change *worse* to *more bad*
   (3) change *worse* to *worst*
   (4) change *worse* to *worser*
   (5) no correction is necessary

10. **If I were more smarter, I would have bought this television last week. That sale was better than the sale this week.**

    What correction should be made to these sentences?

    (1) change *more smarter* to *most smarter*
    (2) change *more smarter* to *smarter*
    (3) change *better* to *more better*
    (4) change *better* to *best*
    (5) no correction is necessary

11. **That basketball player has scarcely any competition. Watch how he sets up the play so easy.**

    What correction should be made to these sentences?

    (1) change *That* to *Those*
    (2) change *has* to *hasn't*
    (3) change *any* to *no*
    (4) change *easy* to *easily*
    (5) no correction is necessary

12. **That computer is less expensive than this one. However, it isn't hardly the best one that I have ever seen.**

    What correction should be made to these sentences?

    (1) change *less* to *least*
    (2) change *this* to *these*
    (3) change *isn't* to *is*
    (4) change *best* to *better*
    (5) no correction is necessary

13. **Waving frantically, the hungry, shipwrecked sailor screamed loud at the passing ship.**

    What correction should be made to this sentence?

    (1) change *frantically* to *frantic*
    (2) remove the comma after *frantically*
    (3) change *hungry* to *hungrily*
    (4) change *loud* to *loudly*
    (5) no correction is necessary

14. **Patty seemed extremely happy when she was given those tickets there.**

    What correction should be made to this sentence?

    (1) change *extremely* to *extreme*
    (2) change *happy* to *happily*
    (3) change *those* to *them*
    (4) remove *there*
    (5) no correction is necessary

Answers are on pages 234–235.

CHAPTER 4

Sentence Structure

Combining Ideas in Sentences

Read the following two paragraphs. Which do you like better?

> The U.S. Army is dumping tanks into the Gulf of Mexico. They are trying to improve fishing. Old tanks are cleaned up. The army no longer wants them. All poisonous chemicals are removed. Then the tanks are taken out to sea on ships. The tanks are dumped overboard. This part of the gulf is flat. It has few natural hiding places for fish. Dumping the tanks creates artificial places. Fish can hide and reproduce.

> The U.S. Army is dumping tanks into the Gulf of Mexico in order to improve fishing. Old tanks that the army no longer wants are cleaned up, and all poisonous chemicals are removed. Then the tanks are taken out to sea on ships and dumped overboard. This part of the gulf is flat; it has few natural hiding places for fish. Dumping the tanks creates artificial places where fish can hide and reproduce.

Both paragraphs are correct, and both give the same information. The first one, however, is made up entirely of simple sentences. When you read it, it sounds choppy. In the second paragraph, the sentences have been combined to create more variety in sentence length and structure. Ideas are also more closely linked so you know how they are related.

Forming Compound Sentences

The most basic form of a sentence is the **simple sentence**. It contains one subject and one predicate and expresses a complete thought.

> Yolanda wanted a radio for her birthday. She got two.

Simple sentences like these can often be combined to make a more interesting sentence.

> Yolanda wanted a radio for her birthday, and she got two.

This new sentence has two subject-predicate sets. In fact, the two original simple sentences were not changed at all. They were linked by the word *and*. The result is a compound sentence.

A **compound sentence** contains two or more connected simple sentences.

Conjunctions

Compound sentences are most often linked by a **conjunction.** These are words like *and, or, but,* and *yet.*

Mr. Ruiz does not have a lawn mower. He doesn't want one.

<u>becomes</u>

Mr. Ruiz does not have a lawn mower, and he doesn't want one.

Please bring the cooler. The soda will become warm.

<u>becomes</u>

Please bring the cooler, or the soda will become warm.

Conjunctions link sentences by showing how ideas are related. Each conjunction shows a certain kind of connection between ideas.

Conjunctions and Their Uses	
Conjunction	**Use**
and	adds extra information
but, yet	shows how ideas are different
or	shows a choice between ideas
nor	shows a rejection of both ideas
for	connects an effect to a cause
so	connects a cause to its effect

Here are some examples of compound sentences. Notice that when two simple sentences are combined using a conjunction, the original sentences are not changed. The only exception is *nor.* Then the subject and verb in the second sentence are reversed.

Laura bought a coat, and Sara bought a pair of gloves.

Pan hated painting, yet he finished the whole room.

The Tuckers had a long trip before them, so they left early.

Jim's baby wouldn't be quiet, nor would she keep still.

MIND ON MECHANICS

Commas Used Before Conjunctions

A comma is used before the conjunction in most compound sentences. Remember, however, that a compound sentence has two subject-verb sets, and each expresses a complete thought. If either part of the compound sentence does not express a complete thought or does not have a subject-verb set, then don't use a comma before the conjunction.

> Jerry bought flowers but forgot to give them to Julie.

> Jerry bought flowers, but he forgot to give them to Julie.

The second part of the first sentence does not have a subject, so no comma is needed. The second sentence has two complete subject-verb sets, so a comma is needed.

Other Conjunctions

Some conjunctions made up of two parts are used in pairs.

both ... and	either ... or
not only ... but also	neither ... nor

These conjunctions are often used in the pairs listed below. Place them next to the words they are connecting.

Not only do I take sugar in my coffee, **but** I **also** take milk.

Either it rains when I go fishing, **or** it's sunny when I work.

A comma is used when conjunctions connect two subject-verb sets.

Joining Ideas with a Semicolon

Semicolons with Conjunctive Adverbs

Simple sentences can also be joined using a semicolon and a conjunctive adverb. A **conjunctive adverb** is a word or phrase that works like a conjunction. As with conjunctions, it is important to choose the right conjunctive adverb to say what you mean.

Conjunctive Adverbs		
To show contrast	however otherwise	nevertheless on the other hand
To explain	for example furthermore besides	in other words in fact moreover
To show a result	consequently as a result	then therefore

These words are used like conjunctions to join sentences. Place a semicolon before the conjunctive adverb. Put a comma after all conjunctive adverbs except *then.*

Food prices keep rising; **in fact,** our weekly grocery bill is ten dollars higher than last year.

Noriko took tennis lessons; **then** she beat me all the time.

Semicolons Without Conjunctions

You can also join two simple sentences without using a conjunction or a conjunctive adverb. A semicolon shows the ideas are linked.

Benito likes to barbecue; ribs are his specialty.

Forming Compound Sentences

A compound sentence can be formed in three ways:

1. Using a conjunction and a comma
2. Using a conjunctive adverb and a semicolon
3. Using a semicolon alone

One common error in forming compound sentences is caused by forgetting to use one of these methods. The result is a **run-on sentence.**

Incorrect: Hieu needed new shoes he bought some at the sale.

Run-ons can be corrected with one of the methods you've learned for forming compound sentences.

Correct: Hieu needed new shoes, so he bought some at the sale.

Correct: Hieu needed new shoes; consequently, he bought some at the sale.

Correct: Hieu needed new shoes; he bought some at the sale.

A second common error in forming compound sentences is caused by stringing several sentences together with the word *and.*

Incorrect: He went on vacation to New Mexico and visited Pueblo villages and saw hot-air balloons and rode on a tram up the mountain.

Correct: He went on vacation to New Mexico and visited Pueblo villages; he also saw hot-air balloons and rode on a tram up the mountain.

A third common error in forming compound sentences is caused by a **comma splice.**

Incorrect: I keep sneezing, I think I'm catching a cold.

Correct: I keep sneezing, so I think I'm catching a cold.

Correct: I keep sneezing; I think I'm catching a cold.

EXERCISE 1

Directions: Rewrite each of the following pairs of simple sentences as a compound sentence. Use the conjunction, conjunctive adverb, or semicolon shown in parentheses to connect the sentences. Add correct punctuation.

Example: Bill likes sports. He especially enjoys touch football. *(and)*

Bill likes sports, and he especially enjoys touch football.

1. Ann starts a new job soon. She hasn't told her present boss. *(but)*

_____

_____

2. There are no good movies in town. A great rock band is playing. *(however)*

_____

_____

3. My house is a mess. I never seem to have time to clean it. *(semicolon)*

_____

_____

4. The plane's wings were covered with ice. The departure was delayed. *(as a result)*

_____

_____

5. The server took their orders. She brought us coffee. *(then)*

_____

_____

6. I could never keep the washer fixed. I bought a new one. *(so)*

_____

_____

7. Snow is forecast for tonight. We should change our travel plans. *(therefore)*

_____

_____

8. Max is a good dog. I don't want him eating off the table. *(nevertheless)*

_____

_____

Answers are on page 235.

Forming Complex Sentences

Another kind of sentence is the **complex sentence.** It is made up of two or more clauses. Remember that a clause is a group of words that contains a subject and a predicate. A clause may express a complete thought, or it may not. In a complex sentence, only one clause expresses a complete thought and can stand alone as a sentence. Look at the clauses in the following sentence:

While Rosa loaded the car, Michael got the kids ready to go.

The first clause in this sentence is not a complete thought. When you read it, you want to know what happened while Rosa loaded the car. This clause is called a **dependent clause** because it depends on the second clause. It needs the second clause to explain it. The second clause is an independent, or main, clause. An **independent clause** expresses a complete thought and can stand alone.

A complex sentence is made up of one or more dependent clauses linked to one independent clause.

Simple sentences can be combined to form complex sentences. One simple sentence will be the independent clause. A second sentence will be linked to it by a type of conjunction that makes it dependent. The dependent clause can come before or after the independent clause. If it comes after the independent clause, no comma is needed.

You are such a good friend. I'll help you out.

becomes

Because you are such a good friend, I'll help you out.

or

I'll help you out because you are such a good friend.

Marty grilled some hamburgers. Denise fixed a salad.

becomes

While Marty grilled some hamburgers, Denise fixed a salad.

or

Denise fixed a salad while Marty grilled some hamburgers.

Elmer likes to visit Greece. Peter prefers Italy.

becomes

Although Elmer likes to visit Greece, Peter prefers Italy.

or

Peter prefers Italy although Elmer likes to visit Greece.

Here is a list of conjunctions that make dependent clauses.

Conjunctions	
To show time	
before after while when whenever until as soon as as long as	**Before** I got out my camera, the bear had Manuel up a tree. Sylvia hurried home **while** it was still light.
To show reason	
because in order that since so that	Alicia went home early **because** she was sick.
To show conditions	
if unless whether	**Unless** you want trouble, don't pester that bee.
To show contrast	
though although even though in spite of the fact that despite the fact that whereas	**Even though** Pak Ku was tired, he helped fix dinner. Jennifer went to the meeting **despite the fact that** she had lost the election.
To show similarity	
as though as if	The day looked **as if** it would be clear and warm.
To show place	
where wherever	Jan went **wherever** her sister went.

When you are combining sentences, be careful to choose the conjunction that says what you mean. Which conjunction would you use to combine these two clauses?

Phillip forgot to open the door _____ he saw the ghost following him.

When and *because* make sense here. Try some other conjunctions, like *unless* or *as though.* They do not make sense at all. Make sure your sentence makes sense when you use a conjunction. Here is another example. Think what relationship there is between the clauses.

Lana went to the show _____ she hated gangster movies.

Several conjunctions would work here — *although, even though, in spite of the fact that, despite the fact that.* All of them show contrast between the ideas. Try other conjunctions from the list. Do you see that they do not make sense here?

Dependent Clauses

When a dependent clause comes at the beginning of a sentence, use a comma to separate it from the independent clause. If the dependent clause comes after the independent clause, no comma is needed.

Because Jerry arrived late, he was criticized.

Jerry was criticized because he arrived late.

Although it was still dark out, Maria was getting ready for work.

Maria was getting ready for work although it was still dark out.

EXERCISE 2

Directions: Complete each complex sentence below. In the blank, write one of the conjunctions from the chart of conjunctions on page 107 to link the clauses.

Example: _When_ the hurricane approached, people left the island.

1. _____ backing into the garage, Sarah loaded the truck.

2. Melissa wants to go to the zoo _____ the weather turns cold.

3. _____ the bats still live in Carlsbad Caverns, there are fewer of them today.

4. Gilbert cast his fly _____ he had seen the large trout jump.

5. _____ I tell Santwana I saw a spider, she will want to leave.

6. Few salmon live in the Snake River _____ huge dams were built.

7. _____ that dog has a loud bark, it's really very friendly.

8. _____ you said the dog was friendly, I tried to pet him.

9. _____ you were bitten, I still say the dog is gentle.

10. The doctor says the wound will heal _____ I keep it bandaged.

Answers are on page 235.

Combining Ideas in Sentences

Directions: Choose the best way to write the underlined part of each sentence below. If the underlined part is the best way, choose option (5).

1. <u>Since</u> Mrs. Tenorio saw her unharmed son, tears of relief streamed down her face.

   (1) As though
   (2) Where
   (3) As soon as
   (4) Until
   (5) no correction is necessary

2. I usually read a magazine <u>as soon as</u> I eat lunch.

   (1) when
   (2) since
   (3) although
   (4) even though
   (5) no correction is necessary

3. You will receive only one more issue <u>so that</u> you renew your subscription.

   (1) because
   (2) in spite of the fact that
   (3) whether
   (4) unless
   (5) no correction is necessary

4. Michiko bought healthy plants, <u>but</u> all of them are wilted now.

   (1) and
   (2) so
   (3) for
   (4) or
   (5) no correction is necessary

5. Will you please answer the phone <u>despite the fact that</u> I am in the shower?

   (1) whether
   (2) while
   (3) as soon as
   (4) unless
   (5) no correction is necessary

6. He won't pay his bills on time <u>whether</u> he didn't get his paycheck.

   (1) while
   (2) so that
   (3) because
   (4) as though
   (5) no correction is necessary

Answers are on page 235.

Sentence Problems

Misplaced Modifiers

Modifiers—whether they are words, phrases, or clauses—should be placed as close as possible to the words they modify. When they are not, confusing ideas sometimes result. What does the following sentence mean?

Julian is following a stray cat wearing yellow sneakers.

The writer probably meant that Julian, not the cat, was wearing yellow sneakers. However, that is not what the sentence says. This is an example of a misplaced modifier.

A **misplaced modifier** is a word or phrase whose meaning is unclear because it is out of place.

To correct a misplaced modifier, move the modifier closer to the word it modifies.

Wearing yellow sneakers, Julian is following a stray cat.

Here are some other examples:

Incorrect: Carmen bought milk from the grocery store **that was spoiled.**

Correct: Carmen bought milk **that was spoiled** from the grocery store.

Incorrect: Sharon read a story about a woman who won the lottery **in the elevator.**

Correct: **In the elevator,** Sharon read a story about a woman who won the lottery.

Dangling Modifiers

Another sentence problem is the dangling modifier. This error is sometimes more difficult to identify than the misplaced modifier.

A **dangling modifier** is a phrase or clause that does not modify any word in the sentence.

While entering the cave, bats flew out of the darkness.

Who entered the cave? The bats? You probably know what the writer means, but the message isn't quite clear. *While entering the cave* does not modify a word in the sentence.

There are two ways to correct a dangling modifier. One way is to change the dangling modifier into a dependent clause. (Add a subject to the phrase.)

While I was entering the cave, bats flew out of the darkness.

A second way to correct a dangling modifier is to add a word for the phrase to modify. When rewriting the sentence, place the modifier as close as possible to the word it modifies.

While entering the cave, I **heard** bats fly out of the darkness.

Here is another example:

Incorrect: **To get home quickly,** a creepy path by the river was taken. (*Who wants to get home quickly?*)

Correct: To get home quickly, **they took** a creepy path by the river.

Correct: **Because they wanted to get home quickly,** a creepy path by the river was taken.

EXERCISE 3

Directions: Underline the misplaced or dangling modifier in each sentence below. Then rewrite the sentence to correct it. If there is no error, write *C* in the blank.

Example: While reading an exciting book, Gretchen's telephone rang.
While Gretchen was reading an exciting book, her telephone rang.

1. Your bill should be paid before going on vacation.

   _____

   _____

2. Hanging on the wall, Javier stared at the beautiful painting.

   _____

   _____

3. After cooking breakfast, the fan had to be turned on to remove the smoke.

   _____

   _____

4. To remember my childhood stories, I wrote them in a diary.

   _____

   _____

5. The parade included clowns, elephants, and bands beginning on Bradford Road.

   _____

   _____

Sentences Without Parallel Structure

Many sentences have compound parts that are connected by a conjunction such as *and* or *or*. These parts may be adjectives, verbs, adverbs, phrases, or other sentence parts. Compound parts should always have the same form.

> Combining ingredients, stirring the mixture, and kneading the dough are steps in making bread.

The words *combining, stirring* and *kneading* have the same form. The sentence has **parallel structure**. Using parallel structure makes a sentence easier to read. Now look at the following sentence:

> Jerome's goal is to build a boat, quit his job, and sailing around the world.

This sentence does not have parallel structure. The words *build, quit,* and *sailing* do not have the same form. Here are two ways to correct this sentence:

> Jerome's goal is **to build** a boat, **to quit** his job, and **to sail** around the world.

> Jerome's goal is **building** a boat, **quitting** his job, and **sailing** around the world.

In the first correction, each verb refers back to the word *to: to build, to quit, to sail.* In the second correction, each verb ends in *ing: building, quitting, sailing.*

Nonparallel structure can occur with compound verbs, nouns, adjectives, and adverbs.

> **Incorrect:** This morning I **did** the grocery shopping, *bought* a bus pass, and **had looked** for a job.

> **Correct:** This morning I **did** the grocery shopping, *bought* a bus pass, and **looked** for a job.

In the incorrect sentence above, *did* and *bought* are in the simple past tense. The other verb, *had looked,* is in the past perfect tense. The corrected sentence changes them all to the simple past.

> **Incorrect:** The clothes were **wrinkled, smelly,** and **needed washing.**

> **Correct:** The clothes were **wrinkled, smelly,** and **dirty.**

The incorrect sentence includes two adjectives and a verb phrase. The corrected sentence changes them all to adjectives.

EXERCISE 4

Directions: Rewrite each sentence below to create parallel structure.

Example: Veronica told me to sit back, relax, and enjoying the afternoon.

Veronica told me to sit back, relax, and enjoy the afternoon.

1. I spent the weekend working in the yard, painting a door, and to fix a cracked window.

    _____

    _____

2. Regina said she would fix supper, set the table, and that she would clean up afterward.

    _____

    _____

3. That candidate has energy, concern, and she is honest.

    _____

    _____

4. When Taro got home, he found mud on the carpet, scratch marks on the furniture, and having broken glass on the floor.

    _____

    _____

5. Jo likes people who are kind, thoughtful, and when they are funny.

    _____

    _____

6. The fortune-teller told Ana that she would get a great job, that she would lose money, and she would move to another city.

    _____

    _____

7. The workshop leader explained how to speak clearly, appearing skilled, and how to ask for a raise.

    _____

    _____

Answers are on pages 235–236.

Incorrect Verb Sequence

Sequence of Verbs

As you learned in Chapter 2, verbs have tenses to show when actions occur. When a sentence has more than one verb, the verbs must work together to tell when the different actions happened. This is called the **verb sequence.** What's wrong with the verb sequence in the following sentence?

It **rained** for five days before the sun **had come** out.

Rained is the simple past tense. *Had come* is the past perfect tense. The past perfect tells that an event occurred in the past before another event in the past. Here, the verb tenses say that the sun came out before it rained for five days. That doesn't make sense. Here is the correct verb sequence:

It **had rained** for five days before the sun **came** out.

To check verb sequence, first decide if the action of each verb occurs in the past, present, or future. If both actions are in the past, decide if they happened at the same time or if one happened before another. Here are some examples of correct verb sequence:

I **eat** too much when I **worry.**
(Both verbs are in the present tense.)

I **ate** too much yesterday because I **worried** about work.
(Both verbs are in the past because both actions, were completed in the past and happened at the same time in the past.)

I **had eaten** three sandwiches before I **realized** it.
(Both actions happened in the past. One action—eating the sandwiches—took place before the other action—realizing it. The earlier action is correctly shown by the past perfect tense.)

Conditionals

A **conditional** clause is one that begins with the word *if.*

If Marie Valdez is elected, taxes will increase.

Sentences with conditional clauses must have certain verb sequences. In the example above, the conditional clause uses the present tense verb *is.* The main clause uses the future tense verb *will increase.* Here are some examples using the past, subjunctive, and past perfect tenses in the conditional clause.

If you **had** a million dollars, you **could buy** any car.

If Jim **were** rich, he **would give** his money to charity.

If Nancy **had been** more careful, this accident **would have been** avoided.

The following chart summarizes the correct verb sequences to use in sentences containing conditional clauses.

Conditional Verb Tenses	
Form of verb in *if* clause	**Form of verb in main clause**
present *(is elected)*	future *(will increase)*
past *(had)*	*would, could,* or *should* plus the base form of the verb *(could buy, would give)*
subjunctive *(were)*	
past perfect *(had been)*	*would have, could have,* or *should have* plus the past participle *(would have been)*

Problems with Helping Verbs

A **helping verb** is a verb such as *is, was, have, has,* or *had.* A helping verb is used to form different tenses of a verb. These helping verbs must be used in the correct combination with verbs in the rest of the sentence. Some cannot be used when another verb in the sentence is in the past tense.

Helping Verbs	
Not used in past tense	**Can be used in past tense**
can	could
may	might
must	had to
will	would
shall	should

Incorrect: When I **looked** at my study habits, I **decided** that I really *can work* harder.

Correct: When I **looked** at my study habits, I **decided** that I really **could work** harder.

In the example, *looked* and *decided* are both in the past tense. *Can,* therefore, is an incorrect choice as a helping verb with *work.* The helping verb *could* is correct. Try some other verbs from the chart that can be used in the past tense. All of them could be used correctly in this sentence.

EXERCISE 5

Directions: In each of the following sentences, a verb is underlined. If the verb shows correct verb sequence, write *C* in the blank. If the verb shows incorrect verb sequence, write the correct form of the verb.

Example: I am sure that I <u>would be</u> a better soccer player if I go to the training camp. _*will be*_

1. Toni was convinced that she <u>will get</u> lost. _____

2. We were so hungry at noon that we ate the meal we <u>had prepared</u> for supper. _____

3. Leroy finally realized that he <u>locked</u> himself out of his apartment.
   _____

4. Maria's neighbor asked her whether he <u>can</u> borrow a hammer.
   _____

5. We would buy a new refrigerator if we <u>are</u> able to afford one.
   _____

6. Sonia says that she <u>would</u> wash her hair before the party.
   _____

7. The police officer said he <u>will</u> give the driver a warning ticket.
   _____

8. If Bert had known it was you who found his wallet, he <u>had not panicked</u>. _____

9. Tamara <u>is pleased</u> that she will receive an award. _____

10. Vince decided that he <u>could</u> interview for the job tomorrow morning. _____

Answers are on page 236.

Confusing Pronoun References

Pronouns are words that take the place of nouns or refer to nouns. Errors in using pronouns occur when it is not clear what noun the pronoun refers to. This happens in two situations: when more than one noun comes before the pronoun and when there is no noun before the pronoun.

Pronouns with More Than One Preceding Noun

Read the following example. Who is entering the room?

> Amy glanced at Sara as **she** entered the room.

To which noun does the pronoun *she* refer? You cannot tell whether it is to *Amy* or *Sara*. This sentence is an example of an unclear pronoun reference.

There are different ways to correct sentences with unclear pronoun references. Here are two ways to correct the example:

> Amy glanced at Sara as **Amy** entered the room.

> As she entered the room, Amy glanced at Sara.

Here is another example of a sentence with an unclear pronoun reference:

> **Confusing:** I'm reading a story in this book, **which** is very good.

> **Clear:**   I'm reading a very good story in this book.

Pronouns Without a Preceding Noun

Sometimes pronouns are used without any noun preceding them.

> After we put seeds in the birdfeeder, **they** never came around.

What is probably meant is that the birds never came around. However, it is better to be specific.

> After we put seeds in the birdfeeder, the **birds** never came around.

Another common mistake is to use a pronoun to refer to a general idea.

> The Changs give a lot of money to charity, which is admirable.

Here, *which* refers generally to giving money to charity. However, pronouns should refer to specific nouns. Then the sentence's meaning cannot be misunderstood.

> The Changs give a lot of money to charity; **this generosity** is admirable.

One other common problem occurs with the use of pronouns like *they, you,* and *it*.

> **They** say that too much salt is not good for **you.**

Who are *they?* Who is *you?* Notice how the following sentence makes the meaning more exact.

> **Health experts** say that too much salt is bad for **people.**

EXERCISE 6

Directions: Decide if each of the following sentences has a clear pronoun reference. If it does, write *C* in the space. If the reference is not clear, rewrite the sentence correctly.

Example: Mr. Berg and his son David took his car to the mechanic.

Mr. Berg and his son David took David's car to the mechanic.

1. When I saw Ms. Rivera standing with her son, I thought he looked tall.

   _____

   _____

2. Cathy told her son to clean his closet and his room since it was a mess.

   _____

   _____

3. The walls were bright green and the carpeting pale gray, which we thought was really ugly.

   _____

   _____

4. People are actually living without heat and hot water, and this must be taken care of.

   _____

   _____

5. They say that crime is increasing in our city.

   _____

   _____

6. Rosa told her daughter that she would be able to drive in two weeks.

   _____

   _____

7. Thaddeus helped Steve move into his new house.

   _____

   _____

8. Beth talked with them as they walked down the street.

   _____

   _____

Answers are on page 236.

Sentence Problems

Directions: Choose what correction should be made to each sentence below. Then choose the best correction for each sentence. If the sentence is correct, choose option (5).

1. **It had snowed overnight, but the sun had come out by 7:00 A.M. Looking outside, Juan told his son that it would be great skiing.**

   (1) change *had snowed* to *snowed*
   (2) change *had come* to *came*
   (3) change *his son* to *Juan's son*
   (4) change *would be* to *can be*
   (5) no correction is necessary

2. **If Marsha had gone to the movie, she will take her little sister with her.**

   (1) change *had gone* to *has gone*
   (2) change *she* to *Marsha*
   (3) change *will take* to *would have taken*
   (4) change *with her* to *with Marsha*
   (5) no correction is necessary

3. **Isabel told her daughter that she would go on vacation after all.**

   (1) change *told* to *tells*
   (2) change *her daughter* to *Isabel's daughter*
   (3) change *she* to *Isabel*
   (4) change *would go* to *goes*
   (5) no correction is necessary

4. **Mr. Ho likes to read as he rides to work. Yesterday he read a short story about a haunted house on the train.**

   (1) change *rides* to *has ridden*
   (2) change *he read* to *Mr. Ho read*
   (3) change *he read* to *he would have read*
   (4) move *on the train* so it comes right after *Yesterday*
   (5) no correction is necessary

5. **If you will go to the store, pick up some milk, and rent a movie, I will cook dinner.**

   (1) change *will go* to *had gone*
   (2) change *will go* to *could go*
   (3) change *rent* to *renting*
   (4) change *will cook* to *would cook*
   (5) no correction is necessary

6. **Barry told Boris that he is a better athlete because he can run faster.**

   (1) change *told* to *tell*
   (2) change *is* to *am*
   (3) change *because* to *although*
   (4) change the first *he* to *Barry*
   (5) no correction is necessary

Answers are on page 236.

Style and Diction

Sometimes problems with writing are not caused by errors in grammar or sentence structure. In fact, writing can be grammatically and mechanically correct, and yet the meaning may still be unclear. These problems can result from poor style or mistakes in diction.

Style is how you use words and sentences to express your meaning. **Diction** refers to your choice and use of words.

Economy and Precision in Writing

When you write, your most important goal should be to make your meaning clear. To write clearly, do not confuse your reader with more words than are necessary. Choose words that are as exact as possible. Here is an example of a sentence in which too many words make the meaning unclear:

> An article in a book that Sue was reading states that walking in which the walker moves briskly is exercise that is excellent.

Grammatically, there is nothing wrong with this sentence. However, to know what is said, you must read carefully. The problem is too many words. To make this kind of writing easier to understand, simplify it.

> An article in a book Sue was reading states that brisk walking is excellent exercise.

Even more simplification makes the meaning clearer.

> An article states that walking is excellent exercise.

When the sentence was made so brief, some ideas were lost. However, this information is probably not important to the reader. The message in the final revision is what the writer really wants readers to understand.

Here are some suggestions for making writing more economical and precise.

Avoid Repeating Ideas

Writers often unnecessarily repeat ideas. For example:

> Lemonade is **equally as refreshing as** orange juice.

Equally refreshing and *as refreshing as* mean the same thing.

> **Better:**   Lemonade is as refreshing as orange juice.
>
> <u>or</u>
>
> Lemonade and orange juice are equally refreshing.

A common example of repetition occurs when writers want to avoid sounding too sure of themselves. Then phrases like *I think* creep into the writing.

In my opinion, I think you should use a hammer.

In my opinion and *I think* repeat the same idea. Sometimes this is important information. Often it is not, because it is already understood that the writer is expressing a personal opinion.

Better: I think you should use a hammer.

Best: You should use a hammer.

Repetitious: In my opinion, it seems to me that nowadays there's too much violence on TV.

Better: In my opinion, nowadays there's too much violence on TV.

Best: There's too much violence on TV.

Use the Active Voice

Most verbs have both an active and a passive form. Remember that the subject of an **active verb** is the performer of the action. The subject of a **passive verb** has the action done to it. Sentences using passive forms usually need more words to say the same thing. To identify a verb in the passive voice, look for a phrase beginning with *by*. It tells who performs the action.

Passive: The bread was baked by Maya.
Active: Maya baked the bread.

Besides needing fewer words, active verbs make sentences more direct and forceful.

Passive: The speech had been given by the world-famous civil rights leader Dr. Martin Luther King, Jr.

Active: The world-famous civil rights leader Dr. Martin Luther King, Jr. gave the speech.

Passive: Soap operas are loved by people all over the world.

Active: People all over the world love soap operas.

Passive: The lamp was broken by me.

Active: I broke the lamp.

Passive: The movie was enjoyed by the whole audience.

Active: The whole audience enjoyed the movie.

Passive: Carrie's column is read by many people each day.

Active: Many people read Carrie's column each day.

EXERCISE 7

Directions: Rewrite each sentence to state the idea more precisely and economically.

Example: My neighborhood has several new buildings that were recently built near my house last year.

In my neighborhood, several buildings were built last year.

1. Heatwise, the temperature should get to eighty degrees warm.

2. People's names are often forgotten by me all the time.

3. The first step is to make a detailed list of each of the necessary ingredients right away.

4. The reason I don't write letters is because I never have enough time to write them.

5. He said that he thought the new salespeople were ready to go out into the field for further training.

Answers are on page 236.

Common Problems with Diction

Idioms are groups of words that have been used together so often that they have developed a special meaning. For example, *to keep up with, to come between,* and *to make believe* are idioms. You wouldn't know exactly what the phrases mean just by knowing what the separate words mean.

Idioms, like other words, have to be used precisely. Sometimes problems occur because idioms are used incorrectly.

Problems with Prepositions

1. Use *different from,* not *different than.*

   Incorrect: Pecans are **different than** walnuts.

   Correct: Pecans are **different from** walnuts.

2. Use the preposition *at* or *in* with the verb *to be,* not the preposition **to.**

   Incorrect: Juan was **to** the game yesterday.

   Correct: Juan was **at** the game yesterday.

3. Use the preposition *as* when a subject-verb combination follows, even if the verb is implied. Use the preposition *like* in all other cases.

   Incorrect: My daughter looks **as** me.

   Correct: My daughter looks **like** me.

   Incorrect: **Like** you know, she is already as tall as I am.

   Correct: **As** you know, she is already as tall as I am.

4. Use *between* when referring to only two things. Use *among* when referring to more than two things.

   Incorrect: The argument was **among** the two brothers.

   Correct: The argument was **between** the two brothers.

   Incorrect: The four couples divided the cost **between themselves.**

   Correct: The four couples divided the cost **among** *themselves.*

5. Use the preposition *from* after the word *borrow,* not the preposition *off* or *off of.*

   Incorrect: I will borrow the bicycle **off** Melissa.

   Incorrect: I will borrow the bicycle **off** of Melissa.

   Correct: I will borrow the bicycle **from** Melissa.

6. Use the preposition *off,* not *off of.*

   Incorrect: Warner got **off of** the train from Kansas City.

   Correct: Warner got **off** the train from Kansas City.

7. After the verbs *could*, *should*, and *would*, do not use the preposition *of*. The correct phrase is *could have*, *would have*, or *should have*. A contraction is also acceptable.

> **Incorrect:** I **should of** known the answer.
>
> **Correct:** I **should have** known the answer.
>
> **Correct:** I **should've** known the answer.

Problems with Verbs

Be alert for incorrect and unidiomatic uses of verbs. The following are a few of the more common errors.

1. Do not use the phrase *try and*. Use *try to* instead.

> **Incorrect:** Ms. Clemente says she will **try and** be here by three.
>
> **Correct:** Ms. Clemente says she will **try to** be here by three.

2. Use an infinitive after the word *ought*. *Should* means the same thing but does not need an infinitive.

> **Incorrect:** The team **ought try** to recruit a really tall center.
>
> **Correct:** The team **ought to try** to recruit a really tall center.
>
> **Correct:** The team **should try** to recruit a really tall center.

Problems with Comparisons

1. Be sure you are comparing similar things.

> Dep's bowling score was better than his partner.

Look closely. This sentence is comparing a *bowling score* with a *partner*. Here is what the writer means:

> Dep's bowling score was better than his partner's (bowling score).

2. Don't confuse *any* with *any other*.

> Katie is a better swimmer than **any** girl in her class.

Katie is a girl, so she cannot be a better swimmer than any girl. The writer means she is better than any *other* girl.

> Katie is a better swimmer than **any other** girl in her class.

EXERCISE 8

Directions: Decide if each of the following sentences contains an incorrect usage. If there is an error, rewrite the sentence correctly. If there is no error, write *C*.

Example: Julie's dog is very different than my dog.

Julie's dog is very different from my dog.

1. Lee told us that Greg should of received the package by now.

   _____

   _____

2. Like I've said before, most people never know how well off they are.

   _____

   _____

3. Sarah divided the remaining cake between the three of us.

   _____

   _____

4. Roland will certainly be to the game Saturday to see his brother play.

   _____

   _____

5. When she got up off of the ground the last time, Yoko gave up skating.

   _____

   _____

6. Tina's got a sharper memory than any person I know.

   _____

   _____

7. The actors in that movie were worse than the movie I saw last week.

   _____

   _____

8. Sid said he knew someone who would try and get us tickets.

   _____

   _____

Answers are on page 236.

Style and Diction

Directions: Choose the most effective revision of each sentence. If you think the original sentence is the best way, choose option (5).

1. **The new baby was brought home from the hospital by the parents.**

   (1) The new baby was brung home from the hospital by her parents.
   (2) The parents brought the new baby home from the hospital.
   (3) By the parents, the new baby was brought home from the hospital.
   (4) The new baby that was just born the other day was brought home from the hospital where it was born by the parents who had it.
   (5) no correction is necessary

2. **The mother divided the box of chocolates between her four children.**

   (1) The mother could of divided the box of chocolates between her four children.
   (2) The mother divided the box of chocolates to her four children.
   (3) Between her four children, the mother divided the box of chocolates.
   (4) The mother divided the box of chocolates among her four children.
   (5) no correction is necessary

3. **In my opinion, it seems to me as if the amount of traffic in this town has increased rapidly over the past ten years.**

   (1) The amount of traffic in this town has increased rapidly over the past ten years.
   (2) In my opinion, it seems to me as if the amount of traffic in this town had increased rapidly over the past ten years.
   (3) It seems to me, in my opinion, that the amount of traffic in this town has increased rapidly over the past ten years.
   (4) Over the past ten years, it seems to me as if the amount of traffic in this town has increased rapidly in my opinion.
   (5) no correction is necessary

4. **The first candidate's campaign speech was much better than the second candidate's.**

   (1) The first candidate's campaign speech was much more good than the second candidate.
   (2) The first candidate's campaign speech was much better than the second candidate.
   (3) Much better was the first candidate's campaign speech than the second candidate.
   (4) The campaign speech of the first candidate was much better than the second candidate.
   (5) no correction is necessary

Answers are on page 237.

Chapter Review

Directions: Choose the <u>one best answer</u> to each question. Some of the sentences may contain errors in sentence structure. A few sentences, however, may be correct as written. Read the sentences carefully and then answer the questions based on them. For each question, choose the answer that would result in the most effective writing of the sentence or sentences.

1. **Taro is <u>different from Tamara because he would of been</u> nervous speaking before a large group.**

   Which is the best way to write the underlined portion of the text? If the original is the best way, choose option (1).

   (1) different from Tamara because he would of been
   (2) different than Tamara because he would have been
   (3) different than Tamara because they would have been
   (4) different from Tamara; because he would have been
   (5) different from Tamara because he would have been

2. **Barb <u>was upset when she has discovered that she had forgotten</u> her keys.**

   Which is the best way to write the underlined portion of the text? If the original is the best way, choose option (1).

   (1) was upset when she has discovered that she had forgotten
   (2) was upset when she discovers that she had forgotten
   (3) was upset when she discovered that she had forgotten
   (4) was upset; although she had discovered that she had forgotten
   (5) was upset because she has discovered that she had forgotten

3. **Rhode Island <u>not only is the smallest state but also near the ocean</u>.**

   Which is the best way to write the underlined portion of the text? If the original is the best way, choose option (1).

   (1) not only is the smallest state but also near the ocean
   (2) is both the smallest state but also near the ocean
   (3) not only is the smaller state but it is also near the ocean
   (4) not only is the smallest state but also is near the ocean
   (5) is not only the smallest state but near the ocean

4. **<u>The hurricane brought high winds and driving rains the</u> damage was not severe.**

   Which is the best way to write the underlined portion of the text? If the original is the best way, choose option (1).

   (1) The hurricane brought high winds and driving rains the
   (2) Although the hurricane brought high winds and driving rains, the
   (3) Although the hurricane brought high winds and driving rains the
   (4) The hurricane brought high winds and driving rains, however, the
   (5) The hurricane brought high winds and driving rains and

5. **The climate in the Caribbean is considered <u>tropical even though it has</u> lots of sun and rainfall.**

   Which is the best way to write the underlined portion of the text? If the original is the best way, choose option (1).

   (1) tropical even though it has
   (2) tropical, even though it has
   (3) tropical; however, it has
   (4) tropical since it has
   (5) tropical, since it consists of

6. **John's brother and his mother <u>took his injured dog</u> to the veterinarian.**

   Which is the best way to write the underlined portion of the text? If the original is the best way, choose option (1).

   (1) took his injured dog
   (2) took the dog that had been injured
   (3) took John's injured dog
   (4) took her injured dog
   (5) took his or her injured dog

7. **<u>In the future time before us, world leaders around the globe</u> must make tough decisions.**

   Which is the best way to write the underlined portion of the text? If the original is the best way, choose option (1).

   (1) In the future time before us, world leaders around the globe
   (2) In the future, world leaders
   (3) In the future time, world leaders
   (4) In the time before us, world leaders around the globe
   (5) World leaders of the future that's before us

8. **<u>If you pay that fine you will</u> lose your driver's license.**

   Which is the best way to write the underlined portion of the text? If the original is the best way, choose option (1).

   (1) If you pay that fine you will
   (2) Unless you pay that fine, you will
   (3) Unless you pay that fine you will
   (4) If you pay that fine, you would
   (5) However you pay that fine you will

9. **Cheryl's serve <u>is faster than any other tennis player</u> in the league.**

   Which is the best way to write the underlined portion of the text? If the original is the best way, choose option (1).

   (1) is faster than any other tennis player
   (2) is the fastest of any other tennis player
   (3) is faster than the serve of any other tennis player
   (4) is faster than any tennis player
   (5) is more fast than any other tennis player

10. **Murray Mugford bought a <u>used car at an auto dealership that was on sale for $2,000.</u>**

    Which is the best way to write the underlined portion of the text? If the original is the best way, choose option (1).

    (1) used car at an auto dealership that was on sale for $2,000.
    (2) car, at an auto dealership that was on sale for $2,000
    (3) car at an auto dealership selling for $2,000
    (4) car, that was at an auto dealership for $2,000
    (5) car that was on sale for $2,000 at an auto dealership

11. **Like Mr. Murray said, about two hundred people applied for this job.**

    Which is the best way to write the underlined portion of the text? If the original is the best way, choose option (1).

    (1) Like Mr. Murray said, about
    (2) Like Mr. Murray said, around
    (3) As Mr. Murray said, about
    (4) As Mr. Murray said about
    (5) Like Mr. Murray said around

12. **The trio is singing tonight in spite of the fact that the lead singer has a bad cold.**

    Which is the best way to write the underlined portion of the text? If the original is the best way, choose option (1).

    (1) tonight in spite of the fact that the
    (2) tonight, in spite of the fact that the
    (3) tonight, because the
    (4) tonight, since the
    (5) tonight, in spite of the fact that, the

13. **If Marie Rosello were mayor, this city would not have been in debt.**

    Which is the best way to write the underlined portion of the text? If the original is the best way, choose option (1).

    (1) mayor, this city would not have been
    (2) mayor, this city will not be
    (3) mayor, this city were not
    (4) mayor, this city would not be
    (5) mayor this city would not be

14. **Clean water, clean air, and protecting our other natural resources should be the goal of every elected official.**

    Which is the best way to write the underlined portion of the text? If the original is the best way, choose option (1).

    (1) clean air, and protecting our other natural resources
    (2) cleaning the air, and protecting our other natural resources
    (3) clean air, and to protect our other natural resources
    (4) to clean the air, and protecting our natural resources
    (5) clean air, and protection for our other natural resources

15. **After months of work on the construction project, at last it was finally completed by Jim.**

    Which is the best way to write the underlined portion of the text? If the original is the best way, choose option (1).

    (1) at last it was finally completed by Jim.
    (2) at last, it was finally completed by Jim
    (3) at last Jim finally completed it
    (4) Jim finally completed it
    (5) Jim finally completed it at last

16. <u>**Wanting so badly to own a sheep farm in Australia**</u>**, Ted and his wife Sonia packed up their things and left the country.**

Which is the best way to write the underlined portion of the text? If the original is the best way, choose option (1).

(1) Wanting so badly to own a sheep farm in Australia,
(2) Because they wanted so badly to own a sheep farm in Australia,
(3) Although they wanted so badly to own a sheep farm in Australia,
(4) Wanting so badly to own a sheep farm in Australia;
(5) Their want of a sheep farm in Australia was great, so

17. <u>**The bitter disagreement among Dr. Freud and Dr. Jung**</u> **developed gradually over many years.**

Which is the best way to write the underlined portion of the text? If the original is the best way, choose option (1).

(1) The bitter disagreement among Dr. Freud and Dr. Jung
(2) The bitter disagreement, which was among Dr. Freud and Dr. Jung,
(3) Because the bitter disagreement among Dr. Freud and Dr. Jung
(4) The bitter disagreement between Dr. Freud and Dr. Jung
(5) As a result of the bitter disagreement among Dr. Freud and Dr. Jung

18. <u>**Calmed by the doctor and because he was under medication**</u>**, Manuel finally was able to sleep.**

Which is the best way to write the underlined portion of the text? If the original is the best way, choose option (1).

(1) Calmed by the doctor and because he was under medication,
(2) Calmed by the doctor, because he was under medication,
(3) The doctor having arrived, and because he was on medication,
(4) Calmed by the doctor and quieted by the medication,
(5) Having been calmed by the doctor, and because he was on medication,

19. **Wendy's speech** <u>**was both dramatic and it also inspired the audience**</u>**.**

Which is the best way to write the underlined portion of the text? If the original is the best way, choose option (1).

(1) was both dramatic and it also inspired the audience
(2) not only was dramatic but it was also inspiring to the audience
(3) was both dramatic and inspiring to the audience
(4) was both dramatic and it inspired the audience
(5) being both dramatic and inspirational to the audience

Answers are on page 237.

Evaluate Your Progress

On the following chart, circle the number of any item you answered incorrectly in the Chapter 3 Review on pages 99–100 or in the Chapter 4 Review on pages 128–131. Next to each group of item numbers, you will see the pages you can review to learn how to answer the items correctly. Pay particular attention to reviewing skill areas in which you missed half or more of the questions.

Skill Area	Chapter 3 Review Item Number	Chapter 4 Review Item Number	Review Pages
SENTENCE STRUCTURE			
Run-on sentences/ comma splices		4	103–104
Wordiness/repetition		4	121–127
Coordination/subordination		3, 5, 12, 15	102–110
Modification	6, 7, 8, 9, 10, 11 12, 13	9, 10, 11	81–100, 111–112
Parallelism		14	113–114
USAGE			
Verb tense/form	2	1, 2, 13	53–66, 115–117
Pronoun reference/ antecedent agreement	3, 4, 5, 14	6	30–47, 118–119
MECHANICS			
Punctuation (commas)	1	8	20

CHAPTER 5

Mechanics

Capitalization

Read the passage below. What's wrong with it?

> herman melville spent five years on a whaling boat between 1839 and 1844 he sailed the atlantic ocean and on other oceans too drawing upon this experience melville wrote several masterpieces of american literature you have probably heard of moby dick it was melville's most famous novel it is the story of captain ahabs vengeful search for the white whale which had maimed him on one level the book can be read as an exciting adventure story at a deeper level the book is an in-depth study of mans struggle against nature and the forces of evil for decades melvilles book went unnoticed but after world war I students of american literature rediscovered melville today his works enjoy a wide audience

You probably noticed that capitalization and punctuation are missing. Although neither punctuation nor capitalization will make poor writing great, both help make all writing clear and understandable.

You know that the first word in every sentence should be capitalized. In addition, nouns that name specific people, places, and things are capitalized. For example, Herman Melville is a specific person. His masterpiece, *Moby Dick,* is a specific book. The Atlantic Ocean is a specific ocean.

Nouns that name general people, places, or things are not capitalized. The word *ocean* is a general name. It could refer to any ocean. Some other general nouns in the passage are *masterpieces, whaling boat,* and *novel.*

When to Capitalize

Geographic Locations
Stick to this rule: Capitalize specific names; do not capitalize general names. The rule applies to names of geographic places.

General: My friend lives in a large **city.**

Specific: My friend lives in **San Francisco.**

Note that the rule also applies to specific names that are used as adjectives but not to general names used as adjectives.

General: I ordered bread.

Specific: I ordered **French** bread.

General: I ordered **garlic** bread.

Directions, such as north, southeast, easterly, and western, are not capitalized when they refer to a direction. They should be capitalized when they name a specific region of the country or of a city.

General: We drove **south** to the coast and then **northeast** into Georgia.

Specific: We visited **Sante Fe,** which is in the **Southwest.**

Titles and Names

Capitalize words used as titles that refer to a specific person.

When **Senator** Jones spoke, the audience listened carefully.

I asked **Doctor** Basulto to look at my arm.

Sometimes titles are used by themselves as though they were a name. This occurs when you are speaking directly to someone.

Will it heal, **Doctor?**

Tell me how you will reduce crime, **Mayor.**

If a title is used only to refer to an occupation, do not capitalize it.

The judge gave her decision.

EDITING TIP

If you are not sure whether a title that stands by itself should be capitalized, try replacing it with the person's name. If the sentence makes sense, capitalize the title. If it does not make sense, do not capitalize the title.

I wrote a letter to my aunt. ⟶ I wrote a letter to my Maria.

Thank you for the letter, Aunt. ⟶ Thank you for the letter, Maria.

Capitalize the first word and all important words in titles of books, plays, poems, or other written works.

I read the book ***Death Comes for the Archbishop.***

Did you see the play ***The Importance of Being Earnest***?

He memorized the poem ***Jazz Fantasia.***

Buildings and Other Places

Capitalize the names of buildings and other places when they stand for specific buildings or places.

Empire State Building   White House
Lottie's Laundromat   Grand Avenue

Words like *building, house, laundromat,* and *avenue* are not always capitalized. Capitalize them only if they are part of the specific name. Look at how the words are used in the sentence to decide.

That **building** is one of the tallest in the city.

Let's visit the Empire State **Building**.

She washes her clothes every Saturday at the **laundromat**.

Her favorite place to wash her clothes is Lottie's **Laundromat**.

There's a **white house** on the corner of our block.

The Mendez family toured the **White House**.

Madison Street is a **grand avenue**.

Grand Avenue is lined with stately oak trees.

EXERCISE 1

Directions: One of the underlined words in each sentence below has incorrect capitalization. Write the word, with correct capitalization, on the line.

Example: <u>Mr. Wang</u> is a <u>Congressman</u> from <u>Missouri.</u>

congressman

1. To get to the <u>supermarket</u>, turn <u>East</u> on <u>Riverdale Road</u>.

   _____

2. A famous <u>monument</u> to <u>president</u> Lincoln is in <u>Springfield</u>, Illinois.

   _____

3. The <u>english</u> <u>highways</u> are crowded with <u>automobiles</u> traveling at unbelievable speeds.

   _____

4. A <u>production</u> of the play <u>*My Fair Lady*</u> will be presented by <u>southeast</u> High School.

   _____

5. <u>langston hughes</u> is one of <u>America's</u> greatest <u>poets</u>.

   _____

Answers are on page 237.

Other Capitalization Rules

Quotations

The first word of every sentence is capitalized. When you are writing a quotation, follow the same rule.

> Celeste asked, "**Should** we buy groceries now, or wait till later?"

In the example, the quotation would stand alone as a complete sentence. It should begin with a capital letter. If the quotation is not a complete sentence, do not begin it with a capital letter.

> Ken described the color of Cindy's new car as a "**seasick** green."

In the following sentence, the quotation makes up a complete sentence. However, it is divided by words introducing the speaker. Capitalize the first part of the quotation because it begins a complete sentence. Do not capitalize the second part of the quotation because it is a fragment.

> "**A** fire broke out this morning," the newscaster reported, "**and** three people were injured."

Abbreviations and Initials

Capitalize the letters that make up abbreviations of titles and organizations and initials.

> **CPA** (Certified Public Accountant)
>
> **NFL** (National Football League)
>
> Kathy Chung, **Ph.D.** (Doctor of Philosophy)
>
> Samuel Dickens, **Jr.** (junior)

Dates

Capitalize the names of days of the week and months. Do not capitalize seasons.

> My vacation begins next **Friday, October 3.**
>
> I love to take my vacations in the **autumn.**

Capitalize the names of holidays.

> I always think of **Memorial Day** as the first day of summer.

School Subjects

Capitalize the names of school subjects only when you refer to specific courses. If you are referring to a general kind of class, do not capitalize it.

> I am taking a **biology** class and **History** 101.

Note that you always capitalize words that name a specific language, like *English* and *Spanish.*

Organizations

Names of government and social organizations are always capitalized.

> Anna's father works for the **Department of Transportation.**

> All profits will be donated to the **American Diabetes Association.**

EXERCISE 2

Directions: One of the underlined words in each sentence below has incorrect capitalization. Write the word using correct capitalization on the line.

Example: My favorite <u>month</u> is <u>December</u> because I love <u>christmas.</u>

*Christmas*_____

1. Last <u>Wednesday</u>, members of the <u>PTA</u> formed a special committee that will meet <u>Weekly</u> until the end of the school year.

   _____

2. "<u>Don't</u> drink water from the spring," my <u>sister</u> warned, "<u>Unless</u> you want to get sick."

   _____

3. On <u>Friday</u>, <u>April</u> 24, I will be in Minneapolis for a meeting of the <u>aclu</u> (American Civil Liberties Union).

   _____

4. My father, John S. Haynes, <u>sr.</u>, will retire next <u>spring</u> after thirty years with the <u>NYPD</u> (New York Police Department).

   _____

5. Susan Cordova, <u>Ph.D.</u>, teaches <u>biology 340</u> on <u>Wednesday</u> evenings.

   _____

6. "Of course I'll be there," Maria answered, "<u>if</u> the <u>event</u> benefits the <u>children's aid society</u>."

   _____

Answers are on pages 237–238.

Capitalization

Directions: Choose what correction should be made to each sentence below. If you think the sentence is correct, choose option (5)

1. **Lonnie and Felicia went to a Los angeles Lakers basketball game.**

   (1) change *Felicia* to *felicia*
   (2) change *Los angeles* to *Los Angeles*
   (3) change *Lakers* to *lakers*
   (4) change *basketball* to *Basketball*
   (5) no correction is necessary

2. **When you told me you were from New York, you never mentioned the East Side, which is the area where my Grandmother grew up.**

   (1) change *New York* to *new york*
   (2) change *East Side* to *east side*
   (3) change *area* to *Area*
   (4) change *Grandmother* to *grandmother*
   (5) no correction is necessary

3. **Whenever Lucha's sister hears "Moon River," she cries because that song reminds her of her first boyfriend.**

   (1) change *sister* to *Sister*
   (2) change *Moon River* to *moon river*
   (3) change *song* to *Song*
   (4) change *boyfriend* to *Boyfriend*
   (5) no correction is necessary

4. **I want you to know, Dad, that I really enjoyed going to the Baseball game at Tiger Stadium.**

   (1) change *Dad* to *dad*
   (2) change *Baseball* to *baseball*
   (3) change *game* to *Game*
   (4) change *Tiger Stadium* to *tiger stadium*
   (5) no correction is necessary

5. **The coach, Joe Stearns, EdD., recommended a book on Physical Fitness.**

   (1) change *coach* to *Coach*
   (2) change *EdD.* to *edd*
   (3) change *book* to *Book*
   (4) change *Physical Fitness* to *physical fitness*
   (5) no correction is necessary

6. **Bill's Rusty Spoon Restaurant was closed before the Memorial Day holiday by an administrator for the department of health.**

   (1) change *Restaurant* to *restaurant*
   (2) change *Memorial Day* to *memorial day*
   (3) change *administrator* to *Administrator*
   (4) change *department of health* to *Department of Health*
   (5) no correction is necessary

7. **Dr. Debra Samrit, a psychiatrist from the Northwest side of Denver, gave a lecture on guilt.**

   (1) change *psychiatrist* to *Psychiatrist*
   (2) change *Northwest* to *northwest*
   (3) change *lecture* to *Lecture*
   (4) change *guilt* to *Guilt*
   (5) no correction is necessary

Answers are on page 238.

Punctuation

There are many types of punctuation, and there are specific rules for each type. Using punctuation correctly will help you make your writing clearer and more effective.

Using End Punctuation

A sentence can be ended in three ways: with a period, a question mark, or an exclamation point.

A **period** is used to end a sentence that gives information or states a feeling or wish.

> The Riveras will arrive tomorrow.

A **question mark** is used to end a question.

> Why does Mary Ann always work late?

An **exclamation point** is used to end a sentence that shows strong excitement or emotion.

> Help!

> Please hurry, Doctor!

Pay special attention to how end punctuation is used in quotations.

The period always goes inside the quotation marks.

Incorrect:	"Elephants," he said, "can be dangerous".
Correct:	"Elephants," he said, "can be dangerous."

The question mark and exclamation point can go either inside or outside the quotation marks. To decide which, look at the meaning of the sentence. If the quotation is itself a question, put the question mark inside the quotation marks.

Incorrect:	"Is that elephant loose," Shawna asked?
Incorrect:	"Is that elephant loose" Shawna asked?
Correct:	"Is that elephant loose?" Shawna asked.

But sometimes a quotation is part of a sentence that is a question. Then put the question mark outside the quotation marks.

Incorrect:	Did Charise say, "That elephant is loose?"
Incorrect:	Did Charise say, "That elephant is loose."?
Correct:	Did Charise say, "That elephant is loose"?

When using exclamation points with quotation marks, follow the same rule. If the quotation is an exclamation, put the exclamation point inside the quotation marks. If the quotation is not an exclamation but is part of a sentence that is, put the exclamation point outside the quotation marks.

Incorrect: Kim Soon said, "Run for your life"!

Incorrect: Kim Soon said, "Run for your life."!

Correct: Kim Soon said, "Run for your life!"

EDITING TIP

Never use more than one kind of end punctuation.

Using Abbreviations and Initials

In addition to ending sentences, periods are used in abbreviations and with initials.

Dec. 3 (December 3)
C. S. Lewis
Badger Co. (Badger Company)

When an abbreviation comes at the end of a sentence, use only one period.

Incorrect: Pedro works at Celltine, Inc..

Correct: Pedro works at Celltine, Inc.

EXERCISE 3

Directions: Write the correct punctuation in the blanks in each sentence below. Use either a period, a question mark, or an exclamation point.

Example: Will a week from tomorrow be Feb _._ 23 _?_

1. Mrs____ Rachet completed the annual report____

2. Look out for that bus____

3. Did he pick the winning lottery number____

4. "Did he already spend all the money____" Georgia asked____

5. My uncle named his new business the Rivets Co____

6. "Quick____" shouted the police officer over his car radio____

7. As she looked all over the house, Maxine moaned, "Where are my keys____"

8. Just what do you mean by the term "slacker"____

Answers are on page 238.

Commas

The **comma** has two main uses. First, it separates clauses in compound and complex sentences. (You may want to review compound and complex sentences in Chapter 4.) Second, it separates items in the sentence, such as interrupting phrases and items in a series.

Commas in Compound Sentences

Commas with Conjunctions

Remember, a **compound sentence** is made up of two simple sentences, or independent clauses, that are joined together. The most common way to join clauses is by using a comma plus one of these conjunctions: *and, or, nor, but, for, so,* and *yet.*

> The shark swam toward the shore, **but** the swimmers didn't notice.

When clauses are joined using a conjunction, place a comma before the conjunction. Never join independent clauses using only a comma.

Incorrect: It rained hard all week, the rivers rose out of their banks.

Incorrect: It rained hard all week and the rivers rose out of their banks.

Correct: It rained hard all week, and the rivers rose out of their banks.

Commas with Conjunctive Adverbs

A second way to join independent clauses is by using a **conjunctive adverb.** These are words such as *however, furthermore, nevertheless, for example,* and *moreover.*

> The snow piled up three feet high; **however,** the snowplows had the roads open by noon.

Notice that a semicolon comes before the conjunctive adverb and a comma follows it.

Commas in Complex Sentences

Complex sentences are made up of one main, or independent, clause and one or more dependent clauses. A dependent clause is joined to the main clause by a conjunction such as *when, after, because, if,* and *although.*

> After Kyoko heard the news, she leaped from her chair.

> She couldn't believe her good luck because she had never won anything.

Notice that when the dependent clause comes at the beginning of the sentence, it is followed by a comma. When the dependent clause comes at the end of the sentence, no comma is used.

Commas with Sentence Elements

Commas with Quotations

Use a comma to separate a direct quotation from the rest of a sentence.

> Juan said, "I'm joining a softball team."

> "Maybe you'll be called up to the majors," Stan joked.

If a quotation comes first in a sentence, and if it is a question or an exclamation, do not use a comma to separate the quotation from the rest of the sentence.

Incorrect: "When can I play?", Juan asked.

Incorrect: "When can I play," Juan asked.

Correct: "When can I play?" Juan asked.

Commas with Interrupting Phrases

An **interrupting phrase** is not a necessary part of a sentence. It simply gives additional information. Three types of interrupting phrases should be set off from the rest of the sentence by commas.

1. Renaming Phrases

   In Chapter 3, you learned about phrases that rename the subject or object of a sentence. These interrupters should be set off with commas.

   > Manuel Suarez, **the man behind the desk,** is an accountant.

   The phrase **the man behind the desk** renames or further identifies Manuel Suarez. Set it off with commas.

2. Direct Address

   When a sentence is directed to a specific person, the person's name should be set off with commas.

   > Please hand me that book, **Maria.**

   > If you will go with me, **Amy,** I will buy your dinner.

3. Extra Information

   Some words and phrases interrupt a sentence to give added information. These should be set off with commas.

   > Lydia, **in fact,** refused to accept the gift.

   > **Nevertheless,** we must keep making an effort.

When the phrase is in the middle of the sentence, put commas on both sides of it. When the phrase begins or ends a sentence, separate it with one comma.

One common type of interrupting phrase is made up of a subject and a verb such as *believe, think,* or *know.* Set them off with commas.

The plan, **I believe,** is a good one.

I didn't ask for this, **you know.**

Phrases such as *in fact* and *of course* and phrases used to show contrast are also interrupters. Set them off with commas.

Sandy Davis is, **in fact,** my mother's cousin.

Rene will work on Thursday, **not on Friday.**

Before setting off a phrase with commas, be sure the phrase is not essential to the meaning of the sentence.

Incorrect:	I think, that Mike should become a professional musician.
Correct:	Mike, I think, should become a professional musician.
Correct:	I think that Mike should become a professional musician.

In the first sentence, *I think* is part of the main clause. No commas should be used. In the second sentence, *I think* is an interrupter. It is not necessary to the meaning of the sentence. Use commas to set it off.

Commas with a Series

When more than two nouns or verbs or more than two adjectives or adverbs are used in a series, separate them with a comma. The final item in the series of nouns or verbs is usually introduced by a conjunction, such as *and.* A comma should be used before the conjunction.

That **big, ugly, ill-tempered** dog is a nuisance.

We had **hot dogs, baked beans, and salad.**

Commas should also be used to set off phrases, or even clauses, that are written as a series.

Andrew **grabs the ball, dribbles to his left, pulls up, and shoots.**

Commas with Addresses, Dates, and Greetings

Use a comma to separate parts of an address or of a date.

20 Stanford Street, Dayton, OH 66660

November 7, 2002

December 2002

Notice that no comma is used to separate these items:

* the month and day

* the house number and street name

* the state and zip code

* the month and year when no specific date is given

Also use a comma after the greeting and closing in an informal letter.

Dear family and friends,

We are having a get-together to celebrate the holiday season on Saturday, December 21, any time after 7 P.M. Feel free to bring your favorite snack, dessert, or drink. Please R.S.V.P. by December 14. We look forward to seeing you.

Sincerely,

Christine and Alan

Christine and Alan

EXERCISE 4

Directions: Read the sentences below. If a comma is missing from a sentence, add it. If a comma is not needed, cross it out.

Example: Fran, will you please come here, and help me?

1. When Akiko came by the office she fixed the copy machine.

2. The little boy asked "How can I get home from here?"

3. On January 3, the Bombers will play at Johnson Field, Omaha Nebraska.

4. It was in fact the best cheesecake she had ever had.

5. Jim picked up the trash can and a rat came flying out.

6. Why don't you wear your yellow sweater Tomás?

7. This exercise program is easy for me; moreover I have lost ten pounds.

8. Yolanda the woman who got me this job has now quit.

9. Mr. Chung hurriedly left his house, after getting the telephone call.

10. "Gina will pick you up in an hour" the woman replied.

Answers are on page 238.

Other Types of Punctuation

Colon

Use a **colon** after a complete thought that introduces a list. Do not use a colon if the introduction to the list is not a complete thought.

Incorrect:	We packed: apples, cheese, and a loaf of bread.
Correct:	We packed the following items: apples, cheese, and a loaf of bread.
Correct:	We packed apples, cheese, and a loaf of bread.

Use a colon after the greeting in a formal or business letter.

Dear Sir or Madam:

Use a colon to separate the hour from minutes in written time.

It is now 6:45.

Semicolon

A **semicolon** is used in two ways in forming compound sentences. When the clauses in a compound sentence are linked using a conjunctive adverb, place a semicolon before the adverb.

David is a good tennis player; however, he has never beaten Christy.

You can also link closely related clauses in a compound sentence without using either a conjunction or a conjunctive adverb. Use the semicolon by itself to show that the two clauses are independent.

It is a beautiful day; I should be spending it outdoors.

A semicolon can also be used to separate items in a series when there are already commas within the items.

The contestants in the dog show were Fido, a brown mutt; Fifi, a French poodle; and Farley, a golden retriever.

Quotation Marks

Use **quotation marks** to show the exact words of a speaker in a direct quote.

"Stop yelling," Michael said, "or we will go home."

If the sentence is only a statement about what someone says (an indirect quote), don't use quotation marks.

Michael said that we should stop yelling or we will go home.

Be alert to the use of other punctuation with quotation marks.

- Place commas and periods inside quotations.

- Place question marks and exclamation points outside quotation marks if the entire sentence is a question or exclamation.

- Place question marks and exclamation points inside quotation marks only if the quotation itself is a question or exclamation.

Apostrophe

The **apostrophe** has two main uses. The first of these is to show possession. When used for possession, an apostrophe shows that one thing belongs to another.

Piri's cat is more ferocious than any dog on the street.

The second use for apostrophes is to form contractions. A **contraction** is one word that is made up of two words with one or more letters left out. The apostrophe is used in place of the missing letters.

Common Contractions			
isn't → is not		can't → cannot	
doesn't → does not		we'll → we will	
wouldn't → would not		let's → let us	
they're → they are		she's → she is or she has	
won't → will not		they'd → they had or they would	
hasn't → has not		there's → there is or there has	
I'm → I am		you've → you have	

See the section on spelling that follows for more about contractions.

EXERCISE 5

Directions: Write the correct punctuation in the blanks provided for each sentence below. Watch for blanks that need two kinds of punctuation.

Example: Which would you prefer__:__ a soft drink__,__ a glass of water __,__ or a cup of coffee__?__

1. Teresa really wanted to go to Mexico____ nevertheless____she agreed to spend her vacation at the lake.

2. At the supermarket, we ran into our old neighbors____the Okaras ____who lived next door____Jill and Sean____the ones who gave noisy parties____and Marianne____our babysitter.

3. Keisha cried____He forgot my birthday____then he went to a hockey game____

4. Paulo wished he could remember everything____however____he was already forgetting the details.

5. He gave these reasons for moving____a bigger yard____more bedrooms____lower taxes____and a better school district.

6. It is now 7____00 and Stan just got here____nevertheless____we're still going to the game.

7. Jan yelled to her brother____Who's going to feed the dog____

8. Dear Madam____

   I bought a SlimMachine because I wanted to lose weight____ It____s already broken____Please refund my money____

   Sincerely____

   John Arocha

9. They____re looking for a new car____the one they have is worn out.

10. I want a job downtown____not one out in the suburbs.

Answers are on pages 238–239.

Punctuation

Directions: Choose the best correction for each sentence below. If you think the sentence is correct, choose option (5).

1. **"Is Mark's new company located in Philadelphia," Julie asked.**

   (1) change *Philadelphia,"* to *Philadelphia."*
   (2) change *Philadelphia,"* to *Philadelphia"?*
   (3) change *Philadelphia,"* to *Philadelphia?"*
   (4) change *asked.* to *asked?*
   (5) no correction is necessary

2. **When the engine caught on fire, Sachi yelled, "Get out of the car now"!**

   (1) change *yelled,* to *yelled!*
   (2) change *now"!* to *now."*
   (3) change *now"!* to *now!".*
   (4) change *now"!* to *now!"*
   (5) no correction is necessary

3. **When Trivits, Inc., didn't hire her, Mercedes wanted to know what she had to do to get a job?**

   (1) change *Inc.,* to *Inc,*
   (2) change *job?* to *job.*
   (3) change *job?* to *job!*
   (4) change *job?* to *job!.*
   (5) no correction is necessary

4. **On Feb. 29, Suzanne took the day off. The next day, she innocently asked her boss, "Wasn't that a holiday?"**

   (1) change *Feb.* to *Feb*
   (2) change *off.* to *off!*
   (3) change *boss,* to *boss?*
   (4) change *holiday?* to *holiday.*
   (5) no correction is necessary

5. **Who said, "I want to play basketball?"**

   (1) change *said,* to *said?*
   (2) change *said,* to *said.*
   (3) change *basketball?"* to *basketball"?*
   (4) change *basketball?"* to *basketball."?*
   (5) no correction is necessary

6. **I believe, Melissa will be here in 20 minutes.**

   (1) change *Melissa* to *Melissa,*
   (2) change *here* to *here,*
   (3) change *believe,* to *believe*
   (4) change *minutes.* to *minutes?*
   (5) no correction is necessary

7. **As soon as I finish this task, I will go home.**

   (1) change *task,* to *task*
   (2) change *task,* to *task:*
   (3) change *I will go home* to *"I will go home"*
   (4) change *as soon as* to *as soon as,*
   (5) no correction is necessary

8. **Its too cold to go outside tonight; however, I'll shovel the driveway first thing tomorrow morning.**

   (1) change *tonight;* to *tonight,*
   (2) change *its* to *it's*
   (3) change *however,* to *however;*
   (4) change *I'll* to *Ill*
   (5) no correction is necessary

   Answers are on page 239.

Spelling

As you know, accurate spelling is an important skill in effective writing. The GED Language Arts, Writing Test will test your ability to spell possessives, contractions, and homonyms. A **homonym** is a word that sounds the same as another word but is spelled differently. Several possessives and contractions are homonyms. You saw some homonyms in Chapter 1. Here are some more examples:

All of the forklift operators are good at **their** jobs.

They're good drivers on the open road, too.

Are **there** any questions?

The words *their, they're,* and *there* are homonyms. *Their* is a possessive pronoun meaning "belonging to them." *They're* is a contraction meaning "they are." *There* is an adverb that specifies where something is. All three words have different meanings and different spellings, but they all sound alike. A common writing error is to use the wrong homonym in a sentence. What is the spelling error in the sentence below?

There should be a bonus for they're hard work.

The spelling error in the sentence is the contraction *they're*. *They are* makes no sense in this sentence, but *their*, the possessive pronoun that shows who did the hard work, does.

There should be a bonus for **their** hard work.

Here is a review of some confusing contractions and possessive pronouns that are homonyms. Notice how they follow a simple rule: Contractions need apostrophes; possessive pronouns <u>do not</u> have apostrophes.

Possessive Pronouns	Contractions
its (the cat's)	it's (it is, it has)
theirs (the workers')	there's (there is)
your (belonging to you)	you're (you are)
whose (Maggie's)	who's (who is)

Incorrect:	That cat must be controlled by **it's** owner.
Correct:	**It's** a cat without fear.
Correct:	It knows **its** claws are sharp.

Incorrect:	**Who's** dog wandered onto Piri's street?
Correct:	**Who's** looking for a pet?
Correct:	I know **whose** dog it is.

Another common homonym error is using an apostrophe to form a plural noun. This error is often made because a plural noun sounds just like a possessive noun—but it's spelled differently.

Incorrect:	The **computer's** have all crashed.
Correct:	The **computers** have all crashed.
Correct:	Jane's **computer's** circuits were fried by lightning.
Correct:	All three **computers'** circuits were fried by lightning.

The first sentence is incorrect because it uses an apostrophe in a plural noun that does not show possession. The next three sentences are correct. The first correct sentence shows a simple plural, the next shows a singular possessive, and the last shows a plural possessive.

In the English language, there are many homonyms that are not contractions, possessives, or plurals. Some of these homonyms may appear on the Language Arts, Writing Test as spelling errors. The chart on the next page provides you with just a few examples of the many homonyms that exist.

EXERCISE 6

<u>Part A</u>   **Directions:** Underline the word in parentheses that will correctly complete each sentence below.

Example: What is the (affect, <u>effect</u>) of the new rules?

1. I (brake, break) for unicorns.
2. I (know, no) that you think I'm crazy, but I did see it.
3. The start of the concert season is finally (hear, here).
4. Does it matter (whether, weather) or not it rains if we're going to be indoors?
5. Marta (passed, past) the history book to Alex.

<u>Part B</u>   **Directions:** Find and correct the spelling errors in the passage below.

The founders of the United States didn't no whether they wood succeed in winning independence from Great Britain, but they new they had to try. They're goal was freedom. This country was founded on the principal of equality for all. The founders past on to us there belief in democracy. The Constitution guarantees our write to free speech. That means everyone is allowed to say whatever he or she thinks, weather anyone else wants to here it or not.

Answers are on page 239.

Homonym	Meaning	Example Sentence
affect effect	act upon result	The change will **affect** marketing. The **effect** of the change was minor.
all ready already	completely ready previously	Delores is **all ready** for the meeting. She **already** discussed that issue.
brake break	stop; stopping device fall to pieces; take a rest	Victor repaired the **brake** line. After four hours of work, we get a short **break.**
hear here	listen; use one's ears in this place	I couldn't **hear** the speaker. It's noisy in **here.**
knew new	was aware of not old	Betty **knew** how to use a computer. She didn't know the **new** program.
know no	be aware of opposite of yes	Do you **know** what time it is? **No,** I don't. I forgot my watch.
passed past	went by; succeeded before the present; gone by	The deadline **passed** with no answer. In the **past,** we wouldn't have let that happen.
principal principle	main; most important theory; belief	John's **principal** aim is to do a good job. In **principle,** he believes in honesty.
right write	opposite of left; correct put words on paper or screen	The **right** answer was "none of the above." I'm going to **write** a memo.
through threw	finished; into and out of did throw	They drove **through** the business district. Jan **threw** a stick for the dog to catch.
to two too	word before a verb; in a direction number after one also; more than enough	Steve is going **to** Pittsburgh. He's spending **two** days there. He's going to Cleveland **too.**
weather whether	atmospheric conditions if	The **weather** is warm. We're going **whether** he likes it or not.
week weak	seven days not strong	I learned a lot in just one **week.** Leo's performance was **weak.**
whole hole	entire empty place	The **whole** conference was canceled. That left a **hole** in my schedule.
wood would	product of trees helping verb	The floorboards are old **wood.** Marie **would** help if you asked.

Spelling

Directions: Choose the best correction for each sentence below. If you think the sentence is correct, choose option (5).

1. **Jean's younger sister accidentally hit the baseball threw the window.**

   (1) change *Jean's* to *Jeans*
   (2) change *threw* to *through*
   (3) change *Jean's* to *Jeans'*
   (4) add a comma after *sister*
   (5) no correction is necessary

2. **It's safe to return to you're homes now.**

   (1) change *it's* to *its*
   (2) insert a comma after *homes*
   (3) change *it's* to *they're*
   (4) change *you're* to *your*
   (5) no correction is necessary

3. **Who's coffee grounds have clogged the sink's drain?**

   (1) change *grounds* to *grounds'*
   (2) change *sink's* to *sinks*
   (3) change *Who's* to *Whose*
   (4) change *sink's* to *sinks'*
   (5) no correction is necessary

4. **The Martin familys' house has been affected by all three storms.**

   (1) change *Martin* to *Martin's*
   (2) change *familys'* to *family's*
   (3) change *affected* to *effected*
   (4) change *storms* to *storms'*
   (5) no correction is necessary

Answers are on page 239.

Chapter Review

Directions: Choose the <u>one best answer</u> to each question. Some of the sentences may contain errors in mechanics. A few sentences, however, may be correct as written. Read the sentences carefully and then answer the questions based on them. For each question, choose the answer that would result in the most effective writing of the sentence or sentences.

1. **James said in surprise, "How did you get here so quickly?".**

   What correction should be made to this sentence?

   (1) change the comma after *surprise* to a colon
   (2) remove the comma after *surprise*
   (3) change *quickly?".* to *quickly?"*
   (4) change *quickly?".* to *quickly"?*
   (5) no correction is necessary

2. **When Annie reached home, she found the door wide open. It's lock was broken. She ran to the neighbor's house and telephoned the police.**

   What correction should be made to these sentences?

   (1) change the comma after *home* to a semicolon
   (2) remove the comma after *home*
   (3) change *It's* to *Its*
   (4) add a comma after *house*
   (5) no correction is necessary

3. **"Are you going to the concert, two?"**

   What correction should be made to this sentence?

   (1) add a comma after *going*
   (2) change *to* to *too*
   (3) remove the comma after *concert*
   (4) change *two* to *too*
   (5) no correction is necessary

4. **Lupita plays three sports, tennis, basketball, and softball. She won't say which she likes best, but she's a great softball player.**

   What correction should be made to these sentences?

   (1) change the comma after *sports* to a colon
   (2) change *won't* to *wont'*
   (3) remove the comma after *best*
   (4) change the comma after *best* to a semicolon
   (5) no correction is necessary

5. **That movie was great, I'd love to see it again. I can't remember the star's name; nevertheless, I think she's great.**

   What correction should be made to these sentences?

   (1) change the comma after *great* to a semicolon
   (2) change *can't* to *ca'nt*
   (3) change the semicolon after *name* to a comma
   (4) change the comma after *nevertheless* to a semicolon
   (5) no correction is necessary

6. **The people of the state of Colorado are in fact satisfied with who's running their government.**

   What correction should be made to these sentences?

   (1) capitalize *state*
   (2) begin *Colorado* with a small letter
   (3) place commas before and after *in fact*
   (4) change *who's* to *whose*
   (5) no correction is necessary

7. **"The person who's lucky enough to pick the winning number," shouted the host, "Will be the proud owner of this new car!"**

   What correction should be made to this sentence?

   (1) change *who's* to *whose*
   (2) change *number,"* to *number",*
   (3) change *"Will* to *"will*
   (4) change *car!"* to *car"!*
   (5) no correction is necessary

8. **The three greatest poets of ancient times were Homer, Virgil, and Ovid.**

   What correction should be made to this sentence?

   (1) change *were Homer,* to *were: Homer,*
   (2) add a comma after *were*
   (3) remove the comma after *Virgil*
   (4) change both commas to semicolons
   (5) no correction is necessary

9. **Dad, will you tell me a story about your Uncle, the one who went gold prospecting in Alaska?**

   What correction should be made to this sentence?

   (1) remove the comma after *Dad*
   (2) change *Uncle* to *uncle*
   (3) remove the comma after *Uncle*
   (4) change the question mark to an exclamation point
   (5) no correction is necessary

10. **The old saying that money does'nt grow on trees is a good one to remember.**

    What correction should be made to this sentence?

    (1) place quotation marks before *money* and after *remember*
    (2) change *money* to *Money*
    (3) change *does'nt* to *doesn't*
    (4) change the period to an exclamation point
    (5) no correction is necessary

11. **Whenever Renee and Julie eat out, they choose the french restaurant.**

    What correction should be made to this sentence?

    (1) remove the comma after *out*
    (2) replace the comma after *out* with a semicolon
    (3) change *out, they* to *out, and they*
    (4) change *french* to *French*
    (5) no correction is necessary

12. **"When is Judy due to have her baby," asked Jack, "and what will they choose for a name"?**

    What correction should be made to this sentence?

    (1) change the comma after *baby* to a question mark
    (2) change *Jack, "and* to *Jack "And*
    (3) change *Jack, "and* to *Jack, "And*
    (4) change *name"?* to *name?"*
    (5) no correction is necessary

13. **Sumari is going on a bicycle trip this Fall, and she plans to camp out.**

What correction should be made to this sentence?

(1) change *Fall* to *fall*
(2) change the comma after *Fall* to a semicolon
(3) add a comma after *and*
(4) change the period to a question mark
(5) no correction is necessary

14. **The administrator of the Department of Natural Resources has an important job; he manages the state's public lands.**

What correction should be made to this sentence?

(1) capitalize *administrator*
(2) change *Department of Natural Resources* to *department of natural resources*
(3) change the semicolon to a comma
(4) change the semicolon to a colon
(5) no correction is necessary

15. **When Dr. Mendez announced her retirement, the Doctors at the hospital organized a party.**

What correction should be made to this sentence?

(1) change *Dr. Mendez* to *dr. Mendez*
(2) change the comma to a semicolon
(3) add a conjunction after the comma
(4) change *Doctors* to *doctors*
(5) no correction is necessary

16. **Is your date of birth June, 12, 1961, or am I confusing you with Phil? I know his birthday is in June.**

What correction should be made to this sentence?

(1) remove the comma after *June*
(2) remove the comma after *1961*
(3) change the comma after *1961* to a semicolon
(4) add a comma after *I know*
(5) no correction is necessary

17. **The schedule couldn't be changed, because many of the club members are from out of town.**

What correction should be made to this sentence?

(1) change *couldn't* to *could'nt*
(2) remove the comma after *changed*
(3) change the comma to a semicolon
(4) add a comma after *because*
(5) no correction is necessary

18. **When you consider how much money the club raised, I suppose, that all your work was worthwhile.**

What correction should be made to this sentence?

(1) remove the comma after *raised*
(2) change the comma after *raised* to a semicolon
(3) remove the comma after *suppose*
(4) change *your* to *you're*
(5) no correction is necessary

19. **Curtis couldn't decide which to visit first; the National Gallery, the Washington Monument, or the men's room.**

    What correction should be made to this sentence?

    (1) change the semicolon to a colon
    (2) change *National Gallery* to *national gallery*
    (3) change both commas to semicolons
    (4) change *men's* to *mens'*
    (5) no correction is necessary

20. **Most of the program's fund's come from federal taxes, local charities, and donations from businesses.**

    What correction should be made to this sentence?

    (1) change *program's* to *programs'*
    (2) change *fund's* to *funds*
    (3) add a colon after *from*
    (4) change all the commas to semicolons
    (5) no correction is necessary

21. **As the building was about to collapse, a firefighter yelled, "Quick! Put this towel over your face and jump"!**

    What correction should be made to this sentence?

    (1) remove the comma after *collapse*
    (2) remove the comma after *yelled*
    (3) replace the exclamation point after *Quick* with a comma
    (4) change *jump"!* to *jump!"*
    (5) no correction is necessary

22. **Students who apply to this Junior College are given credit for the following: high school courses, work experience, and military service.**

    What correction should be made to this sentence?

    (1) change *Junior College* to *junior college*
    (2) add a comma after *College*
    (3) remove the colon after *following*
    (4) change the commas to semicolons
    (5) no correction is necessary

23. **"Why doesn't he scold the girls when they don't eat they're breakfast?" asked Jane.**

    What correction should be made to this sentence?

    (1) add a comma after *girls*
    (2) change *don't* to *dont'*
    (3) change *they're* to *their*
    (4) replace the question mark with a comma
    (5) no correction is necessary

24. **The stranger handed the girl's mother a torn envelope and a rusty key when she asked him what he wanted?**

    What correction should be made to this sentence?

    (1) change *girl's* to *girls*
    (2) capitalize *mother*
    (3) add a comma after *key*
    (4) change the question mark to a period
    (5) no correction is necessary

25. **I wood think twice about turning in their report with your name on it.**

    What correction should be made to this sentence?

    (1) change *wood* to *would*
    (2) change *their* to *they're*
    (3) add a comma after *report*
    (4) change *your* to *you're*
    (5) no correction is necessary

Answers are on pages 239–240.

Paragraph Organization

Paragraph Structure

A **paragraph** is a group of sentences that work together to communicate one idea. An effective paragraph states a clear main idea and then goes on to give more information about it.

Is the following paragraph an example of effective writing?

> I have been learning to search for information on the Internet. My supervisor tells me I need to use different search engines. My supervisor is a nice guy, but he doesn't understand how hard this is for me. He's so young! He grew up using computers, and I never touched a computer until I was thirty. I liked the job I had then. Life was simpler.

Although there are no errors in grammar or usage, this paragraph is <u>not</u> effective writing. The first sentence tells you that you will be learning about searching for information on the Internet. But then the writer wanders off into a discussion of her supervisor and moves even further afield remembering a job she used to have. The rest of the paragraph does not support its main idea.

Is the paragraph below an improvement over the one you just read? Why or why not?

> I have been learning to search for information on the Internet. I found out that different search engines provide different information about the same subject, so now I use two or three engines for every search. For example, I wanted to find out more about credit ratings. The search engine Google led me to several interesting Web sites. One explained what a credit rating is and why it's important, and another gave tips on how to improve your credit rating. Then I tried the search engine Lookoff.com, which directed me a to site where I could find my own credit rating. I've learned that two search engines are better than one (no matter how good the one is).

This paragraph is an example of effective writing. The first sentence tells you that you will be learning about searching for information on the Internet, and all the other sentences in the paragraph support that main idea.

To succeed on the Language Arts, Writing Test, you need to be able to tell the difference between an effective paragraph and an ineffective paragraph. Further, you need to know how to revise a paragraph to make it more effective.

EXERCISE 1

Directions: Read each paragraph below. If it is an effective paragraph, write *effective* in the space provided. If it is not, write *ineffective*.

1.   Your car will perform more reliably if you take a few simple steps to prepare it for winter. Change the antifreeze. Make sure there's enough windshield-wiper fluid. You know how messy the roads can get in the wintertime. Snow becomes dirty slush, and every time a truck passes you, slush winds up on your windshield. I'm thinking of moving to Florida to avoid the whole hassle.

_____

2.   My husband gave me a shrub for the garden last Mother's Day. It's a hydrangea, and it has the most beautiful blue flowers. We planted it in a spot where I can see it from the living room window. We added aluminum to the soil because that makes the flowers a brighter blue. The flowers dry beautifully, too. They turn from sky blue to slate blue, and they make a great year-round arrangement.

_____

3.   Starting next Monday, there will be a new procedure for signing in for the restaurant staff. For both the lunch and dinner shifts, all servers will need to sign in at least thirty minutes before we open. They must already be in uniform when they sign in. And speaking of uniforms, could servers please make sure their uniforms are clean at the beginning of their shifts? That's why we provide machine-washable clothing. Fabrics are so much easier to care for than they once were.

_____

4.   Alessandro bought an answering machine for his telephone. He plugged the AC adapter into an electrical outlet on the wall. Then he inserted the small plug into the adapter jack on the base of the machine. He also attached the phone jack to the answering machine and the answering machine's jack to the wall jack. Finally, he set the date/time stamp.

_____

5.   Elayne took her puppy to obedience school. The puppy's name was Zoe. The instructor taught the "stay" command first. Zoe was a sweet, friendly border collie. She wanted to play, not stay. Elayne got the puppy for her children. Zoe had been abandoned. Elayne was happy to give her a good home, but her husband liked cats better than dogs.

_____

Answers are on page 240.

Effective Topic Sentences

The **topic sentence** of a paragraph, which is often the first sentence, tells what the rest of the paragraph is about. It gives the **main idea** of the paragraph. All of the other sentences in the paragraph are **supporting sentences.** They add details to support that main idea.

What kind of sentences would you expect to see after the topic sentence below?

Tomas has a wonderful recipe for a fruit tart.

You are correct if you thought the rest of the paragraph would probably give the recipe for a fruit tart.

Tomas has a wonderful recipe for a fruit tart. He starts with a sheet of ready-made puff pastry. Then he spreads fruit-flavored yogurt on the pastry. He cuts kiwi, cantaloupe, apples, and bananas into slices. He soaks the apple and banana slices in orange juice for a few minutes so they won't turn brown. Then he arranges all the fruit slices on the pastry in rows.

The paragraph is effective because every sentence in it contributes to the main idea.

Suppose you read a paragraph that had only supporting details. Could you choose the most effective topic sentence to add to it? Look at the following example.

You can give them to the children of your friends. You can donate them to a library. You can take them to the children's ward at your local hospital and read aloud to the kids. Whatever you do, don't throw out old books.

Which sentence below would be most effective at the beginning of the paragraph?

(1) It's time to clean house.
(2) Reading is one of the most important skills that a child can master.
(3) There are many things you can do with books when your kids outgrow them.
(4) Old books can still be interesting.
(5) Children's books get more expensive every year.

To answer this type of organization question, you need to read the paragraph and understand what the main idea is. Each of the first three sentences gives a use for old children's books, and the final sentence tells what not to do with them. The sentence that best describes the main idea is option (3).

Remember, a sentence is not necessarily an effective topic sentence just because it relates to the other sentences. For example, why is option (5) not correct? It relates to children's books, just as the rest of the paragraph does. But *children's books* is too broad a subject to be the main idea of the other sentences. Instead, *what to do with old children's books* is the main idea. Look at all answer choices closely to see which is the <u>best</u> match, not just sort of a match.

EXERCISE 2

Directions: Make each group of supporting sentences below into a complete paragraph by adding a topic sentence. Make sure your topic sentence states the main idea of the paragraph and is a complete sentence.

1. _____

First, we recommend conducting a survey of current customers. Find out what they like about the company's products and what they don't like. Then, management must decide which customer complaints can be addressed cost effectively. Studies show that 20 percent of your customers buy 80 percent of your products. Our goal is to identify that 20 percent and provide excellent service to those customers. The end result will be an increase in sales and therefore an increase in profits.

2. _____

Andrea picked up several chairs and tables in various sizes for a few dollars each at flea markets. She bought irregular sheets for far less than the material would have cost at a fabric store. She used one of the sheets, in a green and blue paisley pattern, as a slipcover to cover the rather beat-up sofa in her living room. She draped part of another over a coffee table and used the scraps to make pillows.

Answers are on page 240.

Effective Topic Sentences

Directions: Choose the best answer to each question below.

1.   Menchu is a Maya Indian from a farming family in Guatemala. In 1979, her younger brother was kidnapped and killed by the Guatemalan army. His crime was trying to help peasants keep their land. The same year, Menchu's parents were also killed by the army for speaking out. Rigoberta Menchu fled to Mexico, where she continued to fight for the rights of Indian peasants. She was awarded the Nobel Peace Prize in 1992.

Which sentence below would be most effective at the beginning of this paragraph?

(1) Life can be dangerous for Guatemalan peasants.
(2) Rigoberta Menchu is a brave woman with a vision.
(3) The rich get richer.
(4) Rigoberta Menchu emigrated from Guatemala to Mexico.
(5) The Nobel Peace Prize brings worldwide attention to important causes.

2.   It was written by Jonathan Swift nearly three hundred years ago. Gulliver is a ship's surgeon who gets shipwrecked and stranded several times in his career. First he finds himself in a place called Lilliput, where the people are so tiny they can stand on his hand. Then he lands in a country called Brobdingnag, where the people are as tall as church steeples. Finally, he winds up in a land where horses are the rulers and humans are slaves.

Which sentence below would be most effective at the beginning of this paragraph?

(1) *Gulliver's Travels* was a best-seller.
(2) *Gulliver's Travels* is long.
(3) *Gulliver's Travels* was one of the first science fiction novels.
(4) *Gulliver's Travels* features a wide range of characters.
(5) *Gulliver's Travels* is a political satire.

3.   CGI creates realistic-looking characters and locations that aren't real at all. They're digitally "painted" onto film using computer software. The dinosaurs in the *Jurassic Park* series are CGI. The same is true of the monsters in *The Mummy* and elements of hundreds of other movies. With the widespread use of CGI, audiences today can have the experience of feeling they're right in the middle of a totally alien landscape.

Which sentence below would be most effective at the beginning of this paragraph?

(1) More and more movies are using computer-generated graphics, or CGI.
(2) The velociraptors were the coolest thing in *Jurassic Park.*
(3) CGI stands for computer-generated graphics.
(4) With CGI, soon the movie business won't need live actors at all.
(5) Audiences have responded to computer-generated graphics.

Answers are on page 240.

Correct Text Divisions

How would you improve the paragraph below?

(1) The chief executive officer, Carla Yagarin, will be making a statement to the press this afternoon, but she wanted to let all employees know ahead of time what she will be saying. (2) As you all know, Lightbearer Technologies has been going through some difficult times lately, as has nearly every other company in our industry. (3) Our solution is two-pronged. (4) First, it is with regret that we announce a layoff of 200 employees. (5) This was a very difficult decision to make, but the time has come when we must retrench if we are to survive. (6) For those who are laid off, be assured that it is no reflection on you as a person or on the quality of your performance. (7) The company will support you fully in your search for another job. (8) The human resources department is setting up a job-search center equipped with computers and supplies. (9) Employees can use those resources to research other companies on the Internet, as well as to update and print their resumes. (10) HR staffers will be available to help you with your resume and to conduct mock job interviews, which can be videotaped so you can critique and improve your performance. (11) The second part of the solution is that the company is offering early retirement to eligible employees. (12) Anyone who has been here for twenty years or more is eligible. (13) The amount of your pension will be determined by a formula based on your years of service and your current salary. (14) Human resources will be happy to meet with you to discuss the details. (15) We hope the generous retirement package will allow Lightbearer to trim the payroll by another 200 employees without causing undue hardship.

You probably noticed that this paragraph is very long. You may also have noticed that it contains two important main ideas. The best way to improve this paragraph is to divide it into two separate paragraphs.

Some questions on the Language Arts, Writing Test will ask you to decide where a new paragraph should begin. Here is an example using the paragraph above.

Which revision would make the paragraph more effective?

Begin a new paragraph

(1) with sentence 7
(2) with sentence 10
(3) with sentence 11
(4) with sentence 12
(5) with sentence 14

Can you see that two main ideas are discussed in the original paragraph? One is the layoffs. The other is the early retirement package. The best place to start a new paragraph is with the first sentence of the second main idea— sentence 11.

Sometimes, dividing a paragraph is only one of the possible answers to a question. Look at the following example:

(1) I've always liked both cats and dogs; that's one reason I took a job working for a veterinarian. (2) But I've been amazed at how many people like only one kind of pet. (3) Cat people say that felines are very intelligent. (4) They can be taught all kinds of entertaining and even useful tricks. (5) They're easy to care for in an apartment because they don't take up much room and they can use a litterbox instead of needing to be walked in all kinds of weather. (6) Dog people say that canines are friendlier than cats. (7) They are loyal and devoted to their humans. (8) Dogs can learn tricks, too. (9) You can play catch and fetch with them. (10) Playing with dogs and walking them is good exercise for their owners as well.

Which revision should be made to sentence 6 to make this paragraph more effective?

(1) move sentence 6 to follow sentence 4
(2) move sentence 6 to follow sentence 7
(3) remove sentence 6
(4) begin a new paragraph with sentence 6
(5) no revision is necessary

The writer of this paragraph is comparing cats and dogs, so it makes sense to divide the paragraph into these two main ideas. Beginning a new paragraph with sentence 6 would be an effective revision of the original paragraph. Option (4) is correct.

To figure out where to divide a long paragraph, look for a change in topic or the appearance of a new idea. If the paragraph describes steps in doing something or a series of events, begin a new paragraph with each major step or event.

EXERCISE 3

Directions: The following paragraph contains more than one main idea. Decide which sentence should begin a new paragraph and draw a paragraph mark (¶) at the beginning of it.

There are two main types of trees, coniferous and deciduous. Coniferous trees get that name because they have cones. They also have needlelike leaves that don't fall off in the winter in temperate regions. There are a few exceptions to that rule. Both larches (also known as tamaracks) and bald cypress are conifers, but they do shed their needles for winter. Coniferous trees are pine trees and their relatives. The pine family includes spruce, fir, and hemlock trees, among many others. Deciduous trees are also called broad-leaved trees. Their leaves do fall off, so the trees are bare in winter. There are hundreds of species of deciduous trees. A few examples are oaks, maples, beeches, and poplars. Most deciduous leaves turn bright colors before they fall off. Maples, for example, usually turn red, while tulip poplars turn yellow.

Answers are on page 240.

Correct Text Divisions

Directions: Choose the best answer to each question below.

1.   (1) Georgia O'Keeffe was a twentieth-century American artist. (2) She spent the early years of her career living in New York City. (3) Her work was first exhibited in 1916. (4) She socialized with other artists of all kinds: painters, photographers, writers, and musicians. (5) New York was filled with people with whom she could discuss art and share ideas. (6) During this period, O'Keeffe painted mostly cityscapes with towering skyscrapers and crowds of people. (7) She also filled her canvases with huge renderings of flowers: pink sweet peas, purple petunias, and white calla lilies. (8) In 1931, O'Keeffe moved to New Mexico. (9) She had burned out on city life and had begun to crave peace and quiet. (10) She turned her attention to painting other subjects. (11) Cattle skulls nestled in the desert sand were a favorite subject. (12) Sometimes she combined them with flowers. (13) O'Keeffe lived in New Mexico until her death at age 98, although she returned to New York regularly for long visits.

Which revision would make the paragraph more effective?

Begin a new paragraph

(1) with sentence 4
(2) with sentence 5
(3) with sentence 8
(4) with sentence 11
(5) with sentence 13

2.   (1) Businesses are affected by both microeconomic and macroeconomic forces. (2) Just as "micro" means "tiny," microeconomics studies, up close, the behavior of individual people (buyers) and specific companies (sellers). (3) The place where buyers and sellers bargain over goods and services is called a market, so microeconomics studies how markets work. (4) The two main microeconomic forces that affect business are supply/demand and competition. (5) In contrast, "macro" means "huge," and macroeconomics studies the entire economy of a nation. (6) It deals with the nation's economic growth, inflation, interest rates, and unemployment. (7) When the economy is growing, most people have more money to spend on products or services. (8) When inflation increases rapidly, the costs of products in general go up and people have less money left over after they buy the necessities. (9) When unemployment goes up, people usually cut back on their spending in case they get laid off. (10) When interest rates are high, the cost of buying on credit goes up and people cut back.

Which revision would make the paragraph more effective?

Begin a new paragraph

(1) with sentence 3
(2) with sentence 5
(3) with sentence 7
(4) with sentence 8
(5) with sentence 9

Answers are on page 240.

Unity and Coherence

Every paragraph should have both unity and coherence. **Unity** means that each sentence in the paragraph unites to support the main idea. **Coherence** means that all the sentences in the paragraph relate to each other and flow logically from one to the next. They cohere, or pull together.

If a paragraph lacks unity, you need to either remove any sentence that does not support the topic sentence or rewrite it by adding details that do support the topic sentence.

What improvement would you make to the paragraph below?

The Auroras: Nature's Light Show

(1) The Northern Lights are displays that light up the night sky with beautiful colors. (2) Rainbows are beautiful, too. (3) The lights are also called the Aurora Borealis. (4) They are formed when the sun sends flares of particles into space. (5) Some of the particles loop around Earth's magnetic fields and hit air molecules, causing them to glow. (6) There are Southern Lights as well. (7) The auroras appear around bóth the North and South Poles as halos of fire. (8) When the sun is especially active or the solar wind especially strong, the Northern Lights can be seen much farther south than usual.

The main idea of this paragraph is the auroras and what causes them. All the sentences in the paragraph should tell more about this main idea. One sentence, however, does not do this. Which one?

You are correct if you thought that sentence 2 does not support the main idea of the paragraph. Although the sentence conveys a valid opinion, and although it is somewhat related to the topic of the auroras, it is not related closely enough to belong in this paragraph. To make this piece of writing more effective, sentence 2 should be removed.

If a paragraph lacks coherence, you can achieve it by rearranging the order of some sentences within the paragraph or by moving them to another paragraph, which sometimes means combining two paragraphs. (Another way to achieve coherence is by using an appropriate pattern of organization to start with. Chapter 7 discusses several different patterns of organization.) On the next page is an example of how the rearranging/combining type of revision might appear on the Language Arts, Writing Test.

To: All Employees of the 10th St. Chicken World Store
From: Alan Kowalski, Manager

(A)

(1) I'm sure you've all seen Chicken World's new ad campaign. (2) I want to call your attention to the part where the cashier says, "If we forget your free rolls, your whole order is free." (3) At this store, we have to abide by the national ad's promises. (4) However, giving out free meals would really cut into our profit margin. (5) So it's very important that everyone remember to include free rolls with every meal.

(B)

(6) The ad campaign also promotes Chicken World's newest offering, the chicken caesar salad. (7) We've trained the kitchen staff to make this meal. (8) I just want to remind everyone that the romaine lettuce must be absolutely fresh. (9) You may think you're saving us money by using up wilted lettuce, but if it drives away customers, it's not worth it.

(C)

(10) Since we're asking people to pay $6.99 for a meal whose ingredients cost a small percentage of that, wilted lettuce definitely would drive away customers.

(D)

(11) You're the best crew we've ever had. (12) Every one of you is smart, hardworking, and dedicated. (13) I know you won't need to be reminded again about either the rolls or the lettuce. (14) Keep up the good work.

Is there a sentence in this memo that should be moved? You are correct if you chose to move sentence 10 to the end of paragraph B. The main idea of paragraph B is that the quality of the salad must be kept high. Sentence 11 explains more about why that goal is important, so it is an effective addition to that paragraph.

Now try adding unity and coherence to another piece of writing. Read the example below and answer the questions that follow.

How to Grow Tomatoes

(A)

(1) What could be tastier than a tomato picked fresh from your own garden? (2) If you don't have a garden, a balcony will do. (3) Many city dwellers have everything from flowers to grass to trees growing on their balconies. (4) Tomatoes are easy to grow, and they're an indispensable addition to summer salads.

(B)

(5) The first thing to do is make sure you have good-quality soil. (6) Tomatoes don't do well in acidic soil, so it's wise to test yours and make sure it has a pH of 5.5 to 7.5 (close to neutral). (7) To prepare the garden, scatter about a pound of fertilizer for every 15 feet. (8) Dig it in thoroughly.

(C)

(9) Now it's time to choose which tomato to plant. (10) Most modern varieties are resistant to several diseases. (11) Some gardeners, nevertheless, choose a nonresistant variety because they like its flavor enough to risk disease. (14) In the northeast, Better Boy bears fruit in about 70 days and Beefeater in 75 days. (12) In most temperate climates, you'll want a variety that matures well before frost. (13) Better Boy and Beefeater are both good choices.

(D)

(15) You can start seedlings indoors in early spring or scatter them directly in the ground after it warms up, but the easiest approach is to buy small tomato plants. (16) Strip their bottom leaves and lay the plants sideways in your prepared soil. (17) New roots will form along the stem where the leaves were, strengthening the plants. (18) Tamp down the soil around each plant and water thoroughly.

(E)

(19) Spread a mulch of grass clippings or old hay around the base of each plant.

Which revision would make paragraph A more effective?

(1) move sentence 1 to follow sentence 3
(2) remove sentence 3
(3) move sentence 4 to follow sentence 1
(4) remove sentence 4
(5) move sentence 4 to the beginning of paragraph B

In paragraph A, sentence 3 does not belong, so option (2) is the correct answer. A sentence about growing plants other than tomatoes does not belong in instructions for growing tomatoes. Moving the sentence to another spot in the paragraph will not make the piece more effective.

Which revision would make paragraph C more effective?

(1) move sentence 9 to the end of paragraph B
(2) move sentence 10 to follow sentence 11
(3) move sentence 14 to follow sentence 13
(4) remove sentence 12
(5) move sentence 13 to the beginning of paragraph D

In paragraph C, sentence 14 is out of place. The sentence that tells how long Better Boy and Beefeater tomatoes take to bear fruit should follow the sentence that says both varieties are good choices; it explains why they're good choices. Moving sentence 14 to follow sentence 13 makes the paragraph more effective, so option (3) is the correct answer.

Which revision would make this piece of writing more effective?

(1) move sentence 2 to follow sentence 4
(2) move sentence 8 to the beginning of paragraph C
(3) remove sentence 17
(4) move sentence 18 to the beginning of paragraph E
(5) move sentence 19 to the end of paragraph D

Sentence 19 is the final step in planting: mulching. Because sentence 19 continues the main idea of paragraph D, it should be part of that paragraph. Combining the two paragraphs makes the piece more effective.

EXERCISE 4

Directions: The following paragraph contains a sentence that is not placed correctly. Underline the sentence and draw an arrow to where it should be placed correctly.

We will have a brief agenda for the Civic Club's April 7 meeting. The main subject is the community center. We're in negotiations with the Blackburn family, who have offered to donate their building at 925 Ridge Avenue. That brings us to fundraising. Plans are progressing for the History Dinner in June. Now the Civic Club needs only to raise enough money to renovate the building and bring it up to code. Jessie Grey is organizing the dinner. She's looking for volunteers to help with publicity, programs, and preparations. So check your schedule and come prepared to volunteer.

Answers are on page 240.

Unity and Coherence

Directions: Choose the best answer to each question below.

Questions 1–4 refer to the article below.

The Royal Family of the Sky

(A)

(1) The stars in the night sky were very important to our ancestors. (2) Millions of stars could be seen when there was no artificial light or smog to dim them. (3) The ancients gazed at them long enough to identify shapes in the way you might gaze at a cloud and say, "It looks like a rabbit." (4) Then they made up stories about those shapes.

(B)

(5) One of the best-known constellations is Cassiopeia, the queen of Ethiopia. (6) The ancient Greeks looked at the stars and imagined they saw the queen sitting on her throne. (7) Actually, the constellation is shaped like a *W*. (8) Cassiopeia is in the far northern sky, almost directly across the sky from the Big Dipper.

(C)

(9) Queen Cassiopeia was very vain. (10) She bragged that she was even more beautiful than the sea nymphs. (11) The god of the sea, Poseidon, ruled the nymphs. (12) He heard of Cassiopeia's boast.

(D)

(13) Poseidon sent a sea monster named Cetus to destroy the coast of Ethiopia.

(E)

(14) Cassiopeia and her husband, King Cepheus, had a daughter named Andromeda. (15) So the people chained Andromeda to rocks at the edge of the sea. (16) The gods told them the only way to stop Cetus was to sacrifice their daughter. (17) Just as Cetus was about to consume her, the hero Perseus swooped down from the sky to rescue her. (18) He killed the sea monster and cut Andromeda's chains with his sword.

(F)

(19) To this day, every character in the story is immortalized in a constellation. (20) Once you find Cassiopeia in the sky, you can find Cepheus next to her, Andromeda just beyond them, and Perseus beyond her. (21) Cetus the sea monster is even a constellation that stretches across the sky south of them.

1. **Which revision would make paragraph D more effective?**

   (1) move sentence 13 to the beginning of paragraph C
   (2) move sentence 13 to the end of paragraph C
   (3) move sentence 13 to the beginning of paragraph E
   (4) remove sentence 13
   (5) no revision is necessary

2. **Sentence 15: So the people chained Andromeda to rocks at the edge of the sea.**

   Which revision should be made to sentence 15?

   (1) move sentence 15 to the end of paragraph C
   (2) move sentence 15 to the beginning of paragraph D
   (3) move sentence 15 to follow sentence 16
   (4) remove sentence 15
   (5) move sentence 15 to follow sentence 17

Answers are on page 240.

Tone and Diction

Which sentence does not belong in the paragraph below?

(1) This letter is in regard to my year 2001 income tax return. (2) I received a letter from your office of the Internal Revenue Service claiming that I under-reported my income last year. (3) I sent my W2 forms when I filed my tax return, but I'm enclosing copies of them here. (4) Can't you guys get anything right? (5) As the enclosed information clearly shows, my figures were correct. (6) I would appreciate it if you would check your records.

You may have noticed right away that one sentence "leaps out" at you as not belonging. Sentence 4 does not match the rest of the paragraph in its tone and diction. **Tone** is how the writer uses language to make his or her point. The tone of sentence 4 is much more casual (and hostile) than that of the rest of the paragraph. Its word choice, or **diction**, differs from the word choice in the other sentences. It does not fit into the paragraph and should be removed.

A writer's choice of tone and diction depends on the type of document being written and the audience who will be reading it. A letter to the IRS will use a different tone and diction from a note to friends. An office memo will use a different tone and diction from an advertisement.

Look at the following e-mail message from a teenager to some friends. Which sentence does not belong?

(1) Hey, what are you guys doing Friday night? Do you want to go to the new Drew Barrymore movie? (3) I hear it's way cool. (4) Then we could go hang at the diner. (5) I'll be wearing a funky fuchsia sweater I just bought. (6) I can't wait to show it to you. (7) I look forward to hearing your response to my suggestion.

You are correct if you decided that sentence 7 does not fit into the paragraph. It uses a formal tone and businesslike diction, while the rest of the paragraph uses a casual tone and slangy diction. The writer might want to include the idea that she looks forward to a response, but she might want to revise the way she said it.

EXERCISE 5

Directions: In each paragraph below, there may be a sentence that does not belong due to its tone and diction. Cross out any sentence that does not belong. If all the sentences in the paragraph belong, write *effective* in the space provided.

1.　　Hey, did you watch the baseball game last night? Our whole family went to see it. I believe that, if one analyzes it, baseball is a sport that reflects the great American values of teamwork and sportsmanship. It was the season opener, so the kids were all excited. This was the first game Sarah's ever seen live. The game was really close, but finally the Pirates beat the Dodgers by one run. That new pitcher has a great arm.

_____

2.　　Four hundred years ago, most people believed that disease was caused by evil spirits. Then a Dutchman named Antony Leeuwenhoek began to experiment with lenses. This was a hobby for him; he was uneducated and worked as a janitor. But in his spare time, he invented the microscope. He was the first person to see the tiny bacteria and viruses that cause disease. It was so cool to look at a drop of water and see a bunch of tiny animals living in it.

_____

3.　　In 1630, a Spanish countess named Ana de Osorio and her husband moved to Peru. After only a few months there, they both came down with malaria. None of Ana's home remedies worked, but she heard that the local people used the bark of a tree as medicine. That tree contained quinine, which fought off the disease. In 1638, the de Osorios were called back to Spain. Ana threw some quinine bark into her luggage. When they arrived, Spain was in the middle of a malaria epidemic—and no cure was known. Her medicine saved the day and ended the epidemic.

_____

4.　　Many parts of Africa have not achieved free and democratic elections. Now an unexpected tool may help: mobile phones. Communication has always been difficult on that continent. All of sub-Saharan Africa put together has fewer fixed phone lines than New York City. Even after lines have been installed, it's hard to keep them in place because looters take them down to sell the copper. What a racket they've got going! Mobile phones keep the lines of communication open and keep the public informed. During elections poll watchers use mobile phones to report the true vote counts to the people throughout the day.

_____

Answers are on page 240.

Chapter Review

Directions: Choose the one best answer to each question. Some of the sentences may contain errors in organization. A few sentences, however, may be correct as written. Read the sentences carefully and then answer the questions based on them. For each question, choose the answer that would result in the most effective writing of the sentence or sentences.

Questions 1–6 refer to the following instructions.

The Five Functions of Management

(A)

(1) The five basic functions of management are planning, organizing, staffing, directing, and controlling. (2) These functions must be performed by all managers in all businesses. (3) However, the scope of each function and the time it requires differ. (4) Usually, first-line supervisors spend most of their time directing and controlling. (5) All managers need to plan, but top executives spend the most time planning. (6) That can be hard to believe when you consider the thick-headed plans they so often come up with.

(B)

(7) Planning basically means figuring out what should be done in the future. (8) It involves setting goals, objectives, policies, procedures, and other plans for achieving the company's purposes. (9) It includes collecting and sorting information from many sources to make decisions.

(C)

(10) Managers must be careful not to get so caught up in solving daily crises that they don't have time to plan.

(D)

(11) The organizing function answers the question, "How will the work be divided and accomplished?" (12) Part of a supervisor's job is to group various activities and job duties into separate sections or teams. (13) Organizing involves assigning these activities and delegating the authority that employees need to perform them. (14) Staffing is the task of selecting, orienting, and training employees. (15) The manager must conduct performance appraisals and make promotion decisions. (16) He or she must also devise and set in place pay systems and rates (often working with the human resources department).

(E)

(17) Whatever it's called, directing is very important to employee morale, job satisfaction, productivity, and communication. (18) In the directing function, the supervisor encourages employee satisfaction while meeting the department's objectives. (19) Directing is the day-to-day process of guiding, coaching, and supervising employees. (20) It's what first-line supervisors spends most of their time doing. (21) Coaching your child's sports team can be very rewarding.

(F)

(22) Controlling means deciding whether or not plans are being met and progress is being made toward objectives. (23) It also involves correcting any blocks to achieving those objectives. (24) Without planning, none of the other four functions of management could be done (25) It would be impossible for supervisors to control if there weren't a plan to check against.

1. **Which revision would make paragraph A more effective?**

   (1) move sentence 3 to follow sentence 4
   (2) remove sentence 4
   (3) begin a new paragraph with sentence 3
   (4) move sentence 6 to the beginning of paragraph B
   (5) remove sentence 6

2. **Sentence 10: Managers must be careful not to get so caught up in solving daily crises that they don't have time to plan.**

   Which revision should be made to sentence 10?

   (1) move sentence 10 to follow sentence 8
   (2) move sentence 10 to follow sentence 11
   (3) move sentence 10 to the end of paragraph B
   (4) move sentence 10 to the beginning of paragraph D
   (5) remove sentence 10

3. **Which revision would make paragraph D more effective?**

   Begin a new paragraph

   (1) with sentence 12
   (2) with sentence 13
   (3) with sentence 14
   (4) with sentence 15
   (5) with sentence 16

4. **Which sentence below would be most effective at the beginning of paragraph E?**

   (1) Directing is also called leading or motivating.
   (2) Not enough managers appreciate the importance of employee morale.
   (3) A satisfied employee is a productive employee.
   (4) First-line supervisors must know how to direct.
   (5) Communication is so important in the business world.

5. **Which revision would make paragraph E more effective?**

   (1) move sentence 17 to the end of paragraph D
   (2) remove sentence 18
   (3) move sentence 20 to follow sentence 21
   (4) move sentence 21 to the beginning of paragraph F
   (5) remove sentence 21

6. **Sentence 24: Without planning, none of the other four functions of management could be done.**

   Which revision should be made to sentence 24?

   (1) move sentence 24 to the end of paragraph E
   (2) move sentence 24 to the beginning of paragraph F
   (3) move sentence 24 to follow sentence 22
   (4) move sentence 24 to follow sentence 25
   (5) remove sentence 24

Questions 7–12 refer to the following article.

An English Teacher at the Court of Siam

(A)

(1) Anna Crawford was born in Wales, Great Britain, in 1845. (2) She attended school in her homeland, but her mother and stepfather were living in India. (3) As soon as Anna graduated, she traveled to India to live with them. (4) It was a long and difficult journey by ship in the days before air travel. (5) Now a jet can carry you that far in a matter of hours.

(B)

(6) Before she was twenty, Anna had already traveled widely and learned several Eastern languages. (7) She had also married a British major named Thomas Leonowens. (8) Their first child died and Anna grew ill. (9) Doctors prescribed a change of climate, common advice in a time when medical knowledge was limited. (10) Anna and Thomas moved to Australia. (11) Unfortunately, their ship wrecked on the way there. (12) They were so bummed by their bad luck that they scoped out another place to live. (13) They moved to London, England, next. (14) Then they tried Singapore in the Far East.

(C)

(14) After two years in Singapore, Anna's husband died. (15) She was twenty-eight now and had two surviving children. (16) She opened a school to support them and herself. (17) The king of Siam (the country now called Thailand) heard about her work and summoned her. (18) That might sound easy, but the king had sixty-seven children. (19) He wanted her to give a European education to his children.

(D)

(20) He wanted Anna to teach Western knowledge to their mothers and various slaves also.

(E)

(21) Anna stayed in Siam for six years. (22) She taught her pupils English, math, science, and, as much as she could manage, morality. (23) In 1867, she became ill again and went to America to live. (24) She corresponded with her Siamese students for the rest of her life. (25) When one of them became king at his father's death, she watched proudly as he abolished slavery and guaranteed religious freedom. (26) Anna's experience was immortalized seventy-five years after the fact in the book *Anna and the King of Siam*. (27) The 1945 book was based on the memoirs she wrote, called *The English Governess at the Siamese Court*. (28) A hit musical followed, and then the movie *The King and I* was made.

7. **Which revision would make paragraph A more effective?**

   (1) move sentence 2 to follow sentence 3
   (2) move sentence 4 to follow sentence 5
   (3) remove sentence 4
   (4) move sentence 5 to the beginning of paragraph B
   (5) remove sentence 5

8. **Sentence 12: They were so bummed by their bad luck that they scoped out another place to live.**

   Which revision should be made to sentence 12?

   (1) move sentence 12 to the beginning of paragraph B
   (2) move sentence 12 to follow sentence 7
   (3) move sentence 12 to follow sentence 13
   (4) move sentence 12 to the beginning of paragraph C
   (5) remove sentence 12

9. **Which revision would make paragraph C more effective?**

   (1) move sentence 14 to the end of paragraph B
   (2) move sentence 15 to follow sentence 16
   (3) move sentence 16 to follow sentence 17
   (4) move sentence 18 to follow sentence 19
   (5) move sentence 19 to the beginning of paragraph D

10. **Sentence 20: He wanted Anna to teach Western knowledge to their mother and various slaves also.**

    Which revision should be made to sentence 20?

    (1) move sentence 20 to the end of paragraph C
    (2) move sentence 20 to the beginning of paragraph E
    (3) move sentence 20 to follow sentence 16
    (4) move sentence 20 to follow sentence 21
    (5) remove sentence 20

11. **Which sentence below would be most effective at the beginning of paragraph E?**

    (1) Anna remained sickly.
    (2) Anna was a dedicated letter writer all her life.
    (3) Anna had a very productive time at the king's court.
    (4) Anna believed children should learn high moral standards.
    (5) Anna believed in religious freedom.

12. **Which revision would make paragraph E more effective?**

    Begin a new paragraph

    (1) with sentence 23
    (2) with sentence 24
    (3) with sentence 25
    (4) with sentence 26
    (5) with sentence 27

Answers are on page 241.

Evaluate Your Progress

On the following chart, circle the number of any item you answered incorrectly in the Chapter 5 Review on pages 153–156 or in the Chapter 6 Review on pages 172–175. Next to each group of item numbers, you will see the pages you can review to learn how to answer the items correctly. Pay particular attention to reviewing skill areas in which you missed half or more of the questions.

Skill Area	Chapter 5 Review Item Number	Chapter 6 Review Item Number	Review Pages
ORGANIZATION			
Text divisions		2, 3, 10, 12	162–164
Topic sentences		4, 11	159–161
Unity/coherence		1, 5, 6, 7, 8, 9	165–171
MECHANICS			
Capitalization	7, 9, 11, 13, 15, 22		133–138
Punctuation	1, 4, 5, 6, 8, 12, 14, 16, 17, 18, 19, 21, 24		20, 139–148
Spelling (possessives, contractions, and homonyms)	2, 3, 10, 20, 23, 25		27–28, 149–152

CHAPTER 7

Patterns of Organization

You know how to write a good sentence. You can make subjects and verbs agree and keep the tenses clear. Your pronoun references make sense and you've got punctuation mastered.

You also know how to write a paragraph. You can create a topic sentence to express a main idea. You can develop sentences to support a main idea. However, there is still more to good writing.

What's wrong with the following paragraph?

> You can buy good pizzas, but the ones you make at home can be even better. Some people like grated cheeses. When you've got your pizza loaded up, put it in the oven at 350°F for about 12–15 minutes. Add your favorite ingredients. Pour on the tomato sauce and spread it around. Spread out the pizza dough on a well-greased baking sheet. Myself, I like sliced cheese. Pile on the ingredients; the more the better. Add the cheese.

Although the sentences are correctly written, the paragraph doesn't make much sense. There is a definite main idea—how to make a homemade pizza. However, the ideas that support the main idea are not written in correct time order, so you don't get a clear idea about how to make a pizza.

Here's one important rule to remember about writing a paragraph.

A good paragraph must be well organized and coherent.

There are four basic ways to organize writing. One of these **patterns of organization** will bring order to almost any writing.

- order of importance
- time order
- cause-and-effect order
- comparison-and-contrast order

Order of Importance

When you organize ideas in **order of importance,** you give examples or characteristics to support a main idea. You rank those details either from most important to least important or from least important to most important.

When to Use Order of Importance

You should use order of importance when you want to convey information quickly or persuade someone of your opinion. Order your ideas from most important to least important when you want to get your main point across fast. Order your ideas from least important to most important when you want to build suspense. For example, you might want to talk your family into spending a holiday the way you want to. Your idea of a fun family day might involve sleeping in a little, taking a picnic lunch to the park, where everyone can play pickup baseball, running some errands, and then going to a movie in the evening. You know the part your kids will like best is the trip to the park, so you start with that. After they decide your main idea is a good one, you add the details about activities that may not excite them as much.

When To Use Order of Importance
Uses
1. To convey information quickly
2. To persuade someone of your opinion
3. To build suspense
4. To tell about an event
Examples
What are the dangers of drinking and driving?
Why does our neighborhood need a community center?
Guess what I saw on my way home?

Organizing Details in Order of Importance

To organize ideas in order of importance, it helps to make a **cluster map**. Put the topic of your paragraph in the center and draw a circle around it. Then put three or four (or more) details about the topic in circles around the central circle. Look at them for a minute and decide which detail is the most important. Put a *1* next to it. Rank and number the other ideas by importance.

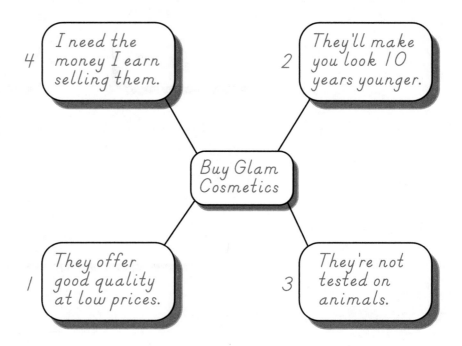

EXERCISE 1

Part A   **Directions:** Create a cluster map for a paragraph about things you want to do to fix up your house or apartment.

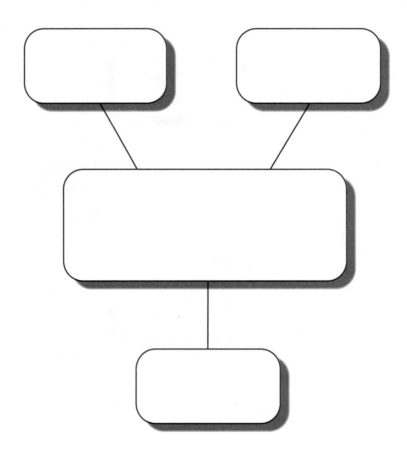

Part B   **Directions:** Look at the cluster map you created in Part A. Rank the details in order of importance. Number them from *1* to *4*.

Answers are on page 241.

Time Order

When you organize ideas in **time order**, you tell about them in the order in which they occur.

When to Use Time Order

Time order is one of the easiest organization patterns to use. Simply tell about events in the order in which they happen. Time order is very useful for telling a story or explaining to someone how to do something, such as making a pizza.

When to Use Time Order
Uses
1. To list steps in a process
2. To explain how something works
3. To describe a routine
4. To tell about an event
Examples
How do you make a pizza?
How does an electric switch work?
How do you spend Sunday morning?
What happened in the accident?

Organizing Details in Time Order

Organize details in time order in two steps. First make a list of all the details you want to tell about. Then go back and number the details in the order they happen. Here is an example of how the details of the confused paragraph that opened this chapter might be organized.

How to Make a Pizza

1. Grease a baking sheet.
2. Spread out the pizza dough on the baking sheet.
3. Pour on tomato sauce.
4. Spread the tomato sauce around.
5. Add the cheese.
6. Add your favorite ingredients.
7. Bake it at 350° F for about 12-15 minutes.

Using the ordered list as a guide, the paragraph might be written like this:

You can buy good pizzas, but the ones you make at home can be even better. First, grease a baking sheet and spread out the pizza dough on it. Then pour on the tomato sauce and spread it around. Next, add the cheese. Some people like grated cheeses. Myself, I like sliced cheese. It covers better. Next, add your favorite ingredients. Pile them on; the more, the better. When you've got your pizza loaded up, put it in the oven at 350° F for about 12-15 minutes.

This paragraph makes sense. Anyone can follow the directions step by step and make a pizza.

Besides putting the details in time order, the writer has added **transition words**. These are words such as *first, next, then, after,* and *when.* Transition words give the reader clues about the order of events. They make the writing even clearer.

EXERCISE 2

Directions: Number the items in each list in time order. The items in List 1 have been done for you.

1. Getting ready for work

    _(2)_ I take a quick shower.

    _(4)_ I eat breakfast.

    _(3)_ I get dressed.

    _(5)_ I leave the house.

    _(1)_ The alarm goes off.

2. Making pancakes

    _____ Flip the pancakes.

    _____ Add 1/3 cup of milk.

    _____ Measure the mix into a bowl.

    _____ Pour the mixture onto griddle.

    _____ Mix well.

3. How to plant a tree

    _____ Put the tree in the hole.

    _____ Give the newly planted tree plenty of water.

    _____ Holding the tree straight, fill the hole with dirt.

    _____ Dig a hole.

    _____ Spread the roots out in the hole.

4. Wars in American history

    _____ World War I

    _____ Vietnam War

    _____ American Revolution

    _____ Civil War

    _____ World War II

Answers are on page 241.

Cause-and-Effect Order

When you use **cause-and-effect order**, you tell what happened because of something else.

When to Use Cause-and-Effect Order

Cause-and-effect order is useful whenever you want to tell why something happened or what will happen because of something. You might choose cause-and-effect order to tell what happened at work the day twelve inches of snow fell in two hours. You might use it to tell what will happen because the star center of a basketball team is injured.

When to Use Cause-and-Effect Order
Uses
1. To explain why an event happened
2. To explain the results of an event
3. To predict what will happen because of some event
Examples
Why did a local business close down and lay off 300 workers?
What happened because the Mississippi overflowed its banks?
What will happen now that a new industry is moving to town?

Organizing Details in Cause-and-Effect Order

There are two ways to organize ideas in cause-and-effect order. You might look at an effect, or result, and then explain what caused it. Or you might look at a cause, or situation, and tell what effects it has had or will have.

It's important to remember that one cause can have many effects. Likewise, one effect can have many causes.

Often, you will have a string of cause-and-effect events. One event will have an effect. That effect will cause something else to happen, which causes something else to happen, and so on.

cause ⟶ effect		
	cause ⟶ effect	
		cause ⟶ effect
		cause ⟶ effect

Usually cause-and-effect order also follows time order. That is, you tell about the events in the order in which they happened. Telling when events happened is often helpful in explaining how one event caused another.

Recognizing True Cause-and-Effect Details

Be alert to one common mistake in using cause-and-effect order. Don't think one event caused another just because it happened first. Read the following passage. What cause-and-effect relationship does it give?

> The hockey team was on the road for six games. The star player scored seven goals on the trip. The team returned home, so the player broke his leg in practice. He will be out for the season.

This passage contains one cause-and-effect relationship: the player broke his leg, so he will be out for the season. The star didn't break his leg because the team returned home. The word *so* incorrectly suggests a cause-and-effect relationship. When you organize information in cause-and-effect order, be sure the facts are related correctly.

The following is a list of ideas about the effects of higher costs for new cars. Cross out one topic that is not a true effect.

1. People will keep their cars longer.
2. People still want new cars even if they can't afford them.
3. Mechanics have more business because they must keep older cars running longer.
4. To save money, people may buy less well-equipped new cars.

You should have crossed out item 2. It may be true that people still want new cars even if they can't afford them, but it is not an effect of higher-priced cars.

EXERCISE 3

Directions: Put a check in front of the correct answer for each question that follows.

1. Which of the following is <u>not</u> a cause of air pollution?

   _____ (1)   exhaust fumes from cars and trucks

   _____ (2)   electric cars are not practical

   _____ (3)   factories that exhaust smoke out of smokestacks

   _____ (4)   burning leaves and trash

2. Which of the following is <u>not</u> a cause of homelessness?

   _____ (1)   Many factories and other businesses have laid off workers.

   _____ (2)   Some people do not have enough money saved to support themselves or their families while they look for a new job.

   _____ (3)   Single-occupancy hotels have been torn down and replaced with buildings that charge higher rents for their apartments.

   _____ (4)   Every big city in America now has more homeless people on the streets than ever before.

3. Which of the following is <u>not</u> a means of transmitting the HIV/AIDS virus?

   _____ (1)   blood transfusions

   _____ (2)   water fountains

   _____ (3)   hypodermic needles

   _____ (4)   unprotected sex

Answers are on page 241.

EXERCISE 4

Directions: List two causes and two effects for each problem listed below.

Causes

_____
_____
_____
_____

Effects

_____
_____
_____
_____

Violent Crime

_____
_____
_____
_____

_____
_____
_____
_____

Causes

_____
_____
_____
_____

Effects

_____
_____
_____
_____

Lack of Basic Educational Skills

_____
_____
_____
_____

_____
_____
_____
_____

Answers are on page 241.

Comparison-and-Contrast Order

When you use **comparison-and-contrast order**, you show how one item is similar to and different from another item.

When to Use Comparison-and-Contrast Order

Comparison-and-contrast order is helpful whenever you want to tell how two things are alike or different. For example, you might use this organization to make a decision about two job offers.

You might ask yourself how far you want to travel to get to a job. Do you want to work near your home or are you willing to make a longer commute to and from work? What amount of training or educational experience does each job require? What type of work will you be expected to do for each job?

You might also ask yourself if there is a difference in pay between the two jobs. Is there a difference in benefits, such as number of vacation and sick days and insurance coverage? Using comparison and contrast will help you make this kind of decision more easily.

When to Use Comparison-and-Contrast Order

Uses

1. To describe similarities and differences

2. To explain advantages and disadvantages

Examples

How was this year's vacation like the one you took last year?

Which candidate for mayor will do the most for the city?

Whole-to-Whole Pattern

When you use a **whole-to-whole pattern**, you say everything you want to say about one subject. Then you say everything about the other subject. Here's how a writer used this pattern to compare two restaurants.

Jake's Grill has the best barbecue in the city. The food is fresh, hot, and spicy, and there's lots of it. Jake's doesn't have the greatest atmosphere. It has tile floors, bare tables, and bright lighting. Of course, the food's cheap, so who's complaining? If you want atmosphere, go to Chez Paris. The French food is good, fresh, and mildly spicy, but the servings are small. Chez Paris has all the atmosphere you could want, though. The dining room is elegant. It has soft lighting, and classical music plays in the background. If you want to impress someone, Chez Paris is the place, but it is expensive.

Point-by-Point Pattern

You can also organize your writing by using a **point-by-point pattern**. With this organization, you tell one thing about one subject. Then you compare the same point of the other subject. After that, you tell about the next point, and so on. Here's how the writer compared the restaurants using the point-by-point pattern.

> Both Jake's Grill and Chez Paris have good food. Jake's has the best barbecue in town. Chez Paris has French cooking. The food at Jake's is fresh, hot, and spicy, and the helpings are huge. Chez Paris offers good food that's fresh and mildly spicy. The servings, however, are small. Don't go to Jake's for the atmosphere. It has tile floors, bare tables, and bright lights. Chez Paris has an elegant dining room. It is softly lit, and classical music plays in the background. The atmosphere makes Chez Paris expensive, however. Jake's is cheap.

Planning a Comparison-and-Contrast Paragraph

A chart is a useful way to organize ideas when using comparison-and-contrast order. Set it up in columns like the ones shown below.

Items to Discuss	Jake's Grill	Chez Paris
Type of food	American barbecue	French
Quality of food	fresh, hot, very spicy, very filling	fresh, mild spices, small servings
Atmosphere	plain, tile floors, bright lighting, no tablecloths	elegant dining room, classical music, soft lighting
Price	cheap	expensive

EXERCISE 5

Directions: Complete the comparison-and-contrast charts below.

1.

Items to Discuss	Dogs	Cats
Care	_____	_____
	_____	_____
	_____	_____
	_____	_____
Behavior	_____	_____
	_____	_____
	_____	_____
	_____	_____

2.

Items to Discuss	Women	Men
Personality	_____	_____
	_____	_____
	_____	_____
	_____	_____
Appearance	_____	_____
	_____	_____
	_____	_____
	_____	_____

Answers are on page 241.

EXERCISE 6

Directions: Compare and contrast two friends. Tell how they are alike and how they are different.

Friend 1: _____   **Friend 2:** _____

How are they alike?

_____
_____
_____
_____
_____
_____
_____
_____
_____

How are they different?

_____	**Their looks**	_____
_____		_____
_____	**Their interests**	_____
_____		_____
_____	**Their families**	_____
_____		_____
_____	**Type of home**	_____
_____		_____
_____	**Type of work**	_____
_____		_____

Answers are on page 241.

Writing a GED Essay

Directions: Write one paragraph on the following GED essay topic. Make sure your paragraph follows a pattern of organization.

---————————————————— T O P I C ——————————————————---

Why do you want to get your GED certificate?

In your essay, explain why you are studying for the GED Test. Give reasons to support your explanation. Use your personal observations, experience, and knowledge.

---

1. *Choose your pattern of organization.*

   Read the essay topic and decide which pattern of organization you will use. Write the name of the pattern of organization on the line below.

   _____

2. *Organize your details.*

   Think of details to support your response. Use the space below to arrange your details according to the pattern of organization you chose in step 1.

3. *Write your paragraph.*

   Use your organized ideas to write your paragraph. Make sure your paragraph contains a topic sentence as well as several supporting sentences. Follow your pattern of organization as you write.

   _____

   _____

   _____

   _____

   _____

   _____

   _____

   _____

   _____

   _____

   _____

   _____

   _____

   _____

   _____

   _____

   _____

   _____

4. *Revise your paragraph.*

Check your paragraph using the following list.

- [ ] 1. Does your paragraph answer the question that is asked in the writing prompt?
- [ ] 2. Does your paragraph follow a pattern of organization?
- [ ] 3. Does your paragraph contain details that support your explanation?
- [ ] 4. Are the sentences in your paragraph written correctly?
- [ ] 5. Does your paragraph have a consistent tone throughout?

Answers are on page 241.

CHAPTER 8

The Writing Process

Often, the hardest part of writing is getting started. You may know what your topic is. You may even know what information to include. Nevertheless, putting the first words down on paper can seem impossible. What do you say first? What's most important? How can you get your reader interested? How can you make your reader understand?

Prewriting

Fortunately, there is a way to get past these first problems in writing. It is the **prewriting** process. This process will help you develop and organize ideas and prepare to write.

Steps In Prewriting
1. Thinking about what you are writing
2. Brainstorming (listing ideas)
3. Organizing ideas

Thinking About What You Are Writing

Answer the following questions about your writing. Your answers will help you see more clearly what you are trying to do and how to go about doing it.

- What am I writing about?
- Who is going to read my writing?
- What is the purpose for my writing?

For example, imagine that a writer wants to write about how her neighborhood turned a vacant lot into a playground. The lot was overgrown with weeds. There was trash, broken glass, and an abandoned car in the lot. Neighborhood kids played in the lot because there wasn't a park nearby. People in the neighborhood worked together to make it into a playground. Here's how the writer answered the questions about her topic.

- *What am I writing about?*

  a neighborhood project to turn a vacant lot into a playground

- *Who is going to read my writing?*

  the editor and readers of our local newspaper

- *What is my purpose?*

  to tell how my neighborhood turned an ugly lot into a place for kids to play

The writer did not do research to answer these questions. She simply thought about why she was writing. Answering the questions made the writing process more concrete. She knew what she had to do.

Brainstorming

Brainstorming is a way of gathering ideas to write about. When you brainstorm, you jot down every idea that comes to mind about your topic. You don't worry about spelling or writing in complete sentences. You don't even think whether an idea is good or bad. All you're trying to do is to get ideas.

Below is a list of ideas the writer came up with by brainstorming about the vacant lot.

The Vacant Lot

city donated lot
kids played in lot
my nephew suggested the park
kids needed playground
neighbors volunteered to clean it up
lot was an eyesore—weeds broken glass, and cans
collected money to buy equipment

EXERCISE 1

Directions: On a separate sheet of paper, brainstorm a list of ideas about each of the following topics. Spend a few minutes on each. You will be using one of these lists later on for a piece of writing, so save your work.

1. My best vacation
2. My oldest friendship
3. What I'll be doing five years from today
4. An exciting sports event
5. Someone I admire
6. My favorite restaurant
7. A dream come true

Answers are on page 241.

Organizing Ideas

The third step in prewriting is **organizing** information. When you organize, you look at the list of ideas you brainstormed and decide what ideas you want to include. Then you add any new ideas that you think of.

Next decide on a pattern of organization. You might choose order of importance, time order, cause-and-effect, comparison-and-contrast, or any other order that makes sense. If you need a review of patterns of organization, turn to Chapter 7. When you have chosen a pattern, number your ideas in the order in which you will write about them.

Look how the person writing about the vacant lot organized her list.

> *The Vacant Lot*
> 4. city donated lot
> 2. kids played in lot full of glass and trash
> ~~my nephew suggested the park~~
> 3. kids needed playground
> 5. neighbors volunteered to clean it up—city provided trash truck
> 1. lot was an eyesore—weeds, broken glass, and cans
> 6. collected money from local businesses to buy equipment
> 7. put in basketball court, playground equipment

Notice the changes the writer made. She crossed out one idea and added to some of her other ideas. Then she numbered them in a time order. She wanted to tell about the park in the order in which events happened.

EXERCISE 2

Directions: Choose one of your lists from Exercise 1 on page 196. Make any changes you wish to the list. You can add new ideas or scratch out ideas you don't want to use. Then number the ideas in the order in which you want to write about them. Keep in mind that you'll be using this work later, so be sure to save it.

Answers are on page 241.

Writing

Now that you have completed prewriting, you are ready to put your ideas down on paper. This is done most easily if you do it in stages, just like prewriting. The main goal in **writing** is to create a rough draft.

The purpose of the **rough draft** is to turn your list of ideas into sentences and paragraphs. Don't worry too much about grammar or spelling. You can fix those mistakes later. Just try to get your ideas down in the proper order. Use your list as a guide, but if you think of new ideas or want to change the order of ideas, go ahead.

Your writing will have three parts: an introduction, a body, and a conclusion.

Introduction

The **introduction** does three things:

- tells what the topic is

- gives the main idea, or point, of the writing

- gives the reader some idea of what will be discussed

When the writer began drafting the story of the vacant lot, she wrote this introduction. Notice how she achieved the three goals of an introduction.

> There used to be a vacant lot down the street. It was filled with trash, broken glass, and cans. Besides being an eyesore, it was dangerous. Kids played there. They often cut themselves on broken glass and rusty cans. Finally, people got together and did something. Now it's a park and playground for neighborhood kids.

Here are some hints that will help you write a good introduction.

1. **State your main idea clearly.** If your readers know what to expect, they will understand your ideas better. Also, if you clearly state your main idea, you can look back at it as you write. You can make sure that what you say in the body supports your main idea.

2. **Give your readers an idea of the content and organization.** Then they won't become confused by how you present your ideas. If you can't explain the content and organization, you may not be quite ready to begin writing. Go back to Step 1 of prewriting.

3. **Get your readers interested so they will keep reading.** There are many ways to do this. You could begin with an odd or interesting fact. You could explain why your information is important. The first introduction to "The Vacant Lot" uses this method. You could begin with a question. Here's how a question could be used to introduce "The Vacant Lot."

> *What do you do with a vacant lot? Our neighborhood had that problem. One lot was empty and ugly. Everyone talked about it. No one knew what to do with it. Then one day, we found the answer. We would turn the lot into a playground.*

EXERCISE 3

Directions: Write an introduction on a separate sheet of paper. Use your list of ideas from Exercises 1 and 2 as a guide. Write on every other line so you will have room to revise later. When you're finished, check your writing. Make sure it gives the topic and main idea. It should also give your readers an idea of the content and organization, and it should get them interested.

Answers are on page 241.

Body

In the introduction, you told what your main idea is. In the **body** of your writing, you give the details and facts that explain the main idea.

Use your numbered list of ideas as a guide while writing the body. If new ideas occur to you, add them as you go. Start a new paragraph for each big idea or topic you want to explain.

On the next page is the body of "The Vacant Lot." Compare the development of ideas to the original list. Also notice how the ideas were divided into paragraphs. The first paragraph tells about the lot the way it was. The second paragraph is about how the neighborhood changed it.

Just a year ago, the lot was covered with weeds. Kids played in the lot. It was dangerous, though, because of the trash. Broken glass and cans were lying around. However, kids didn't have any other place to play except in the street.

We turned the lot into a playground. A group met with people from the city. They talked the city into donating the land. Other people talked local businesses into donating playground equipment and money. We put in a basketball court and some playground equipment. Then everyone in the neighborhood pitched in to clean up the lot. The city provided a trash truck to haul the junk away.

As you write, look back at your introduction from time to time. Check that you are giving the information you said you wanted to include.

EXERCISE 4

Directions: Now begin the body of your writing. Continue to use the list of ideas from Exercise 2 as your guide in writing. Add details as you think of them. Create new paragraphs for each big idea. Write on every other line so you will have room to revise later.

Answers are on page 241.

Conclusion

Your **conclusion** is the ending for your writing. It's not new information. It is a wrap-up of what you have already said. The length of your conclusion depends on the length of the whole piece of writing. It might be one or two sentences or one or more paragraphs.

There are many ways to write a conclusion. You can summarize what you have said. Your conclusion will be a reminder for your reader. It says again, in a different way, the main idea you gave in your introduction. Here is how the writer of "The Vacant Lot" might have used a summary as her conclusion.

> *Working together, our neighborhood got rid of an eyesore. In the process, we've given kids a safe place to play.*

Another way to end your writing is to tell your reader the broader truth of what you've said. "The Vacant Lot" might have been ended like this:

> *The vacant lot had been a problem in our neighborhood for years. No one knew what to do with it. We found the answer when we stopped looking at the lot only as a problem. Instead, we looked on it as an opportunity. Now we have a great new park for our kids.*

This conclusion says the story is not just about getting rid of a vacant lot or building a playground. It's about turning problems into opportunities.

EXERCISE 5

Directions: Complete the draft you worked on in Exercises 2, 3, and 4 by writing a conclusion. Write on every other line so you will have room to revise later. Before you start, read the introduction and body you have already completed, just to refresh your memory.

Answers are on page 241.

Revising and Editing

Revising

Now your rough draft is complete. The next step in the writing process is **revising**. During revision, you make changes to improve your writing. You can change the order of ideas, rewrite sentences or paragraphs, make different word choices, or cut out ideas that you no longer think are important. Take as much time as you want during this stage. You are finished when you are happy with your work. Here are a few specific things to look for.

Improve Word Choices

While writing your rough draft, you were thinking mainly about getting your ideas down on paper. You didn't spend a lot of time choosing the right words. During revision, read each sentence carefully. Ask yourself if you have chosen the best words to say exactly what you mean. More precise words will make your writing clearer and more interesting.

Improve Links Between Paragraphs

When you wrote your rough draft, you started a new paragraph for each big idea. Now check that your reader will see how the ideas in each paragraph are linked.

One way to improve the links between paragraphs is by starting paragraphs with **transition words**. These are words such as *furthermore, then, on the other hand, as a result, in addition,* and *another advantage is.* Transition words show that ideas are connected. They help your writing to be coherent.

Add Details and Examples

Ask yourself if your ideas are clear. Can your reader picture what you are saying? If not, your writing might need more details or examples. Use facts, descriptive words, or examples to support what you are saying.

On the next page is a revised draft of "The Vacant Lot." Notice how the writer has improved word choices, added details, and made the links between paragraphs stronger.

The Vacant Lot

What do you do with a vacant lot? Our neighborhood had that problem. One lot was empty and ugly. Everyone talked about it. No one knew what to do with it.

Then one day, we found the answer. We would turn the lot into a playground. The lot was covered with weeds. Children played in the lot. It was dangerous, though, because broken glass and cans were lying around. However, children didn't have any other place to play except for in the street.

A group met with people from the city. They talked the city into donating the land. Other people talked local businesses into donating playground equipment and money. Then everyone in the neighborhood pitched in to clean up the lot. The city provided a trash truck to haul the junk away. We put in a basketball court and some playground equipment.

Working together, our neighborhood got rid of an eyesore. In the process, we've given children a safe place to play.

EXERCISE 6

Directions: Revise your draft. Look for ways to make your ideas clearer. You might want to change words, put ideas in a different order, or add transition words. Keep changing your draft until you are happy with your writing.

Answers are on page 241.

Editing

After you have finished your revised draft, the next step is editing. **Editing** is proofreading your writing for mistakes in grammar, punctuation, capitalization, and spelling. Follow these steps during editing.

1. **Read your writing out loud.** Listen for words or sentences that sound wrong or awkward. Mark these places. You can come back and figure out what is wrong after you have finished reading aloud.

2. **Look at each sentence by itself.** Look for anything that is wrong. Be especially alert for fragments and run-ons.

3. **Read your writing several times.** Each time, look for a certain kind of error. Choose two or three mistakes you sometimes make. For example, if you have trouble with using commas, look closely at all the commas. If you have trouble with pronoun agreement, look at the pronouns.

EXERCISE 7

Directions: Edit your draft. Look for errors in spelling, grammar, capitalization, and punctuation. Then make a clean copy of your writing. You may want to read your finished draft one more time to make sure you have not made an error while copying it.

Answers are on page 241.

The GED Essay Scoring Guide

As you revise and edit your essay, you'll want to keep in mind the GED Essay Scoring Guide. The guide rates essays from 1 *(inadequate)* through 4 *(effective)*. Your goal is to write an essay in which readers can easily follow your expression of ideas. An effective essay achieves the following:

- It presents a clearly focused main idea that addresses the prompt.

- It establishes a clear and logical organization.

- It achieves coherent development with specific, relevant details and example.

- It consistently uses correct sentence structure and good grammar, usage, punctuation, and spelling.

- It shows varied and precise choice of words.

Writing a GED Essay

Part A   **Directions:**   Read the essay topic below. Plan your essay before you write. Use the space below to make any notes, and write your essay on a separate sheet of paper. After you finish writing your essay, reread what you have written and make any changes that will improve it. Make sure your essay is long enough to develop the topic adequately.

--------------------------------- T O P I C ---------------------------------

Where is your favorite place to visit?

In your essay, describe your favorite place to visit. Explain why you like this place. Use your personal observations, experience and knowledge.

Part B   **Directions:**   Look at the Essay Scoring Checklist on page 206. Go over each question with your instructor or someone who is a good writer. Check the box for each question that best describes your essay. Look at the number of each box that you checked. Have you checked mostly 4's? 3's? a combination of 2's and 3's? a significant amount of 1's? For each question that has a checked box of 3 or less, think about how you can improve your essay to get a 4. Pay special attention to questions with a checked box of 1 or 2—these scores indicate that you need some extra practice in certain writing skills.

Answers are on page 241.

Essay Scoring Checklist

A. **Does your essay answer the question that is asked in the writing prompt?**

☐ 1. No, my essay refers to the question, but it doesn't really discuss it or develop a main idea that answers the question.

☐ 2. My essay addresses the question with a main idea, but it also includes some ideas that are not directly related to the question.

☐ 3. Yes, my essay has a main idea that is based on the question, but the main idea could be stated in a better way.

☐ 4. Yes, my essay clearly answers the question with a main idea.

B. **Are the ideas in your essay well organized?**

☐ 1. No, the ideas in my essay are mixed up in order and are hard to follow.

☐ 2. Most of the ideas in my essay are clear and easy to follow, but there are some ideas that are hard to follow.

☐ 3. Yes, the ideas in my essay are clearly organized, but some of the ideas could be organized in a better way.

☐ 4. Yes, the ideas in my essay are clearly organized and easy to follow.

C. **Does your essay contain details or examples that support the main idea?**

☐ 1. No, many of the paragraphs in my essay contain details or examples that don't support the topic sentence, or many of the paragraphs don't have any details or examples at all.

☐ 2. Some of the paragraphs in my essay have a topic sentence and supporting details and examples, but the details and examples could be stronger and more abundant.

☐ 3. Yes, each paragraph in my essay contains a topic sentence and details or examples, but some of the paragraphs have more details or examples than others.

☐ 4. Yes, each paragraph in my essay contains a topic sentence with specific details and examples that support the topic sentence.

D. **Are the sentences and paragraphs in your essay grammatically correct?**

☐ 1. No, the sentences and paragraphs in my essay are not worded correctly, and a majority of the sentences contain errors in grammar and spelling.

☐ 2. Some of the sentences and paragraphs in my essay are worded incorrectly, and there are a noticeable amount of errors in grammar and spelling.

☐ 3. Yes, the sentences and paragraphs in my essay are mostly worded correctly, and there are only a few small errors in grammar and spelling.

☐ 4. Yes, the sentences and paragraphs in my essay are worded correctly, and there are practically no errors in grammar or spelling.

E. **Does your essay display a wide range of words that are used correctly?**

☐ 1. No, my essay displays a very limited choice of words, which are often reused or used incorrectly.

☐ 2. My essay doesn't display a very wide range of word choice, and there are a few words that are used incorrectly.

☐ 3. Yes, my essay displays a word choice that is appropriate to the topic but could be more complex.

☐ 4. Yes, my essay displays a wide range, in which all words are used correctly.

Language Arts, Writing Part I

This Posttest will help you evaluate whether you are ready to move up to the next level of GED preparation. It has two parts. Part I consists of 50 multiple-choice questions that test the grammar, usage, and organization skills covered in this book. Part II contains an essay topic.

Directions: Choose the <u>one best answer</u> to each question. Some of the sentences contain errors in organization, sentence structure, usage, or mechanics. A few sentences, however, may be correct as written. Read the sentences carefully and then answer the questions based on them. For each question, choose the answer that would result in the most effective writing of the sentence or sentences.

Posttest Answer Grid

1 ① ② ③ ④ ⑤	18 ① ② ③ ④ ⑤	35 ① ② ③ ④ ⑤
2 ① ② ③ ④ ⑤	19 ① ② ③ ④ ⑤	36 ① ② ③ ④ ⑤
3 ① ② ③ ④ ⑤	20 ① ② ③ ④ ⑤	37 ① ② ③ ④ ⑤
4 ① ② ③ ④ ⑤	21 ① ② ③ ④ ⑤	38 ① ② ③ ④ ⑤
5 ① ② ③ ④ ⑤	22 ① ② ③ ④ ⑤	39 ① ② ③ ④ ⑤
6 ① ② ③ ④ ⑤	23 ① ② ③ ④ ⑤	40 ① ② ③ ④ ⑤
7 ① ② ③ ④ ⑤	24 ① ② ③ ④ ⑤	41 ① ② ③ ④ ⑤
8 ① ② ③ ④ ⑤	25 ① ② ③ ④ ⑤	42 ① ② ③ ④ ⑤
9 ① ② ③ ④ ⑤	26 ① ② ③ ④ ⑤	43 ① ② ③ ④ ⑤
10 ① ② ③ ④ ⑤	27 ① ② ③ ④ ⑤	44 ① ② ③ ④ ⑤
11 ① ② ③ ④ ⑤	28 ① ② ③ ④ ⑤	45 ① ② ③ ④ ⑤
12 ① ② ③ ④ ⑤	29 ① ② ③ ④ ⑤	46 ① ② ③ ④ ⑤
13 ① ② ③ ④ ⑤	30 ① ② ③ ④ ⑤	47 ① ② ③ ④ ⑤
14 ① ② ③ ④ ⑤	31 ① ② ③ ④ ⑤	48 ① ② ③ ④ ⑤
15 ① ② ③ ④ ⑤	32 ① ② ③ ④ ⑤	49 ① ② ③ ④ ⑤
16 ① ② ③ ④ ⑤	33 ① ② ③ ④ ⑤	50 ① ② ③ ④ ⑤
17 ① ② ③ ④ ⑤	34 ① ② ③ ④ ⑤	

When you have completed the test, check your work with the answers and explanations on pages 218–219. Use the evaluation chart on page 220 to determine which areas you need to review.

POSTTEST

1. **Maya and Tim have'nt yet sent out the invitations to the party they're planning.**

   What correction should be made to this sentence?

   (1) change *have'nt* to *haven't*
   (2) change *invitations* to *Invitations*
   (3) change *they're* to *their*
   (4) change the period to an exclamation point
   (5) no correction is necessary

2. **Floyd's Furniture Store sold three chairs, a bookcase, and two couches today but Floyd says business is bad.**

   What correction should be made to this sentence?

   (1) change *Floyd's Furniture Store* to *Floyd's furniture store*
   (2) remove the comma after *bookcase*
   (3) insert a comma after *today*
   (4) change *says* to *will say*
   (5) no correction is necessary·

3. **The press release said that senator Salazar will, as usual, be in his home district in late summer.**

   What correction should be made to this sentence?

   (1) change *press release* to *Press Release*
   (2) change *senator* to *Senator*
   (3) remove the commas before and after *as usual*
   (4) change *summer* to *Summer*
   (5) no correction is necessary

4. **Our supervisor asked whose responsible for the area east of Chatworth Lane.**

   What correction should be made to this sentence?

   (1) change *Our* to *Are*
   (2) change *supervisor* to *Supervisor*
   (3) change *whose* to *who's*
   (4) change *east* to *East*
   (5) no correction is necessary

5. **Curtis's guest list includes the following: his Mother, the Atoles, and three neighbors.**

   What correction should be made to this sentence?

   (1) change *Curtis's* to *Curtis*
   (2) change the colon to a semicolon
   (3) change *Mother* to *mother*
   (4) remove the comma after *Mother*
   (5) no correction is necessary

6. **The dog <u>growled at Jo and me, then he rubbed</u> his head against my hand.**

   Which is the best way to write the underlined portion of the text? If the original is the best way, choose option (1).

   (1) growled at Jo and me, then he rubbed
   (2) growled at Jo and I, then he rubbed
   (3) growled at Jo and me. Then he rubbed
   (4) growled at Jo and me, then he rubs
   (5) growled at Jo and me than he rubbed

7. **I read in the newspaper, that a group of Greek singers will give a concert next Labor Day in Dayton, Ohio.**

   What correction should be made to this sentence?

   (1) remove the comma after *newspaper*
   (2) change *singers* to *Singers*
   (3) change *will give* to *gave*
   (4) change *Labor Day* to *Labor day*
   (5) no correction is necessary

POSTTEST

8. **"Are you finished with that baseball book,"** **asked Nancy, "Or are you still reading it?"**

   What correction should be made to this sentence?

   (1) change *baseball* to *Baseball*
   (2) change the comma after *book* to a question mark
   (3) change *Or* to *or*
   (4) change the question mark to a period
   (5) no correction is necessary

9. **Dr. Sanford's theory is that it is better to** **deal with a problem than to ignore it; I** **would rather ignore it.**

   What correction should be made to this sentence?

   (1) add a comma before *that*
   (2) add a comma after *problem*
   (3) change the semicolon to a colon
   (4) change the period to an exclamation point
   (5) no correction is necessary

10. **Either William or his <u>wife have taken care</u>** **<u>of Yoko's</u> baby more than I can remember.**

    Which is the best way to write the underlined portion of the text? If the original is the best way, choose option (1).

    (1) wife have taken care of Yoko's
    (2) wive have taken care of Yoko's
    (3) wife has taken care of Yoko's
    (4) wife have took care of Yoko's
    (5) wife have taken care of Yokos

11. **Patricia felt angrily when she learned that** **Howard had quit his job.**

    What correction should be made to this sentence?

    (1) change *angrily* to *angry*
    (2) change *she* to *her*
    (3) change *had quit* to *has quit*
    (4) change *his* to *their*
    (5) no correction is necessary

12. **Those neighbors who don't ever seem to** **sleep have went on a vacation to Finland.**

    What correction should be made to this sentence?

    (1) change *Those* to *Them*
    (2) change *who* to *whom*
    (3) change *have went* to *has went*
    (4) change have *went* to *have gone*
    (5) no correction is necessary

13. **Ms. Stanovich, as well as her two <u>sons,</u>** **<u>never run less than three miles</u> every day.**

    Which is the best way to write the underlined portion of the text? If the original is the best way, choose option (1).

    (1) sons, never run less than three miles
    (2) son, never run less than three miles
    (3) sons, never runs less than three miles
    (4) sons, never run least than three miles
    (5) sons, never run less than three mile

14. **The rules state that each runner must have** **their own number and be at the starting** **line at noon.**

    What correction should be made to this sentence?

    (1) change *rules* to *rule's*
    (2) change *state* to *states*
    (3) change *have* to *has*
    (4) change *their* to *his or her*
    (5) no correction is necessary

15. **Last week, not only Marla and also John** **wrote letters to their town's newspaper** **complaining about poor police protection.**

    What correction should be made to this sentence?

    (1) change *and* to *but*
    (2) change *wrote* to *had written*
    (3) change *town's* to *towns*
    (4) insert a comma after *newspaper*
    (5) no correction is necessary

16. **In today's paper there is several articles about community programs that have received much attention.**

   What correction should be made to this sentence?

   (1) change *today's* to *todays*
   (2) change *is* to *are*
   (3) change *have* to *has*
   (4) change *much* to *most*
   (5) no correction is necessary

17. **The governor feels strongly that solutions to this city's serious problems must come from we citizens.**

   What correction should be made to this sentence?

   (1) change *strongly* to *strong*
   (2) change *serious* to *seriously*
   (3) change *this* to *those*
   (4) change *we* to *us*
   (5) no correction is necessary

18. **The efficiency expert who studied plant operations said the engine room should have more workers and fewest machines.**

   What correction should be made to this sentence?

   (1) change *who* to *which*
   (2) change *fewest* to *fewer*
   (3) insert a comma after *operations*
   (4) change *more* to *most*
   (5) no correction is necessary

19. **Neither Javier nor Craig know how many people have sent in their reservations.**

   What correction should be made to this sentence?

   (1) change *know* to *knows*
   (2) change *many* to *much*
   (3) change *have sent* to *had sent*
   (4) change *their* to *his or her*
   (5) no correction is necessary

20. **Laura was furious when she realized that she canceled her credit card before she could buy Toshio a birthday gift.**

   What correction should be made to this sentence?

   (1) change *furious* to *furiouser*
   (2) change *realized* to *realizes*
   (3) change *canceled* to *had canceled*
   (4) insert a comma after *before*
   (5) no correction is necessary

21. **The man whom you introduced me to last night called to ask if I would have dinner with him.**

   What correction should be made to this sentence?

   (1) change *whom* to *who*
   (2) change *introduced* to *introduce*
   (3) change *me* to *I*
   (4) change *called* to *had called*
   (5) no correction is necessary

22. **The manager sees no reason for <u>my absences, the company has a policy</u> about what excuses are acceptable.**

   Which is the best way to write the underlined portion of the text? If the original is the best way, choose option (1).

   (1) my absences, the company has a policy
   (2) mine absences, the company has a policy
   (3) my absence's, the company has a policy
   (4) my absences. The company has a policy
   (5) my absences, the company have a policy

POSTTEST

23. Of all the hairdressers' I have seen in the past five years, Antoinette is the one whom I like best.

What correction should be made to this sentence?

(1) change *hairdressers'* to *hairdressers*
(2) change *past* to *passed*
(3) remove the comma after *years*
(4) change *whom* to *which*
(5) no correction is necessary

24. Having recovered from a bad cold. Kathy can now enjoy life again.

What correction should be made to this sentence?

(1) change *Having* to *Had*
(2) insert a comma after *recovered*
(3) change the period after *cold* to a comma
(4) change *can* to *could*
(5) no correction is necessary

25. Bring those extra bags over to Terry and I; we will put them to good use.

What correction should be made to this sentence?

(1) change *those* to *them*
(2) insert a comma after *bags*
(3) change *I* to *me*
(4) change *we* to *us*
(5) change *good* to *gooder*

26. Ms. Armillo asked us who repairs our TV set because hers often has wavy lines across the screen.

What correction should be made to this sentence?

(1) change *asked* to *ask*
(2) change *who* to *what*
(3) change *hers* to *her's*
(4) change *has* to *has got*
(5) no correction is necessary

27. After Todd will announce his plans to marry Danita, he bought a ring and planned a big engagement party.

What correction should be made to this sentence?

(1) change *will announce* to *had announced*
(2) change *plans* to *plan's*
(3) insert a comma after *plans*
(4) change *bought* to *buys*
(5) no correction is necessary

28. <u>The belief that many experts think is true is</u> that California will suffer another earthquake within ten years.

Which is the best way to write the underlined portion of the text? If the original is the best way, choose option (1).

(1) The belief that many experts think is true
(2) Many experts believe
(3) It is the distinguished opinion of many experts
(4) The belief held by a majority of experts is beyond a doubt
(5) It is true

29. It bothers Ivan that he works more slowly than her although no one has complained about his performance.

What correction should be made to this sentence?

(1) change *more slowly* to *most slowly*
(2) change *her* to *she*
(3) change *has complained* to *have complained*
(4) change *has complained* to *had complained*
(5) no correction is necessary

30. **Since the rain had been so <u>heavy. City</u> officials advised people to beware of flash floods.**

    Which is the best way to write the underlined portion of the text? If the original is the best way, choose option (1).

    (1) heavy. City
    (2) heavy city
    (3) heavy; therefore, city
    (4) heavy, city
    (5) heavy; city

31. **Although she pretends to be mature, Anna still loves to read trashy <u>novels, singing on a crowded bus, and</u> play hide-and-seek.**

    Which is the best way to write the underlined portion of the text? If the original is the best way, choose option (1).

    (1) novels, singing on a crowded bus, and
    (2) novels; singing on a crowded bus; and
    (3) novels, she sings on a crowded bus, and
    (4) novels, sing on a crowded bus, and
    (5) novels although singing on a crowded bus, and

32. **Postal authorities suggest that you stop mail delivery if they are going to be away from home for a long time.**

    What correction should be made to this sentence?

    (1) change *authorities* to *authorities'*
    (2) insert a comma after *delivery*
    (3) change *they* to *you*
    (4) change *are going* to *were going*
    (5) no correction is necessary

33. **Officials say <u>the cost of the price of train fares</u> will increase next month.**

    Which is the best way to write the underlined portion of the text? If the original is the best way, choose option (1).

    (1) the cost of the price of train fares
    (2) the cost of train fares
    (3) the price of train fares
    (4) train fares
    (5) trains

34. **The soldier <u>shared his dinner in uniform with a stranger and her baby.</u>**

    Which is the best way to write the underlined portion of the text? If the original is the best way, choose option (1).

    (1) shared his dinner in uniform with a stranger and her baby
    (2) shared his dinner; in uniform with a stranger and her baby
    (3) in uniform shared his dinner with a stranger and her baby
    (4) shared his dinner in uniform, with a stranger and her baby
    (5) shared his dinner with a stranger and her baby in uniform

35. **The company is pleased with this year's <u>profits. Instead, it is</u> giving employees a bonus.**

    Which is the best way to write the underlined portion of the text? If the original is the best way, choose option (1).

    (1) profits. Instead, it is
    (2) profits; in fact, it is
    (3) profits, in fact it is
    (4) profits; however, it is
    (5) profits; instead, it is

36. **<u>Because we had planned to fly out today,</u> our flight was canceled.**

    Which is the best way to write the underlined portion of the text? If the original is the best way, choose option (1).

    (1) Because we had planned to fly out today,
    (2) Because, we had planned to fly out today
    (3) Although we had planned to fly out today
    (4) Although we had planned to fly out today,
    (5) As a result, we had planned to fly out today,

37. **The apartment manager and the building owner both signed the letter; <u>he said that he was sorry</u> that the rent had to be raised.**

    Which is the best way to write the underlined portion of the text? If the original is the best way, choose option (1).

    (1) he said that he was sorry
    (2) the letter said that he was sorry
    (3) the letter said that the owner was sorry
    (4) he said that the owner was sorry
    (5) they said that he was sorry

38. **Christy was surprised she heard that she had earned more money than anyone else in her department.**

    What correction should be made to this sentence?

    (1) insert *when* after *surprised*
    (2) insert a comma after *surprised*
    (3) change *heard* to *will hear*
    (4) change *anyone else* to *anyone*
    (5) no correction is necessary

39. **All afternoon the players warmed up, practiced, and prepared for the big game.**

    What correction should be made to this sentence?

    (1) change *players* to *players'*
    (2) change both commas to semicolons
    (3) change *warmed up* to *were warming up*
    (4) insert a comma after *prepared*
    (5) no correction is necessary

40. **Blowing at more than 70 miles per hour, <u>trees were knocked down and cars were tossed around.</u>**

    Which is the best way to write the underlined portion of the text? If the original is the best way, choose option (1).

    (1) trees were knocked down and cars were tossed around
    (2) trees were knocked down, and cars were tossed around
    (3) the wind knocked down trees, and tossed around cars
    (4) the wind knocked down trees and tossed around cars
    (5) trees were knocked down and cars will be tossed around

41. **The woman was carrying a basket, some dried <u>flowers, and with four</u> handmade dolls.**

    Which is the best way to write the underlined portion of the text? If the original is the best way, choose option (1).

    (1) flowers, and with four
    (2) flowers, and four
    (3) flowers; and with four
    (4) flowers; furthermore, with four
    (5) flowers and with four

42. **<u>This lovely crocheted afghan was created by the work of an enormously talented son of mine.</u>**

    Which is the best way to write the underlined portion of the text? If the original is the best way, choose option (1).

    (1) This lovely crocheted afghan was created by the work of an enormously talented son of mine.
    (2) My son made this afghan.
    (3) My talented son crocheted this lovely afghan.
    (4) This crocheted afghan was made by my talented son.
    (5) This lovely afghan was created by a very talented son of mine.

POSTTEST

Questions 43–50 refer to the following memo.

To: All Metalcraft Employees

From: Teresa Rodriguez, CEO

Re: Environmental Issues

(A)

(1) I am pleased to announce to all of you that Metalcraft is becoming even more friendly to the environment. (2) But now we are expanding our efforts. (3) As you know, this company has always been concerned about environmental issues.

(B)

(4) Partnering with several conservation groups, the Beechtree River will be cleaned up. (5) Those of you who like to fish will be happy to hear that the state has agreed to stock the river with trout as soon as the water quality improves. (6) Of course, fish is better for you than red meat. (7) We're also looking for volunteers to help work on the wetlands project. (8) We need people now to help build the ponds and over the long term to monitor water quality.

(C)

(9) There will be no more disposable foam coffee cups here, we're providing ceramic coffee mugs for everyone. (10) At the cost of a few minutes to wash out your cup each day, you'll be eliminating tons of landfill garbage. (11) We're using unbleached coffee filters and paper towels to avoid adding more poisonous dioxin to the atmosphere. (12) We're going to reduce the amount of energy we use for heating and to air condition.

(D)

(13) You won't freeze in August because the air conditioner is set too cold. (14) In conclusion, let me say thank you to everyone. (15) Who is ready to put up with a few small inconveniences to yield big improvements. (16) My goal is to see Metalcraft become one of the most environment-friendly companies in the United States. (17) With your help, I know we can reach that goal.

43. Sentence 2: But now we are expanding our efforts.

Which revision should be made to sentence 2 to improve paragraph A?

(1) move sentence 2 to the beginning of paragraph A
(2) move sentence 2 to follow sentence 3
(3) move sentence 2 to the beginning of paragraph B
(4) remove sentence 2
(5) move sentence 2 to the end of paragraph B

44. Sentence 4: Partnering with several conservation groups, <u>the Beechtree River will be cleaned up.</u>

Which is the best way to write the underlined portion of the text? If the original is the best way, choose option (1).

(1) the Beechtree River will be cleaned up
(2) the Beechtree river will be cleaned up
(3) the Beechtree River, will be cleaned up
(4) the Beechtree River cleanup will take place
(5) we will clean up the Beechtree River

POSTTEST

45. Sentence 6: **Of course, fish is better for you than red meat.**

Which revision should be made to sentence 6 to improve paragraph B?

(1) move sentence 6 to the beginning of paragraph B
(2) move sentence 6 to the end of paragraph B
(3) move sentence 6 to follow sentence 4
(4) remove sentence 6
(5) move sentence 6 to follow sentence 7

46. **Which sentence would make the best topic sentence for paragraph C?**

(1) We advise you to cut back on the amount of coffee you drink.
(2) We'll also be making small changes in the workplace to help the environment.
(3) We'll also be changing the workplace.
(4) Do you know how bad foam cups are for the environment?
(5) The process of bleaching paper creates deadly dioxin.

47. Sentences 9 and 10: <u>**There will be no more disposable foam coffee cups here, we're providing**</u> **ceramic coffee mugs for everyone.**

Which is the best way to write the underlined portion of the text? If the original is the best way, choose option (1).

(1) There will be no more disposable foam coffee cups here, we're providing
(2) Their will be no more disposable foam coffee cups here, we're providing
(3) There won't be no more disposable foam coffee cups here, we're providing
(4) There will be no more disposable foam coffee cups, here we're providing
(5) There will be no more disposable foam coffee cups here. We're providing

48. Sentence 12: **We're going to reduce the amount of energy we use for heating and to air condition.**

What correction should be made to sentence 12?

(1) change to *air condition* to *air conditioning*
(2) change *reduce* to *reduced*
(3) insert a comma after *energy*
(4) insert a comma after
(5) no correction is necessary

49. Sentence 13: **You won't freeze in August because the air conditioner is set too cold.**

Which revision should be made to sentence 13 to improve paragraph D?

(1) move sentence 13 to the end of paragraph C
(2) move sentence 13 to the end of paragraph D
(3) remove sentence 13
(4) move sentence 13 to follow sentence 14
(5) move sentence 13 to follow sentence 15

50. Sentences 14 and 15: **In conclusion, let me say thank you to everyone. Who is ready to put up with a few small inconveniences to yield big improvements.**

What correction should be made to sentences 14 and 15?

(1) remove the period after *everyone*
(2) change *me* to *I*
(3) combine them into one sentence
(4) change *is* to *are*
(5) no correction is necessary

Answers are on pages 218–219.

Language Arts, Writing Part II

This part of the Posttest is designed to find out how well you write.

Essay Directions and Topic:

Look at the box on the following page. In the box is your assigned topic.

You must write on the assigned topic ONLY.

You will have 45 minutes to write on your assigned topic. If you run out of time, mark where you were in your essay. Then complete the essay. This will help you determine how much faster you need to work to complete your essay in 45 minutes.

Pay attention to these features as you write:

- Well-focused main points
- Clear organization
- Specific development of your ideas
- Control of sentence structure, punctuation, grammar, word choice, and spelling

As you work, be sure to do the following:

- Write legibly.
- Write on the assigned topic.
- Write your essay on a separate sheet of paper.

POSTTEST

--- TOPIC ---

A century ago, the average human life span was 50 years. Now some scientists believe that children born today could live to be 120 years old. Would you like to live to be 120 years old?

In your essay, tell whether you would want to live to age 120 or beyond. Explain the positive and negative factors of living so long. Use your personal observations, experiences, and knowledge.

Part II is a test to determine how well you can use written language to explain your ideas.

In preparing your essay, you should take the following steps:

- Read the **DIRECTIONS** and the **TOPIC** carefully.
- Plan your essay before you write. Use scratch paper to make any notes.
- After you finish writing your essay, reread what you have written and make any changes that will improve your essay.
- Make sure your essay is long enough to develop the topic adequately.

Evaluation guidelines are on page 221.

POSTTEST

Answer Key

1. (1) The apostrophe in a contraction replaces the missing letter. In this case, the missing letter is the *o* in *not*.

2. (3) This is a compound sentence joined by the conjunction *but*. A comma is needed before the conjunction.

3. (2) *Senator* is used as the title of a specific person, so it should be capitalized.

4. (3) *Whose* shows possession. Here, the meaning is *who is*, so the correct word is the contraction *who's*.

5. (3) In this sentence, *Mother* is not used in direct address or as a substitute for a name, so it should not be capitalized.

6. (3) This is a run-on sentence. To correct it, separate the two independent clauses into two sentences.

7. (1) Because the final clause is essential to the sentence's meaning, it should not be preceded by a comma.

8. (3) The quotations are one sentence separated by *asked Nancy*. The beginning of the second part of the sentence should not be capitalized.

9. (5) This sentence is correct as written.

10. (3) When the parts of a compound subject are separated by *or*, the verb should agree in number with part closer to it, in this case *wife*, which is singular.

11. (1) In this sentence, *felt* is used as a linking verb, so the adjective form, *angry*, should be used.

12. (4) The helping verb *have* tells you to use the past participle. The correct past participle of the irregular verb *go* is *gone*.

13. (3) The subject of the verb *runs* is *Ms. Stanovich*. The phrase *as well as her two sons* is not part of the subject.

14. (4) *Their* is plural, so it cannot refer to the singular noun *runner*.

15. (1) *Not only* and *but also* go together to form a conjunction. *Not only . . . and* is always incorrect.

16. (2) The subject of this sentence is the plural noun *articles*, which requires a plural verb.

17. (4) *We* is a subject pronoun. In this sentence the pronoun is the object of the preposition *from*, so the object pronoun *us* is needed.

18. (2) Two things are being compared, so the *er* form of the adjective is needed, not the *est* form.

19. (1) With *neither ... nor*, make the verb agree with the part of the subject closer to it. Here it should agree with the singular noun *Craig*.

20. (3) The canceling of the credit card occurred in the past before another action, so it should be described in the past perfect tense.

21. (5) This sentence is correct as written.

22. (4) This sentence is a comma splice. Break the two independent clauses into two separate sentences.

23. (1) *Hairdressers'* is a plural possessive noun. Here the word should be plural but not possessive, so no apostrophe is used.

24. (3) *Having recovered from a bad cold* is a fragment. To fix it, attach that dependent clause to the complete sentence that follows.

25. (3) In this sentence, the subject pronoun *I* is used incorrectly. The object pronoun *me* is needed to follow the preposition *to*.

26. (5) This sentence is correct as written.

27. (1) The announcement is a completed action that occurred before another past action. Therefore, it should be described in the past perfect tense.

28. (2) The underlined words are repetitive. Choice (2) gets rid of the repetition without losing any of the meaning.

29. (2) When you see *than*, mentally complete the phrase: *than she does*. *She* is the subject of the verb *does*.

30. (4) The first sentence is a fragment. Changing the period to a comma correctly makes it an introductory dependent clause.

31. (4) *Singing on a crowded bus* is not parallel with the other items in the series. One way to fix the structure is to make it an infinitive (*to sing*) like the other verbs in the series.

POSTTEST

32. (3) The pronoun should refer to *you*, not to *authorities.*

33. (4) *The cost of* and the *price of* say the same thing as *train fares.* Choice (4) gets rid of the repetition without losing any of the meaning.

34. (3) The phrase *in uniform* modifies *soldier,* so it should be placed as close as possible to *soldier.*

35. (2) *Instead* suggests of contradiction of ideas. *In fact* correctly suggests further development of the same idea. The conjunctive adverb should be preceded by a semicolon and followed by a comma.

36. (4) The conjunction *because* suggests an incorrect cause-effect relationship between the two clauses. *Although* correctly expresses a contrast between the two parts of the sentence. The introductory dependent clause must be followed by a comma.

37. (3) It's not clear to whom *he* refers, nor is it clear who was sorry or whether it was said in person or in the letter. Choice (3) makes it clear that *he* refers to the owner and that the apology was in the letter.

38. (1) This is a run-on sentence. One way to fix it is to make the second clause dependent by adding a conjunctive adverb, *when.*

39. (5) This sentence is correct as is.

40. (4) *Blowing at more than 70 miles per hour* is a dangling participle. To fix it, put something in the sentence for it to modify: *the wind.* No comma should separate the two parts of the compound predicate.

41. (2) The series is not parallel. Choice (2) gets rid of the preposition *with* so the items in the series all have the same structure.

42. (3) The sentence is wordy. Choice (3) keeps the meaning but eliminates the wordiness.

43. (2) The information in sentence 3 must come before sentence 2 so the conjunction *but* makes sense.

44. (5) *Partnering with several conservation groups* is a dangling modifier. It needs something to modify: *we.*

45. (4) A sentence about the nutritional value of fish versus red meat does not belong in a paragraph about cleaning up a river so it will support aquatic life.

46. (2) All of the rest of the paragraph, about coffee cups and unbleached towels and heating/air conditioning, can refer back to the new topic sentence in choice (2).

47. (5) The sentence is a comma splice. Choice (5) breaks it into two sentences.

48. (1) The series is not parallel. Changing the second item to *air conditioning* makes both parts of the series end in *ing.*

49. (1) Sentence 13 is about the same subject as paragraph C, not the rest of paragraph D.

50. (1) Sentence 15 is a fragment. Combining it with sentence 14 turns it into a dependent clause.

Part I Evaluation Chart

On the following chart, circle the number of any item you answered incorrectly. Next to each group of item numbers, you will see the pages you can review to learn how to answer the items correctly. Pay particular attention to reviewing skill areas in which you missed half or more of the questions.

Skill Area	Item Number	Review Pages
ORGANIZATION		
Text divisions	49	162–164
Topic sentences	46	159–161
Unity/coherence	43, 45	165–171
SENTENCE STRUCTURE		
Complete sentences, fragments, and sentence combining	24, 30, 50	13–18, 101–110
Run-on sentences/comma splices	6, 22, 38, 47	103–104
Wordiness/repetition	28, 33, 41	121–127
Coordination/subordination	15, 35, 36	102–110
Modification	11, 18, 29, 34, 44	81–100, 111–112
Parallelism	31, 40, 42, 48	113–114
USAGE		
Subject-verb agreement	10, 13, 16, 19	67–77
Verb tense/form	12, 20, 21, 26, 27	53–66, 115–117
Pronoun reference/antecedent agreement	14, 17, 25, 32, 37	30–47, 118–119
MECHANICS		
Capitalization	3, 5, 8	133–138
Punctuation (commas)	2, 7, 9, 39	20, 139–148
Spelling (possessives, contractions, and homonyms)	1, 4, 23	27–28, 149–152

Part II Evaluation Guidelines

If at all possible, give your instructor your essay to evaluate. You will find his or her objective opinion helpful in deciding whether you are ready to begin preparing for the actual GED. If this is not possible, have another student evaluate your essay. If you cannot find another student to help you, review your essay yourself. If you do this, it is usually better to let your essay sit for a few days before you evaluate it. This way you will have similar views as someone reading your essay for the first time. No matter which way you review your work, use the checklist on the next page to review your essay.

After you have evaluated your essay in terms of the criteria in the checklist, look at the number you checked for each question. Pay attention to the questions where you checked a 2 or a 1—these scores indicate that you need some extra practice in certain writing skills. Reviewing the following sections will help you to raise your score:

1. If you had trouble answering the question that is asked in the writing prompt, review pages 195–196.

2. If you had trouble organizing your ideas, review Chapter 7 and page 197.

3. If you had trouble supporting your main idea with details or examples, review pages 196 and 202–203.

4. If you had trouble writing grammatically correct sentences and paragraphs, review Chapters 1–6.

5. If you had trouble using words correctly, review Chapters 4 and 6.

If possible talk to your instructor, another student, or a friend about your feelings as you wrote. Together you will be able to identify your current writing strengths as well as any weaknesses. Based on this combined evaluation, review the sections in this book that will help you most in improving your writing.

POSTTEST
Essay Scoring Checklist

A. Does your essay answer the question that is asked in the writing prompt?

☐ 1. No, my essay refers to the question, but it doesn't really discuss it or develop a main idea that answers the question.

☐ 2. My essay addresses the question with a main idea, but it also includes some ideas that are not directly related to the question.

☐ 3. Yes, my essay has a main idea that is based on the question, but the main idea could be stated in a better way.

☐ 4. Yes, my essay clearly answers the question with a main idea.

B. Are the ideas in your essay well organized?

☐ 1. No, the ideas in my essay are mixed up in order and are hard to follow.

☐ 2. Most of the ideas in my essay are clear and easy to follow, but there are some ideas that are hard to follow.

☐ 3. Yes, the ideas in my essay are clearly organized, but some of the ideas could be organized in a better way.

☐ 4. Yes, the ideas in my essay are clearly organized and easy to follow.

C. Does your essay contain details or examples that support the main idea?

☐ 1. No, many of the paragraphs in my essay contain details or examples that don't support the topic sentence, or many of the paragraphs don't have any details or examples at all.

☐ 2. Some of the paragraphs in my essay have a topic sentence and supporting details and examples, but the details and examples could be stronger and more abundant.

☐ 3. Yes, each paragraph in my essay contains a topic sentence and details or examples, but some of the paragraphs have more details or examples than others.

☐ 4. Yes, each paragraph in my essay contains a topic sentence with specific details and examples that support the topic sentence.

D. Are the sentences and paragraphs in your essay grammatically correct?

☐ 1. No, the sentences and paragraphs in my essay are not worded correctly, and a majority of the sentences contain errors in grammar and spelling.

☐ 2. Some of the sentences and paragraphs in my essay are worded incorrectly, and there are a noticeable amount of errors in grammar and spelling.

☐ 3. Yes, the sentences and paragraphs in my essay are mostly worded correctly, and there are only a few small errors in grammar and spelling.

☐ 4. Yes, the sentences and paragraphs in my essay are worded correctly, and there are practically no errors in grammar or spelling.

E. Does your essay display a wide range of words that are used correctly?

☐ 1. No, my essay displays a very limited choice of words, which are often reused or used incorrectly.

☐ 2. My essay doesn't display a very wide range of word choice, and there are a few words that are used incorrectly.

☐ 3. Yes, my essay displays a word choice that is appropriate to the topic but could be more complex.

☐ 4. Yes, my essay displays a wide range, in which all words are used correctly.

Answer Key

Chapter 1

1. Sarah attacked the chores with enthusiasm.
2. Indira's kitchen table was piled high with fresh-baked bread.
3. High winds broke several windows in downtown buildings.
4. Jevon raced to the telephone in the living room.
5. Mr. Zimmer's house will always be our least favorite.
6. The woman answered the police officer carefully.
7. The doctor arrived at the office at 8:30 A.M.
8. Soon Young prepared a huge meal for her parents.
9. The forest fire had destroyed several thousand acres of trees.
10. Marek's grandmother will turn eighty-five this year.

Exercise 2, page 16

1. The team's manager should win an award.
2. Everyone has ordered something different to eat.
3. Andrej fumbled in his pockets for his car keys.
4. Mr. and Mrs. Hastings complained about the defective lamp.
5. The run-down old bus pulled slowly out of the station.
6. The previous receptionist had been more efficient.
7. Pak Ku runs during his lunch hour every Friday.
8. Christy and Jan became good friends last year.
9. My brother's apartment was burglarized recently.
10. The brilliant writer of this movie has created a suspenseful plot.

Exercise 3, page 17

1. **S** *You* is the subject, and *need three stamps on that envelope* is the predicate. It expresses a complete thought.
2. **S** In this complete thought, the subject is *Sam and his nephew* and the predicate is *fished all morning.*
3. **F** *That thick magazine on the sofa* is a subject, and *fell* is a verb, but this group of words is a fragment. Because the word *when* introduces the sentence, a complete thought is not expressed.
4. **S** This complete thought is made up of the subject *this room* and the predicate is *a mess!*
5. **S** The subject *my client in Dallas* and the predicate *will send you the brochure* make up a complete thought.
6. **F** This group of words lacks a subject to tell you what *rattled and chugged all the way down the street.*
7. **F** This group of words could be a subject. There is no predicate to complete the thought to tell you something about the neighbor and friend.
8. **S** The subject *the workers* and the predicate *walked carefully through the construction area* express a complete thought.
9. **F** *You and your co-workers* is a subject and *are dependable* is a predicate. However, this group of words does not express a complete thought and therefore is a fragment.
10. **S** This group of words expresses a complete thought. *Florentia* is the subject and *received dozens of cards during her illness* is the predicate.

Pre-GED Practice, page 18

1. (1) The original is a fragment because it lacks a predicate. What about people with homes on the Mississippi floodplain? Choice (1) adds the verb *fled* to tell what people with homes on the floodplain did.
2. (4) The original is a fragment because it lacks a subject. What migrated south from Canada? Choice (4) adds the subject *wolves* to tell what migrated.
3. (2) The original is a fragment because it does not express a complete thought. What was a result of the air pollution being so bad? Choice (2) provides a subject, *laws,* and a predicate, *were enacted.*
4. (3) The original is a fragment because it lacks a predicate. What about the car's electric window? Choice (3) adds the verb *became jammed.*
5. (5) The original is a complete sentence.
6. (5) The original is a complete sentence.

Exercise 4, page 21

1. Brian slowly got to his feet _._
2. Be careful with that lawn mower _!_
3. Smoke is coming from the roof _!_
4. Where did you find the book _?_
5. Stop jumping on the bed _!_
6. The train stops here every fifteen minutes _._
7. Have you seen my radio _?_
8. Ms. Luna left here at least twenty minutes ago _._
9. What a nightmare _!_
10. Can you see her yet _?_

Pre-GED Practice, page 21

1. (2) This is a statement of surprise or urgency.
2. (2) This is a question.
3. (5) This sentence is correct as written.
4. (2) This is a statement. No excitement or surprise is shown.

Exercise 5, page 23

1. <u>Hilda</u> says she will return <u>home</u> soon.
2. <u>Construction</u> of the <u>Alaska Highway</u> began in <u>1942</u>.
3. <u>Superman's</u> first <u>home</u> was <u>Cleveland, Ohio.</u>
4. Two high school <u>students</u> created the <u>superhero.</u>
5. Last <u>year,</u> <u>Louis Padilla</u> moved into an <u>apartment</u> in <u>Washington, D.C.</u>

6. <u>Padilla</u> visits the <u>Smithsonian Institution</u> at least twice a <u>month.</u>
7. The <u>Smithsonian</u> is <u>one</u> of the largest <u>museums</u> in the <u>world.</u>
8. <u>Toni</u> is learning to paint <u>landscapes.</u>
9. <u>William</u> wants to capture the <u>beauty</u> of the <u>outdoors</u> in his <u>photos.</u>
10. <u>Shawna</u> captured the <u>colors</u> of the morning <u>sky</u> in her <u>painting.</u>

Exercise 6, page 24

1. The two <u>friends</u> traveled to <u>Chicago</u> and visited the <u>Sears Tower.</u>
2. The <u>salesperson</u> showed <u>Melanie</u> two navy blue <u>jackets.</u>
3. While riding on the <u>train</u>, an <u>attorney</u> read the *St. Louis Post-Dispatch.*
4. The <u>nurse</u> took <u>James's</u> blood <u>pressure</u> and recorded the <u>numbers</u> on the <u>form.</u>
5. My <u>friend</u> <u>Yolanda</u> wants to learn more about <u>Hinduism.</u>
6. Many <u>people</u> go out of <u>town</u> over <u>Memorial Day weekend.</u>
7. A <u>chef</u> from <u>France</u> prepared a fabulous <u>meal</u> for the special <u>event.</u>
8. Let's go into the <u>museum</u> when <u>Mark</u> and <u>Noriko</u> arrive.
9. There are <u>geysers</u> and hot <u>springs</u> in <u>Yellowstone National Park.</u>
10. Can <u>Jeremy</u> stop at the <u>Quikstop Food Store</u> and pick up some <u>milk</u>?

Exercise 7, page 26

1. (3) scratches
2. (5) correct
3. (3) sheep
4. (4) lives
5. (2) spies
6. (5) correct
7. (2) trout
8. (4) skies
9. (3) dishes
10. (1) handkerchiefs

Exercise 8, page 28

1. **country's**   This is a possessive noun. The problem belongs to the country.
2. **women's**   *Women* is a plural noun that does not end in *s*. To make this plural show possession, the apostrophe should precede the *s*.
3. **C**
4. **Millers**   The verb *have* shows possession, so no apostrophe is needed on the noun *Millers*.
5. **C**
6. **books**   This noun is plural, not possessive. No apostrophe is needed.
7. **C**
8. **boss's**   This noun is possessive. A singular noun ending in an *s* is made possessive in the same way as other singular nouns, by adding an apostrophe and an *s*.
9. **years'**   The noun is plural and possessive. Add an *s* to form the plural and an apostrophe to show possession.
10. **citizens'**   This noun is plural and possessive. Add an *s* to form the plural and an apostrophe to show possession.

Pre-GED Practice, page 29

1. (4) There is only one team. Form the possessive by adding an apostrophe and an s.
2. (1) Nouns ending in *ch* are made plural by adding *es*.
3. (2) *Mysteries* is plural but it is not showing possession. Drop the apostrophe.
4. (1) Words ending in *x* are made plural by adding an *es*.
5. (2) The sun possesses the rays. Form the possessive by adding an apostrophe and an s.

Exercise 9, page 32

1. **they**   Since *they* and the *guests* refer to the same people, you should use a subject pronoun.
2. **He and I**   A subject pronoun is needed because *he* is part of the compound subject *he and I.*
3. **Julian and she**   The subject pronoun is used because *Julian and she* is giving more information about the subject, *my two friends.*
4. **they**   *They* is the subject of the verb *sell.*
5. **you and he**   The subject pronoun *he* is correct because it is part of the compound subject of the verb *should plan.*
6. **we**   *We* is the subject of the verb *learned.*
7. **I**   The verb of being, *is*, is the clue that a subject pronoun is correct.
8. **the Porters and we**   A subject pronoun must be used here because *we* is a part of the subject of the verb *have lived.*
9. **he**   The verb of being, *is*, is the clue that a subject pronoun is correct.
10. **I**   *I* is the correct pronoun here because *you* and *I* are part of the subject of the verb *love.*
11. **We**   *We* is the subject of the verb *invited.*
12. **I**   A subject pronoun is needed because *I* is part of the compound subject *Tina and I.*
13. **He**   *He* is the subject of the verb *asks.*
14. **she**   A subject pronoun is needed because *she* is part of the compound subject *William and she.*
15. **You and he**   The subject pronoun *you and he* is used because it is part of the compound subject of the verb *did.*

Exercise 10, page 34

1. her   *Her* is the correct possessive pronoun to show the "ownership" of knowledge.

2. yours   No noun follows the possessive pronoun, so *yours* is correct. *Yours* never has an apostrophe.

3. hers   No apostrophe is used with possessive pronouns.

4. your   *Your* always goes with a noun. Possessive pronouns never have apostrophes.

5. its   No apostrophe is used with a possessive pronoun. Remember that *it's* stands for "it is" or "it has."

6. ours   No noun follows the possessive pronoun, so *ours* is correct. No apostrophe is used with a possessive pronoun.

7. their   *Their* is the correct possessive form because it is followed by a noun, *break time. They* is a subject pronoun and cannot be used to show possession.

8. mine   No noun follows the possessive pronoun, so *mine* is correct. *Mine* never has an *s* at the end.

Exercise 11, page 36

1. us   The pronoun is the object of the preposition *between.*

2. her   *Her* is the object of *followed.* Therefore an object pronoun is needed.

3. him and me   When two or more pronouns are used and one of them is *me, me* always comes last.

4. her   The pronoun *her* tells more about *customers,* which is the object of the verb *asked.* An object pronoun is needed.

5. them   The object pronoun *them* is correct because it answers the question, "For whom is there enough food?"

6. you and me   These pronouns are objects of the preposition *between.*

Exercise 12, page 37

1. ourselves   The correct form of the pronoun is *ourselves.* There is no singular form.

2. she   The subject pronoun is used because *she* is part of the compound subject. Remember that *herself* is not a subject pronoun.

3. I   Use a subject pronoun for the subject of the sentence.

4. themselves   The correct plural reflexive is *themselves. Theirselves* and *themself* are never correct.

5. me   An object pronoun is correct because *me* answers the question, "To whom did the bus driver give transfers?" Remember that *myself* and other reflexive pronouns can never substitute for subject or object pronouns.

6. themselves   This is the correct plural reflexive pronoun.

7. herself   This is the correct singular reflexive pronoun. It refers back to *Yulian.*

8. I   Use a subject pronoun for the subject of a sentence.

Exercise 13, page 40

1. he   Remember that with pronouns after *than* or *as,* you should mentally complete the sentence. Amy is just as qualified as he (is).

2. him   The correct pronoun is the object pronoun *him* because it answers the question, "Whom did we voters want?"

3. me   The object pronoun *me* should be used instead of the reflexive *myself. Me* is the object of the preposition *between.*

4. us   Since *parents* is the object of *give,* the object pronoun *us* is correct.

5. she   The subject pronoun *she* is correct here. I work harder than *she* (works).

6. my   Since a noun follows the possessive pronoun, *my* is the correct pronoun.

7. whomever   The object pronoun *whomever* is correct. It is the object of the verb *brings.*

8. Whoever   Since you can substitute the subject

pronoun *he, Whoever* is the correct
pronoun.

9. **Ted and I** When a noun and the pronoun *I* are
connected by *and* or *or*, the pronoun
I should go last; *Ted and I* continued
laughing.

10. **Correct**

11. **I** The correct pronoun is the subject
pronoun *I* instead of the object
pronoun *me*.

12. **she** The subject pronoun *she* is correct
and not the reflexive pronoun *herself*.

Exercise 14, page 45

1. Someone who forgets to pay *(his or her, their)*
electric bill may end up without lights.
2. The woman *(which, who)* plays the guitar used
to play the drums.
3. When Sergeant York tells you to do something,
he expects *(him, you)* to do it.
4. The players must have *(his, their)* luggage on
the bus by noon.
5. Although I've had *(it, them)* for years, this pair
of scissors is still sharp.
6. If people want to succeed in life, *(you, they)*
must make plans now.
7. The group was sure *(its, their)* performance
would win first prize.
8. The couple giving this party have plenty of
food for *(his, their)* guests.
9. Frank put his sunglasses back in *(its, their)* case.
10. Everything must be put in *(its, their)* place
before the guests arrive.
11. Everyone should sign *(his or her, their)* name to
register for the workshop.
12. Politics has *(its, their)* own set of rules.
13. The pair of pants is missing *(its, their)* belt.
14. The tailor *(which, who)* altered the suit did an
excellent job.
15. Neither Velma nor I can work any harder no
matter how hard *(I, we)* try.

Exercise 15, page 46

1. **that** They have a cat who is always
following them.
2. **We** Us lazy people cannot understand
why he works whenever the boss
asks him.

3. **Correct** She and I told him that everyone
should be well organized.
4. **Correct** He told us that having three jobs
made his life hectic.
5. **Correct** Just between you and me, Sam,
whoever gets this job deserves it.
6. **he** If you were him, would you want this
job?
7. **Correct** When the United States elects its
president, your vote will count as
much as his.
8. **myself** I left me a note so I would remember
to write a letter.
9. **whoever** He will give a ticket to whomever
wants to attend his comedy act.
10. **us** On their vacation, they sent
greetings to we slaves still on the job.
11. **he** That baby showed his parents that it
was ready to walk by pulling himself
up to a standing position.
12. **who** She proved herself the person which
is most qualified.
13. **Correct** They claimed the money that was on
the table was theirs.
14. **I** Do you remember when you and me
visited Washington, D.C.?

Pre-GED Practice, page 47

1. (4) *It's* is a contraction meaning "it is." Here the
possessive pronoun *its* is needed.
2. (2) The subject pronoun is used because *Alicia
and she* is giving additional information
about the subject, *Our friends*.
3. (2) The object pronoun *me* is correct because it
follows the preposition *between*.
4. (1) When *me* and another pronoun are linked,
me always goes last.
5. (2) Reflexive pronouns should not be used as
subject pronouns.

Pre-GED Practice, pages 48–49

1. (4) The original is a fragment. What happened
while the ducks rose? Choice (4) creates a
complete sentence.
2. (3) The original sentence is a fragment because
it lacks a subject. *Himself* is the correct
reflexive pronoun. *Hisself* is always incorrect.

3. (3) The original is a fragment because it does not express a complete thought. What was a result of his cold being so bad? Choice (2) provides a subject, *John,* and a predicate, *stayed home.*

4. (3) The original is a fragment. What happened during that night? The correction adds a simple subject, *fire,* and a predicate, *kept them warm.* (In the original sentence, *fire* is an object.)

5. (4) *Bookshelf* is made plural by changing the *f* to a *v* and adding *es.*

6. (4) *Had jumped over a wall* is a sentence fragment. Adding *They* to the fragment makes it a complete sentence.

7. (4) *It's* means "it is." The possessive form is *its.*

8. (4) The pronoun follows a preposition, *with,* and therefore should be an object pronoun.

9. (2) It's not clear who *she* refers to, so replace it.

10. (3) *Who* is correct because it is a subject pronoun that goes with the verb *ate. Whom* is an object pronoun.

11. (4) This is an exclamatory sentence and needs an exclamation point.

12. (4) Part of this sentence is understood. Read it as "he shoots better than she shoots." *She* is correct because it is a subject pronoun; *her* is an object pronoun.

13. (1) *Us* is an object pronoun. Here the pronoun is the subject, so use *we.*

14. (2) *Somebody* is always a singular pronoun. *Their* is plural. *Somebody* can be either male or female so use *his or her.*

Chapter 2

Exercise 1, page 52

1. Sidney <u>will come</u> to the table when you <u>call</u> him.
2. <u>Did</u> you <u>know</u> that my aunt <u>is</u> still <u>living</u> in Canada?
3. When Veronica <u>saw</u> the picture, she <u>was</u> very <u>surprised.</u>
4. I <u>will be coming</u> to work early tomorrow.
5. When <u>can</u> you <u>come</u> and <u>see</u> my new baby?
6. During our vacation, we <u>camped,</u> <u>cooked</u> and <u>hiked.</u>
7. By the time we <u>finish</u> this job, our boss <u>will have found</u> two new ones for us.

8. <u>Can</u> you <u>describe</u> the man who just <u>left</u> the store?
9. Although her manager rarely <u>talked</u> to her, Akiko <u>liked</u> her job.
10. Cindy <u>has</u> never <u>missed</u> an Elvis Presley movie that <u>has been shown</u> on television.
11. I <u>will</u> always <u>be grateful</u> that I <u>got</u> a good education.
12. Since she <u>came</u> back from her trip, Raisa <u>has felt</u> much more relaxed.
13. After <u>cleaning,</u> <u>shopping,</u> and <u>fixing</u> lunch, Ida <u>took</u> a nap.
14. What <u>will</u> it <u>be</u> like when we <u>arrive</u> in Florida, I <u>wonder</u>?

Exercise 2, page 56

1. **called** The word *yesterday* is the clue that the past tense is necessary.

2. **waits** Use the present form here. It shows an action that is performed regularly. *Every afternoon* is the clue. Remember to add an *s* to the base form for a singular noun, *Stan.*

3. **moved** The past tense of *move* is correct. The phrase *two years ago* tells you that the action occurred in the past.

4. **enjoy** The present form is used for something that is always true.

5. **will work** *Next week* tells you that this verb should be in the future tense.

6. **happened** *Last night* is the clue that the past tense is correct.

7. **demand or are demanding** *Today* shows that this statement is true now. Therefore, use the present tense.

8. **will end** *Next Tuesday* tells you this sentence is in the future tense.

9. **owns** The word *now* tells you that the verb should be in the present tense. The subject *Simon* requires an *s* at the end of the base form of the verb.

10. **talked** *Yesterday* tells you that this happened in the past.

11. **will discuss** *Tomorrow* tells you that the verb is in the future tense.

12. **parked** *Last Sunday* tells you that the verb is in the past tense.

13. **answered** *Last night* tells you that the verb is in the past tense.

14. **will smile** *Next Tuesday* tells you that the verb is in the future tense.

Exercise 3, page 60

1. Brian **threw** out the runner trying to steal second.
2. The rain **freezes** as soon as it hits the pavement.
3. Please **give** this package to the delivery person.
4. I didn't know what she **meant** when she said she was skating home.
5. Jill's babies **clung** tightly to her when she left home.
6. Dilip is the most helpful real estate agent I have ever **dealt** with.
7. Anna **spun** another tale of horror for her young listeners as they squirmed in their seats.
8. If you value your life, don't **set** that can on the table.
9. Ms. Tso **swore** to the judge that she was telling the truth.
10. Javier leaped excitedly as he **pulled** the huge fish ashore.
11. The bread dough had **risen** after a few hours.
12. I **dreamed, dreamt** I won the lottery.
13. He **burst** the balloon with a pin.
14. Mr. Hanley was **bitten** by a dog.

Exercise 4, page 62

1. **will begin** *In two more weeks* tells you that this will happen in the future.
2. **tastes** The present tense is used for action that is always true.
3. **had taken** The past perfect form is correct because this action took place before another action.
4. **will have swum** The future perfect shows that the action will be completed before another future action. By the time they finish the race, the action of swimming twenty miles will be completed.
5. **have said** The present perfect is used to show an action that has taken place in the past and is still true in the present.
6. **has memorized** Use the present perfect tense because the action took place in the past and has continued into the present.
7. **had tried** First Curtis tried to reach the landlady; then he reached her. The past perfect shows the action that took place first.

8. **has ridden** The present perfect tense shows that an event was done in the past and is still being done.
9. **invented** The action was completed in the past.

Exercise 5, page 63

1. complete
2. were
3. be drunk
4. were
5. pay

Exercise 6, page 64

1. My grandparents deserted the old house.
2. Large shrubs hide the doorway.
3. That fallen tree has jammed the cellar door shut.
4. The wrecking crew will tear down the old house.

Exercise 7, page 65

1. rode, rides
2. had bought, discovered
3. began, was
4. will finish *or* will have finished, begins
5. was sweating, returned
6. hope, gave

Pre-GED Practice, page 66

1. (3) John was at the track before Javier crossed the finish line. Therefore, the verb *arrives* should be in the past perfect tense to show that this action occurred before the action of Javier's crossing the finish line.
2. (3) When a verb ends with a *ch*, an *es* instead of an *s* is added to form the simple present tense. *Reachs* should be *reaches*.
3. (2) *Swear* is an irregular verb. The correct spelling of the past participle is *sworn*, not *swore*.
4. (3) Yolanda wrote the address at the same time she stood at the station. Therefore the verbs should be in the same tense. The simple past tense *wrote* agrees with the simple past tense *stood*.
5. (1) This statement takes the subjunctive form of the verb *connect* because it expresses urgency. The subjunctive form does not add an *s* to the base form.

6. (1) The verb *exchange* should be in the past tense, so the correct form is *exchanged*.
7. (3) *After Ted gets his tax return* is in the future tense, so the verb *bought* should be changed to *will buy*.
8. (4) The verb *thank* should be in the past tense, so the correct form is *thanked*.

Exercise 8, page 68

1. Those <u>fish</u> *(has, have)* been jumping since we got here.
2. Our <u>problem</u> *(is, are)* getting the tent set up.
3. <u>We</u> in the jury *(believe, believes)* he is innocent.
4. My <u>muscles</u> *(ache, aches)* from all the exercise.
5. The security <u>guards</u> at the store *(want, wants)* a raise.
6. <u>I</u> *(come, comes)* to all my son's baseball games.
7. The <u>order</u> *(include, includes)* paper clips, folders, and tape.
8. My favorite <u>movie</u> *(is, are)* The African Queen.
9. Michiko's three huge <u>dogs</u> *(pull, pulls)* her helplessly along.
10. The <u>price</u> of those strawberries *(seem, seems)* awfully high.

Exercise 9, page 69

1. **were**	*Mr. Fletcher and Ms. Ortega takes were* because it is a compound subject joined by *and*.
2. **appears**	This compound subject is joined by *not only . . . but also*. The verb should agree with the subject closer to it.
3. **is**	The simple subject is *lunch*, so use the singular verb form. Remember that the verb does not always agree with words following the linking verb.
4. **plans**	The form of the verb ending in *s* is correct because the verb must agree with the part of the subject closer to it, *Jeffrey*.
5. **have**	With compound subjects joined by *either … or*, the verb must agree with the subject closer to it, *they*.
6. **gives**	Both parts of the compound subject, *my roommate and best friend*, refer to the same person. Use the singular verb form.
7. **are**	The subject takes a plural verb because the parts are linked by *and*.
8. **complain**	The plural verb form is correct because the parts of the compound subject are linked by *and*.

Exercise 10, page 72

1. **stand**	The simple subject is *pumps*, so use the plural verb *stand*. If you have trouble finding the simple subject, put the sentence in normal subject-verb order: *Two old water pumps stand at the end of the dusty road.*
2. **are**	Since *there* is neither a noun nor a pronoun, it cannot be the subject. The subject is *clues*, so the correct verb is *are*.
3. **waits**	Don't be confused by the interrupting phrase. *Antonio* is the subject of the sentence.
4. **stretches**	The word order of this sentence is inverted. Change it to *A yellow ribbon stretches across the front windows* and you will see that the subject is *ribbon*.
5. **walk**	Ignore the interrupting phrase, *including my collie*. The subject is *dogs*.
6. **are**	In this inverted sentence, *boots* is the subject and takes a plural verb.
7. **grow**	Ignore the interrupting prepositional phrase, *in the west*. *Clouds* is the subject and takes a plural verb.
8. **do**	*Plants* is the subject of the verb and agrees with the verb *do*.

Exercise 11, page 73

1. **argue**	The pronoun *who* refers to *people*, not *Molly*. Since *people* is plural, the plural verb *argue* is correct.
2. **are**	The pronoun *that* refers to *orders* and is in agreement with the verb *are*.
3. **need**	The pronoun *that* refers to the plural noun *lamps*.
4. **seems**	The pronoun *which* refers to the simple subject *solution*, which takes a singular verb.
5. **require**	The pronoun *that* refers to *books*, a plural noun, which takes the plural verb *require*.

6. appears   *Appears* agrees with the singular noun *plan*.

7. love   The pronoun *who* refers to the plural noun *children*.

8. are   The pronoun *that* refers to the plural noun *computers*.

9. drive   The pronoun *that* refers to the plural noun *inventions*.

10. like   The pronoun *who* refers to the plural noun *brothers*.

11. appears   The pronoun *which* refers to the singular noun *answer*.

12. plans   The pronoun *who* refers to the singular subject *Mr. Lee*, which takes a singular verb.

13. arrive   The pronoun *who* refers to the plural subject *nephews*.

Exercise 12, page 76

1. rides   *Everyone* is a pronoun that is always singular. Always use a singular verb.

2. is   *Most* is a pronoun that refers to the singular noun *meat*. Use the verb form that goes with *he, she, it*.

3. looks   *Everything* is a pronoun that is always singular. Choose the singular verb.

4. laughs   *Crowd* is a collective noun. Here it is used to refer to the whole group acting as a unit. Use a singular verb.

5. are   When *none* is used to refer to a plural noun, as in *voters* in this sentence, use the plural verb.

6. serve   *Few* is always plural. Use the plural verb.

7. was   *Each* is always singular. Use a singular verb.

8. are   *Half* can be plural or singular. Here it refers to the plural noun *people*. Use a plural verb.

Pre-GED Practice, page 77

1. (3) *Neither* is a pronoun that is always singular. It takes the singular verb *wants*.

2. (1) Ignore the interrupter. The verb *jump* should be changed to its singular form to agree with *Rosa*.

3. (4) With *neither ... nor*, the verb agrees with the subject closer to it. Here the closer subject is the singular noun *Andrew*.

4. (5) All the verbs are in agreement with their subjects.

5. (1) *Tickets* is the subject of the sentence, not *here*. The verb must agree with this plural noun.

6. (1) The choir is acting as a group, so the singular verb *performs* is required.

7. (1) Ignore the interrupter. The singular verb *runs* agrees with the singular noun *Jed*.

8. (3) The committee is acting as a group, so the singular verb *decides* is required.

Pre-GED Practice, pages 78–79

1. (5) *Is exhausted* agrees with *guard. Who* is a pronoun that refers to *guard*, so it agrees with the singular verb *walks*.

2. (3) The subject of *are welcome* is the pronoun *everyone. Everyone* is a singular pronoun, so the verb should be *is*.

3. (3) Use the past perfect tense to show that the action of the sale ending happened before Lucinda got to the store.

4. (4) Ignore the clause *whom I do not know* and check the agreement between *somebody* and *send. Somebody* is a singular pronoun and takes a singular verb.

5. (2) The word *while* tells you that both events happened at the same time. Therefore the verbs should show the same tense.

6. (2) *Athletics* is a singular noun, even though it ends with an *s*.

7. (2) This sentence is in the subjunctive mood because it creates a sense of urgency. Therefore the verb *sign* should not end with an *s*.

8. (2) Ignore the interrupting phrase *along with her two little brothers*. The verb agrees with the simple subject *Sonia*, which is singular.

9. (4) The correct past participle of *hide* is *hidden*.

10. (1) When words like *not only ... but also* split up a compound noun, the verb agrees with the noun closer to it. Here the plural noun *cousins* is closer to the verb, so the verb should be plural.

11. (2) Two events occur at different times. *Martha and Kim had never seen such a large roller coaster* occurs before the amusement park opened. Therefore the amusement park opening occurs in the simple past tense to show that it occurred in the past but more recently than the other event.

12. (5) *Jury* is a collective noun. Here it is plural and takes a plural verb, *do look*, because each member looks unhappy. All the action occurs in the present, so the use of present-tense verbs is correct.

13. (3) *Eyeglasses* is a plural noun, so it takes the plural verb form *slip*.

14. (1) The first sentence is inverted. Its subject is *carpenters*, which is plural.

Chapter 3

Exercise 1, page 82

1. **arrived**
   adverb
   Late tells you when the mail arrived. *Arrived* is a verb, so *late* must be an adverb.

2. **dinner**
   adjective
   Late tells you what kind of dinner. *Dinner* is a noun, so *late* must be an adjective.

3. **children**
   adjective
   Four tells you how many children. *Children* is a noun, so *four* must be an adjective.

4. **moved**

   adverb
   Quickly tells you how Andrew moved.

   Moved is a verb, so *quickly* must be an adverb.

5. **amazing**

   adverb
   Absolutely tells you to what extent the discovery is amazing.

   Amazing is an adjective, so *absolutely* must be an adverb.

6. **chair**
   adjective
   This tells you which chair.

   Chair is a noun, so *this* must be an adjective.

7. **played**

   adverb
   Quietly tells you how the music was played.

   Played is a verb, so *quietly* must be an adverb.

8. **lives**
   adverb
   Here tells you where Juan lives.

   Lives is a verb, so *here* must be an adverb.

9. **noise**
   adjective
   Awful tells you what kind of noise. *Noise* is a noun, so *awful* must be an adjective.

10. **car**
    adjective
    New tells you what kind of car. *Car* is a noun, so *new* must be an adjective.

Exercise 2, page 84

1. **rapidly**
   The modifier tells how the runners moved. *Moved* is a verb, so use the adverb *rapidly*.

2. **easily**
   The modifier tells how the calculator should work. *Work* is a verb here, so use the adverb form.

3. **C**

4. **C**

5. **extreme**
   Extremely is an adverb. Here it is used incorrectly to modify a noun, *heat*.

6. **C**

7. **carefully**
   The modifier tells how the contract is being read, so the adverb form is needed.

8. **badly**
   The modifier tells to what extent Molly hurt her foot, so an adverb is needed.

9. **straight**
   Straight does not change form when used as an adverb.

10. **practical**
    Practically is an adverb. It is being used incorrectly to modify a noun, *solution*.

11. **C**

12. **crookedly**
    The modifier tells how the old road winds, so the adverb form is needed.

Exercise 3, page 86

1. **dark**
   Became is a linking verb. *Dark* describes the noun *sky*, so the modifier should be an adjective.

2. **sad**
   Sad modifies *you*, a pronoun. Use the adjective.

3. **quickly**
   The modifier describes the verb *crosses*, telling how Gopal crosses the street. An adverb is correct,

4. **carefully**
   Carefully tells how the doctor felt Ann's arm. It modifies the verb *felt*. An adverb is correct.

5. sure — *Seems* is used as a linking verb. The adjective *sure* is used to modify *Kyle.*

6. happy — The modifier *happy* modifies the pronoun *I,* so use the adjective.

7. brightly — *Brightly* tells how the sun shone. It modifies the verb, so use an adverb.

8. evilly — *Evilly* tells how the robber looked at the woman. *Evilly* modifies the verb *looked,* so use an adverb.

9. C

10. loud — **Loud** modifies the noun *volume,* so use an adjective.

11. slowly — *Slowly* tells how the weeds covered the backyard, so use an adverb.

12. C

Exercise 4, page 90

1. least — Use *least* because more than two things are being compared. The phrase *we have ever had* is the clue that more than two things are being compared.

2. cheapest — The comparison is among more than two things—rice, beans, and macaroni versus all other items bought. Since *cheap* is a one-syllable adjective, use *est* instead of adding *most.*

3. faster — Two people are being compared. Use *er* instead of *more* because *fast* is a short word.

4. best — *Good* is an irregular adjective. Use *best* because more than two people are being compared. *Among all those people* tells you many are being compared.

5. neater or more neatly — Two people are being compared, so the *er* ending or *more* is used for the adverb.

6. fewer — Duties at two jobs are being compared, so the *er* ending is used for this adjective.

7. more serious — Two people are being compared. *Serious* is a longer word, so add *more* to the adjective.

8. most exciting — *Of all the movies* is your clue that more than two things are being compared. Add *most* to the adjective because it is a long word.

9. more — *Much* is an irregular adverb. *More* is used to compare two things.

10. happier — Two time periods are being compared—before and now. Change the *y* to *i* and add *er* to make the correct form of *happy.*

11. best — Use *best* because two or more markets are being compared.

12. farther — Use *farther* because two distances are being compared.

13. worse — Use *worse* because Anita's allergies are being compared for two seasons.

Exercise 5, page 93

1. those — *Them* is a pronoun, so it can't be used to modify a noun. *Those* is an adjective.

2. had scarcely — *Scarcely* is a negative. *Hadn't scarcely* is a double negative.

3. bitter — *Taste* is used as a linking verb in this sentence. *Coffee* is the subject, and it cannot perform the action of tasting. Use an adjective here.

4. well — The modifier refers to health, so use *well,* not *good.*

carefully — *Carefully* describes how the person nursed Jon. Since it modifies the verb *nursed,* use the adverb.

5. an — *An* comes before *easier,* which begins with a vowel sound.

would hardly — *Hardly* is a negative word, so *wouldn't hardly* is a double negative.

6. an — *An* comes before *ideal,* which begins with a vowel sound.

7. any — *Don't* is a negative. Use *any* to avoid the double negative *don't no.*

8. these — *Carrots* is a plural noun, and *this* modifies only singular nouns.

that — *Cup* is a singular noun. *Those* can modify only plural nouns.

9. anything — *Isn't* is a negative, so using *nothing* would create a double negative.

better — Two things are being compared here, how I feel when I'm sick and how I feel when I'm not sick.

10. a — A comes before variety, which begins with a consonant.

11. anywhere — *Couldn't find* is a negative, so using *nowhere* would create a double negative.

12. **this**   *Basket* is a singular noun, and *this* modifies a singular noun.
13. **can hardly**   *Hardly* is a negative word, so *can't* would create a double negative.
14. **an**   *An* comes before *unusual*, which begins with a vowel.

    most angular   *Most angular* is used because many houses are being compared.

Pre-GED Practice, page 94

1. (2) *Careful* is an adjective that is being used to modify the verb *drove*. The adverb is *carefully*.
2. (2) Use *well* to refer to health after a linking verb.
3. (1) *Didn't hardly* is a double negative.
4. (4) The manager is trying to hire the best people of all those available. The comparison, therefore, is among more than two.
5. (1) *Wise* is a short adjective. When comparing two things, add *er*. Never use both *more* and *er*.
6. (2) When comparing two things, add *er*, not *est*.

Exercise 6, page 96

1. **bus**   Louis saw the bus <u>at the corner.</u>
2. **Shen**   <u>Opening the door,</u> Shen looked outside.
3. **smell**   The smell <u>of barbecued chicken</u> made Shawna hungry.
4. **runner**   The exhausted runner, <u>seeing the finish line,</u> speeded up.
5. **sorry**   Julie was sorry <u>to lose the watch.</u>
6. **books**   Jacobo left his books <u>at the library.</u>
7. **Ms. Atole**   <u>Already soaked to the skin,</u> Ms. Atole opened her umbrella.
8. **soon**   The basketball game ended soon <u>after sunset.</u>
9. **left**   The police car left the crime scene <u>in a hurry.</u>
10. **manager**   <u>Hoping to get more customers,</u> the store manager lowered prices.
11. **Mr. Henshaw**   <u>Locking the door,</u> Mr. Henshaw left his apartment.
12. **crossed**   Mrs. Cosmos crossed <u>over the Canadian border.</u>
13. **Lenore**   <u>Sitting between her parents,</u> Lenore felt quite happy.

Exercise 7, page 97

1. Yuri Gagarin, the first human in space, was from the Soviet Union.
2. Ham, a chimpanzee, tested the U.S. spacecraft.
3. Alan Shepard, the first American in space, wrote a book about the early space program.
4. Shepard went into space in *Redstone 3*, a tiny spacecraft.
5. Shepard, an astronaut and test pilot, went to the moon many years later.

Pre-GED Practice, page 98

1. (2) A comma should be used to separate an introductory phrase from the rest of the sentence.
2. (4) Except for introductory phrases and renaming phrases, phrases are not usually separated from the sentence by commas.
3. (3) *An expensive Japanese model* is a renaming phrase that describes *camera*. It should be set off with commas.
4. (5) This sentence is correct as written.
5. (1) An introductory phrase should be set off by a comma.
6. (1) An introductory phrase should be set off by a comma.

Pre-GED Practice, pages 99–100

1. (4) The *produce manager* is a renaming phrase. It should be set off with commas.
2. (1) *Can't hardly* is a double negative.
3. (1) *Them* is always a pronoun. It can never be used to point out a noun.
4. (3) *An* is used before all words that begin with a vowel sound. *A* is used before words that begin with consonant sounds.
5. (3) *That* means "there," so saying *that there* is like saying *there there*.
6. (1) *Looks* is sometimes a linking verb, sometimes an action verb. Here it is used as an action verb. *Nervously* modifies *looks*, telling how the letter carrier looks at the dog. *Nervous* is an adjective.
7. (5) This sentence is correct as written.
8. (3) *I have ever read* is the clue that this book is being compared to all other books. *Funnier* compares only two things.
9. (1) *Well*, not *good*, is used to describe health.

10. (2) The word *more* should not be used with an adjective to which the ending *er* has been added.
11. (4) *Easy* is an adjective. In this sentence it is used to modify the verb *sets,* so an adverb, *easily,* is needed.
12. (3) *Isn't hardly* is a double negative.
13. (4) *Loud* modifies *screamed,* so the adverb, *loudly,* is needed.
14. (4) *Those* means "there," so *there* is not needed in this sentence.

Chapter 4

Exercise 1, page 105

1. Ann starts a new job soon, but she hasn't told her present boss.
2. There are no good movies in town; however, a great rock band is playing.
3. My house is a mess; I never seem to have time to clean it.
4. The plane's wings were covered with ice; as a result, the departure was delayed.
5. The server took their orders; then she brought us coffee.
6. I could never keep the washer fixed, so I bought a new one.
7. Snow is forecast for tonight; therefore, we should change our travel plans.
8. Max is a good dog; nevertheless, I don't want him eating off the table.

Exercise 2, page 109

Sample answers:
1. <u>After</u> backing into the garage, Sarah loaded the truck.
2. Melissa wants to go to the zoo <u>unless</u> the weather turns cold.
3. <u>Although</u> the bats still live in Carlsbad Caverns, there are fewer of them today.
4. Gilbert cast his fly <u>where</u> he had seen the large trout jump.
5. <u>As soon as</u> I tell Santwana I saw a spider, she will want to leave.
6. Few salmon live in the Snake River <u>because</u> huge dams were built.
7. <u>Even though</u> that dog has a loud bark, it's really very friendly.

8. <u>Since</u> you said the dog was friendly, I tried to pet him.
9. <u>In spite of the fact that</u> you were bitten, I still say the dog is gentle.
10. The doctor says the wound will heal <u>if</u> I keep it bandaged.

Pre-GED Practice, page 110

1. (3) *As soon as* shows a time relationship between the two clauses.
2. (1) *When* is the best choice. It says these two events—reading a magazine and eating lunch—happen at the same time. *As soon as* also relates the ideas by time, but it doesn't make sense.
3. (4) *Unless* shows a condition: one thing will happen if something else happens.
4. (5) *But* shows a contrast between the two ideas.
5. (2) *While* shows a time relationship between the ideas.
6. (3) *Whether* doesn't make sense. *Because* introduces the reason why he won't pay his bills on time.

Exercise 3, page 112

Sample answers:
1. before going on vacation
   Your bill should be paid before you go on vacation.
2. Hanging on the wall
   Javier stared at the beautiful painting hanging on the wall.
3. After cooking breakfast
   After breakfast was cooked, the fan had to be turned on to remove the smoke.
4. C
5. beginning on Bradford Road
   The parade, beginning on Bradford Road, included clowns, elephants, and bands.

Exercise 4, page 114

Sample answers:
1. I spent the weekend working in the yard, painting a door, and fixing a cracked window.
2. Regina said she would fix supper, set the table, and clean up afterward.
3. That candidate is energetic, concerned, and honest.

4. When Taro got home, he found mud on the carpet, scratch marks on the furniture, and broken glass on the floor.
5. Jo likes people who are kind, thoughtful, and funny.
6. The fortune-teller told Ana that she would get a great job, lose money, and move to another city.
7. The workshop leader explained how to speak clearly, appear skilled, and ask for a raise.

Exercise 5, page 117

1. **would get** Because *was convinced* is in the past tense, *will get* is not correct.
2. **C**
3. **had locked** *Realized* is in the past tense. Use the past perfect tense to show that Leroy locked himself out before that.
4. **could** *Asked* is in the past tense. *Can* cannot be used with the past tense, so *could* is the correct helping verb.
5. **were** *would* goes with the past tense of the subjunctive *were*.
6. **will** *Says* is in the present tense, and you know that Sonia has not yet washed her hair. Use the future tense *will* in place of *would*.
7. **would** *Said* is in the past tense. *Would* is correct with the past tense.
8. **would not have panicked** The conditional clause is in the past perfect, so you use *would have* with the past participle, *panicked*.
9. **C**
10. **will** *Will* is used with the future tense, since the interview is happening tomorrow.

Exercise 6, page 119

Samples answers:
1. C
2. Cathy told her son to clean his closet and his room since they were a mess.
3. The walls were bright green and the carpeting pale gray, a combination we thought was really ugly.
4. People are actually living without heat and hot water, and this situation must be taken care of.
5. The police department says that crime is increasing in our city.
6. Rosa told her daughter that Rosa would be able to drive in two weeks.

7. Thaddeus helped Steve move into Steve's new house.
8. Beth talked with the girls as they walked down the street.

Pre-GED Practice, page 120

1. (2) The snow occurred during the night, before the sun came out. The simple past shows that the sun came out after the snow fell.
2. (3) This is a conditional statement. The first verb, *had gone*, is the past perfect. It must be paired with a verb such as *would have* along with a past participle.
3. (3) In the original sentence, the pronoun *she* could refer to either Isabel or her daughter.
4. (4) The story is not about a house on the train. *On the train* is a misplaced modifier.
5. (5) This sentence is correct as written.
6. (4) Changing the second use of the pronoun *he* to *Barry* makes the sentence much clearer.

Exercise 7, page 123

Sample answers:
1. The temperature should get to eighty degrees.
2. I often forget people's names.
3. First list the necessary ingredients.
4. I don't write letters because I never have enough time.
5. He said the new salespeople were ready to go into the field for further training.

Exercise 8, page 126

1. Lee told us that Greg should **have** received the package by now.
2. **As** I've said before, most people never know how well off they are.
3. Sarah divided the remaining cake **among** the three of us.
4. Roland will certainly be **at** the game Saturday to see his brother play.
5. When she got up **off** the ground the last time, Yoko gave up skating.
6. Tina's got a sharper memory than any **other** person I know.
7. The actors in that movie were worse than **those in** the movie I saw last week.
8. Sid said he knew someone who would try **to** get us tickets.

Pre-GED Practice, page 127

1. (2) This sentence is written in the active voice and is less wordy than the original.
2. (4) *Between* is used when you are referring to only two things. *Among* is the proper preposition for this sentence.
3. (1) The original sentence is repetitive. This sentence has the same meaning but is less repetitive.
4. (5) This sentence is correct as written.

Pre-GED Practice, pages 128–131

1. (5) *Would of* is incorrect diction. *Would have* is correct. Choice (3) is also incorrect because *different from* is correct. No punctuation is needed.
2. (3) The original sentence has incorrect verb sequence. All the action occurs in the past. *Has discovered* is the present perfect tense, showing that an action is continuing.
3. (4) The original sentence lacks parallel structure.
4. (2) The original sentence is a run-on. Choice (2) turns one of the clauses into a dependent clause. Since it is an introductory clause, it must be followed by a comma.
5. (4) *Even though* is a conjunction showing contrast. Here the writer is telling why the Caribbean is considered tropical.
6. (3) The original sentence leaves it unclear whether the dog belongs to John or to his brother.
7. (2) The original sentence has two repetitive ideas: *the future time before us* and *world leaders around the globe.*
8. (2) *If* says that if the first idea is true, then the second will be true too, which doesn't make sense. *Unless* shows that if you do one thing, then the other won't happen, which does make sense.
9. (3) The original sentence says Cheryl's serve is faster than a tennis player.
10. (5) The original sentence contains a misplaced modifier. It says the auto dealership was on sale.
11. (3) *Like* is incorrectly used with a subject-verb combination: *Mr. Murray said.*
12. (1) The original is correct.

13. (4) The sentence contains an *if* clause with *were*, so the correct form for the main clause is *would* plus the base form *be*. Choice (4) is incorrect because it does not use a comma after the dependent clause.
14. (5) The original sentence has nonparallel structure. The first two items are nouns, but the third is the *ing* form of a verb.
15. (4) *At last* and *finally* are repetitive. Also, the sentence is wordy because it is in the passive voice.
16. (2) The transition word *Because* explains why Ted and Sonia left the country.
17. (4) Use *between*, not *among*, when referring to two people or things.
18. (4) The original sentence contains two nonparallel elements.
19. (3) This sentence has two problems. First, *both … and also* is repetitive and incorrect. Second, the phrases joined by the conjunction are not parallel. *Dramatic* is an adjective and *it inspired* is a subject-verb combination.

Chapter 5

Exercise 1, page 135

1. **east**   Do not capitalize *north*, *south*, *east*, *west* or other directions when used to tell a general direction.
2. **President**   Here *President* is used as a title for a specific person.
3. **English**   *English* is an adjective formed from the proper noun *England*, which names a particular place.
4. **Southeast**   *Southeast High School* is the specific name of a particular high school.
5. **Langston Hughes**   *Langston Hughes* is the name of a specific person.

Exercise 2, page 137

1. **weekly**   Since *weekly* states a general time, not a specific one, it is not capitalized.
2. **unless**   This complete quotation is divided by words telling who the speaker is. *Unless* introduces a clause. It is not a complete sentence by itself and should not be capitalized.

3. **ACLU** Capitalize abbreviations that stand for specific organizations.
4. **Sr.** Capitalize abbreviations of titles.
5. **Biology 340** *Biology 340* is the name of a specific course. It should be capitalized.
6. **Children's Aid Society** The names of specific organizations should be capitalized.

Pre-GED Practice, page 138

1. (2) Names of specific places are capitalized. *Los Angeles* is the specific name for a city.
2. (4) The title does not stand by itself, so *grandmother* should not be capitalized. If *my* were deleted, *Grandmother* would be capitalized.
3. (5) The sentence is correct as written.
4. (2) This could be any baseball game, so *baseball* should not be capitalized.
5. (4) *Physical fitness* is a topic, not the specific title of a book.
6. (4) The names of government organizations are always capitalized.
7. (2) *Northwest* is used as a direction not as the name of a specific place or region.

Exercise 3, page 140

1. Mrs_._Rachet completed the annual report_._
2. Look out for that bus_!_
3. Did he pick the winning lottery number_?_
4. "Did he already spend all the money_?_" Georgia asked_._
5. My uncle named his new business the Rivets Co_._
6. "Quick_!_ shouted the police officer over his car radio_._
7. As she looked all over the house, Maxine moaned, "Where are my keys_?_"
8. Just what do you mean by the term *"slacker"*_?_

Exercise 4, page 144

1. When Akiko came by the office_,_ she fixed the copy machine. (Set off dependent clauses with a comma when they begin a sentence.)
2. The little boy asked_,_ "How can I get home from here?" (Use commas to separate quotations from the rest of the sentence.)
3. On January 3, the Bombers will play at Johnson Field, Omaha_,_ Nebraska. (Separate city from state with a comma.)

4. It was_,_ in fact_,_ the best cheesecake she had ever had. (Interrupters such as *in fact* should be set off from the rest of the sentence with commas.)
5. Jim picked up the trash can_,_ and a rat came flying out. (Use a comma before the conjunction linking clauses in a compound sentence.)
6. Why don't you wear your yellow sweater_,_ Tomás? (Use commas to set off the name of a person addressed in a sentence.)
7. This exercise program is easy for me; moreover _,_ I have lost ten pounds. (When compound sentences are joined by a conjunctive adverb, place a comma after the adverb.)
8. Yolanda_,_ the woman who got me this job_,_ has now quit. (Set off renaming phrases with commas.)
9. Mr. Chung hurriedly left his house after getting the telephone call. (When a nonrestrictive dependent clause comes at the end of a sentence, do not use a comma to set it off.)
10. "Gina will pick you up in an hour_,_" the woman replied. (Use a comma to separate a quotation from the rest of the sentence.)

Exercise 5, page 147

1. Teresa really wanted to go to Mexico_;_ nevertheless_,_ she agreed to spend her vacation at the lake.
2. At the supermarket, we ran into our old neighbors_,_ the Okaras_,_ who lived next door _;_ Jill and Sean_,_ the ones who gave noisy parties _;_ and Marianne_,_ our babysitter.
3. Keisha cried_,_ "He forgot my birthday_;_ then he went to a hockey game _."_
4. Paulo wished he could remember everything_;_ however_,_ he was already forgetting the details.
5. He gave these reasons for moving_:_ a bigger yard_,_ more bedrooms_,_ lower taxes_,_ and a better school district.
6. It is now 7_:_00 and Stan just got here_,_ nevertheless_,_ we're still going to the game.
7. Jan yelled to her brother_,_ "Who's going to feed the dog_?_"
8. Dear Madam_:_
I bought a SlimMachine because I wanted to lose weight_._ It_'_s already broken_._ Please refund my money_._

Sincerely_,_
John Arocha

9. They_'_re looking for a new car_;_the one they have is worn out.
10. I want a job downtown_,_not one out in the suburbs.

Pre-GED Practice, page 148

1. (3) The quotation is a question, so it should end with a question mark inside the quotation marks.
2. (4) The quotation is an exclamation; the exclamation point goes inside the quotation marks. No other end punctuation is needed.
3. (2) This sentence is a simple statement, not a question. It only states that Mercedes had a question. It should end with a period.
4. (5) This sentence is correct as written.
5. (3) The entire sentence is a question, but the quotation by itself is not. Therefore, the question mark should go outside the quotation marks.
6. (3) A comma is not needed between the words *believe* and *Melissa*.
7. (5) This sentence is correct as written.
8. (2) The word *its* in this sentence is the contraction for *it is*. An apostrophe is needed to mark the place of the missing letter *i*.

Exercise 6, page 150

Part A
1. brake
2. know
3. here
4. whether
5. passed

Part B
   The founders of the United States didn't **know** whether they **would** succeed in winning independence from Great Britain, but they **knew** they had to try. **Their** goal was freedom. This country was founded on the **principle** of equality for all. The founders **passed** on to us **their** belief in democracy. The Constitution guarantees our **right** to free speech. That means everyone is allowed to say whatever he or she thinks, **whether** anyone else wants to **hear** it or not.

Pre-GED Practice, page 152

1. (2) The preposition *through* is correct in this sentence.
2. (4) The possessive pronoun *your* is correct in this sentence.
3. (3) The possessive pronoun *whose* is correct in this sentence.
4. (2) The word *family* refers to one family. Therefore, the possessive requires *'s*.

Pre-GED Practice, pages 153–156

1. (3) Only the quotation is a question, so the question mark should be inside the quotation marks. Only one end punctuation mark is needed.
2. (3) *It's* is a contraction meaning "it is." In this sentence, the possessive *its* is needed.
3. (4) The last word in this sentence means "also". It is not a number.
4. (1) Use a colon when a complete thought is used to introduce a list.
5. (1) Use a semicolon to join independent clauses in a compound sentence when a conjunction is not used.
6. (3) *In fact* is used as an interrupting phrase. It should be set off with commas.
7. (3) The two parts of this quotation make one complete sentence. *Will* should not be capitalized because it continues the sentence.
8. (5) This sentence is correct as written.
9. (2) *Uncle* is not used here to replace a name, so it should not be capitalized.
10. (3) Use an apostrophe to show that the *o* in *not* is the missing letter in this contraction.
11. (4) *French* is a word taken from the specific name of a country.
12. (4) Here the quotation itself is a question. The question mark belongs inside the quotation marks.
13. (1) Seasons should not be capitalized.
14. (5) This sentence is correct as written.
15. (4) *Doctors* refers to a general group of people. It is not used as a title for specific people.
16. (1) A comma should not be used to separate the month from the date.
17. (2) A dependent clause that comes at the end of a sentence is not set off with a comma.

18. (3) One complete thought in this sentence is *I suppose that all your work was worthwhile.* No comma is needed.
19. (1) A complete thought introduces a list in this sentence. A colon is needed.
20. (2) *Funds* is used as a plural here. No apostrophe is needed.
21. (4) The quotation is an exclamation. The exclamation point should go inside the quotation marks.
22. (1) *Junior college* is not the name of a specific place.
23. (3) *They're* is a contraction meaning "they are." Here *their* is needed to show possession of the breakfast.
24. (4) The writer is not asking a question but is telling about the mother asking a question.
25. (1) *Wood* is a homonym for the correct word, the helping verb *would*.

Chapter 6

Exercise 1, page 158

1. ineffective
2. effective
3. ineffective
4. effective
5. ineffective

Exercise 2, page 160

Sample answers:
1. Our department has developed a plan to increase profits through improved customer service.
2. Andrea decorated her new apartment elegantly and inexpensively.

Pre-GED Practice, page 161

1. (2) This sentence effectively summarizes the main idea of the paragraph.
2. (3) This sentence effectively summarizes the main idea of the paragraph.
3. (1) This sentence effectively summarizes the main idea of the paragraph.

Exercise 3, page 163

A new paragraph should begin with the sentence *Deciduous trees are also called broad-leaved trees.* This sentence begins the discussion of deciduous trees, which is a new idea.

Pre-GED Practice, page 164

1. (3) The original paragraph contains two main ideas. Beginning a new paragraph with sentence 8 will put each idea in a separate paragraph.
2. (2) The original paragraph contains two main ideas. Beginning a new paragraph with sentence 5 will put each idea in a separate paragraph.

Exercise 4, page 168

The sentence *Now the Civic Club needs only to raise enough money to renovate the building and bring it up to code* is placed incorrectly. It should come directly after the sentence *We're in negotiations with the Blackburn family, who have offered to donate their building at 925 Ridge Avenue.*

Pre-GED Practice, page 169

1. (2) This sentence about the action Poseidon took is part of the sequence of events described in paragraph C.
2. (3) Readers need to find out what the gods told the people to do before they find out what steps the people took.

Exercise 5, page 171

1. Cross out *I believe that, if one analyzes it, baseball is a sport that reflects the great American values of teamwork and sportsmanship.* (This formal tone does not fit a casual, conversational e-mail.)
2. Cross out *It was so cool to look at a drop of water and see a bunch of tiny animals living in it.* (This casual, slangy tone does not belong in a formal paper.)
3. Effective
4. Cross out *What a racket they've got going!* (This sentence is too slangy and too opinionated for a news article.)

Pre-GED Practice, pages 172–175

1. (5) Sentence 6 is too casual and offensive to belong in this objective, informational article.
2. (3) Sentence 10 is about planning, so it belongs in paragraph B, which has planning as its main idea.
3. (3) Paragraph D is trying to cover two subjects: organizing and staffing. It would be more effective to start a new paragraph with the first sentence about staffing.
4. (1) This makes a good topic sentence for paragraph E, since all of the sentences in the paragraph discuss directing.
5. (5) Sentence 21 has nothing to do with the topic of the paragraph or even of the article as a whole. It's about a different kind of coaching, so it does not belong in paragraph E.
6. (4) Sentence 24 wraps up paragraph F, so it should go at the end of the paragraph.
7. (5) Sentence 5 is irrelevant. The paragraph is about Anna's history, not about the present.
8. (5) Sentence 5 is too casual and modern to belong in this historical, informational story.
9. (4) It makes sense to tell why the king summoned Anna right after telling that he summoned her. Also, there is nothing in sentence 17 for "That might sound easy" to refer to.
10. (1) This sentence belongs in the paragraph that talks about what the king wants. It connects so closely to sentence 19 in content that it must be in the same paragraph.
11. (3) All of the other sentences relate to the topic of the paragraph, but only sentence 3 states its main idea.
12. (4) The books and movie about Anna are a different subject from Anna's actual experience, so they belong in a separate paragraph.

Chapter 7

Exercise 1, page 180

Answers will vary for parts A and B.

Exercise 2, page 183

1. The answer is given.
2. 5, 2, 1, 4, 3
3. 2, 5, 4, 1, 3
4. From least to most recent: 3, 5, 1, 2, 4
   From most to least recent: 4, 2, 1, 5, 3

Exercise 3, page 186

1. (2) Electric cars, whether impractical or not, are not a cause of air pollution.
2. (4) The fact that every big city in America now has more homeless people on the streets is not a cause of homelessness.
3. (2) A person cannot transmit HIV/AIDS by drinking from a public water fountain.

Exercise 4, page 187

Answers will vary.

Exercise 5, page 190

Answers will vary.

Exercise 6, page 191

Answers will vary.

Pre-GED Practice, pages 192–194

Answers will vary. Go over your paragraph with your instructor or another student.

Chapter 8

Exercises 1–7, pages 196–204

Answers will vary.

Pre-GED Practice, page 205

Answers will vary. Go over your essay with your instructor or another student.

Glossary

A

action verb   a kind of verb that tells what the subject does

active verb   a verb that shows the subject doing the action

active voice   the way a verb is used to show that the subject does the action

adjective   a word that modifies, or describes, a noun or pronoun

adverb   a word that modifies, or describes, a verb, an adjective, or another adverb

antecedent   the noun or pronoun a pronoun refers to

apostrophe   a kind of punctuation used to show possession or to form contractions

appositive   see **renaming phrase**

B

base form   the most basic form of the verb; the form you begin with when you form all verb tenses

body   the main part of a piece of writing, which gives the details and facts about the main idea

brainstorming   a way of gathering ideas to write about, in which the writer lists every idea that comes to mind

C

cause-and-effect order   a way of organizing information that tells how one event made another event happen

clause   a group of words that contains a subject and a verb

coherence   a logical flow; a paragraph has coherence when all its sentences relate to each other and flow logically from one to the next

collective noun   a noun that names a group of people or things

colon   a kind of punctuation used to introduce items in a list

comma   a kind of punctuation used to separate clauses, interrupting phrases, and items in a series

comma splice   a sentence consisting of two clauses joined incorrectly by a comma without a conjunction

command   a type of sentence that gives an order or makes a request

common noun   a type of noun that names a whole group or general type of person, place, thing, or idea

comparison-and-contrast order   a way of organizing information to show how one thing or idea is similar to or different from another thing or idea

complex sentence   a sentence that contains one independent, or main, clause and one or more dependent clauses

compound sentence   a sentence that contains two or more connected independent clauses or simple sentences

compound subject   a subject of a sentence that is made up of more than one word; the words are connected with words like *and* or *or*

conclusion   the last part of a piece of writing, which summarizes or draws the writing to an end

conditional   a clause that begins with the word *if*

conjunction   a type of word that links parts of a sentence by showing how the parts are related

conjunctive adverb   an adverb or adverb phrase that works like a conjunction

contraction   a word that is made up of two words with some letters left out; an apostrophe is used in place of the missing letters

D

dangling modifier   a modifying phrase or clause that does not modify any word in the sentence

dependent clause   a group of words that contains a subject and a predicate but does not express a complete thought

diction   how words are chosen and used

E

editing   the step in the writing process in which mistakes in grammar, punctuation, capitalization, and spelling are corrected

exclamation   a type of sentence that expresses surprise or excitement; it always ends with an exclamation point

exclamation point   a kind of punctuation that is used to end a sentence that shows strong emotion or excitement

F

fragment   an incomplete sentence

future perfect tense   a verb tense that shows an action that will be completed by a specific time in the future

H

helping verb   a verb that is used with other verb forms to form different tenses

homonym   a word that sounds the same as another word but is spelled differently

I

idiom   a group of words that have been used together so often and for so long that they have developed a special meaning; an idiom cannot be understood just by knowing the meaning of the individual words

independent clause   a part of a sentence that contains a subject and a predicate and expresses a complete thought

infinitive   a verb form that begins with the word *to*

interrupting phrase   a group of words that comes between the simple subject and the verb

introduction   the first part of a piece of writing, which tells what the topic and main idea are

inverted sentence   a sentence in which the usual subject-verb order is reversed, so the verb comes before the subject

irregular verb   a verb that does not form its past and past participle forms in a regular, or predictable, way

L

linking verb   a kind of verb that tells what the subject is or that links the subject with a word or words that describe it

M

main idea   the point that a paragraph discusses or develops

misplaced modifier   word or phrase whose meaning is unclear because it is out of place

modifier   a word or group of words that describes other words in a sentence; adjectives and adverbs are modifiers

N

noun   a word that names a person, place, thing, or idea

O

object pronoun   a type of pronoun that is the object of a verb or a preposition

order of importance   a way of organizing writing that ranks details from most important to least important or vice versa

organizing   the step in the writing process in which a writer puts his or her ideas in order

P

paragraph   a group of sentences that work together to communicate one idea

parallel structure   a correct form of sentence structure in which all elements of a compound sentence have the same form

passive verb a verb that shows the subject being acted upon

passive voice the way a verb is used to show that an action is done to the subject

past perfect tense a verb form that tells that an action was completed in the past before another event or before a certain time in the past

pattern of organization a way to organize writing

perfect tenses verb forms that tell that an action has been completed before a certain time or that will be continuing until a certain time

period a kind of punctuation used to end a sentence that gives information or that states a feeling or wish

phrase a group of words that contains either a noun (or pronoun) or a verb but not both

plural noun a noun that names more than one person, place, thing, or idea

point-by-point pattern a way of organizing comparison-and-contrast writing by telling about one point, or feature, of one item and then comparing and contrasting the same feature of a second item; after that, another feature is compared for the two items, and so on

possessive noun a type of noun that shows that one thing is owned, or possessed, by another person or thing

possessive pronoun a type of pronoun that replaces a noun that shows ownership

predicate the part of a sentence that tells what the subject is or does

preposition a word that connects a noun with another part of the sentence

prepositional phrase a word group that begins with a preposition and ends with a noun or pronoun

present perfect tense a verb form that tells that an action was started in the past and is continuing in the present or that it has just been completed

prewriting the first step in the writing process, during which ideas are found, developed, and organized

pronoun a word that replaces and refers to a noun

proper noun a type of noun that names a specific person, place, thing, or idea; always capitalized

Q

question a type of sentence that asks for or about something

question mark a type of punctuation that is used to end a question

quotation marks a kind of punctuation used to show the exact words of a speaker in a direct quote

R

reflexive pronoun a type of pronoun that shows action is done by the subject to himself or herself

regular verb a verb that forms its past and past participle forms in a regular, or predictable, way

renaming phrase a modifying phrase that gives more information about a noun; it is made up of a noun and other words that modify that noun

revising the step in the writing process in which the rough draft is changed and improved

rough draft the first draft of a piece of writing, in which ideas are put into sentences and paragraphs for the first time

run-on sentence a compound sentence that is incorrectly joined so the ideas run together

S

semicolon a kind of punctuation used in forming compound sentences

sentence a group of words that contains a subject and a predicate and that expresses a complete thought

simple future tense   a verb tense that shows an action that will occur in the future

simple past tense   a verb form that shows actions that occurred at a specific time in the past

simple present tense   a verb form that tells what is happening or is true at the present time, that shows actions that are performed regularly, or that tells what is always true

simple sentence   the most basic, or simple, form of the complete sentence; it has one subject and one predicate and expresses a complete thought

simple subject   the most basic part of the subject of a sentence; it is what or whom the sentence is about but does not include any descriptive words that are part of the subject

singular noun   a noun that names only one person, place, thing, or idea

statement   a type of sentence that gives information or tells something

style   how words and sentences are used to express meaning

subject   whom or what a sentence is about

subject pronoun   a type of pronoun that takes the place of a noun that is used as the subject of a sentence

subjunctive mood   a verb form that expresses a command, wish, or condition that is contrary to fact

supporting sentences   sentences in a paragraph that add details to support the main idea

T

tense   the time shown by a verb

time order   a way of organizing writing according to the order in which events happen

tone   the language used by a writer to make his or her point

topic sentence   the sentence in a paragraph that tells what the rest of the paragraph is about

transition words   words that give the reader clues about the order of events or how the events are connected

U

unity   a single purpose; a paragraph has unity if every sentence in it unites to support the main idea

V

verb   the most important part of the predicate, which tells what the subject is or does

verb phrase   a group of words that begins with a verb and that acts as a modifier

verb sequence   the order and tense of verbs in a sentence; the verbs must work together to tell when the different actions happened

W

whole-to-whole pattern   a way of organizing comparison-and-contrast writing by first telling all about one item and then telling how the other item is alike and different from the first one

writing   the step in the writing process in which a writer puts his or her ideas down on paper

Index